Happy Dads' Day !!
June 1990

A
WATERFALL LOVER'S
Guide to the
PACIFIC NORTHWEST

Second Edition

Where to Find More Than 500 Spectacular Waterfalls in Washington, Oregon and Idaho

Gregory Alan Plumb

The Mountaineers · Books

The Mountaineers: Organized 1906 "...to explore, study, preserve, and enjoy the natural beauty of the Northwest."

Published by The Mountaineers
306 Second Avenue West, Seattle, Washington 98119
Published simultaneously in Canada by Douglas & McIntyre, Ltd.,
1615 Venables Street, Vancouver, B.C. V5L 2H1

Manufactured in the United States of America
Edited by Miriam Bulmer
Cover design by Betty Watson
Layout by Nick Gregoric
Cover Photograph: Salt Creek Falls
Frontispiece: Triple Falls

Library of Congress Cataloging in Publication Data
Plumb, Gregory Alan, 1956-
   A waterfall lover's guide to the Pacific Northwest: where to find more than 500 spectacular waterfalls in Washington, Oregon, and Idaho. — 2nd ed.
      p.   cm.
   Rev. ed. of: Waterfalls of the Pacific Northwest, c1983.
   ISBN 0-89886-191-8
   1. Hiking — Northwest, Pacific — Guide-books.   2. Camp sites, facilities, etc. — Northwest, Pacific — Directories.   3. Waterfalls — Northwest, Pacific — Description.   4. Northwest, Pacific — Description and travel — Guide-books.   I. Title.
GV199.42.N69P58   1989
917.95 — dc20   89-12959
                                                                  CIP

This book is dedicated to my brothers,
Randy and Dennie Plumb

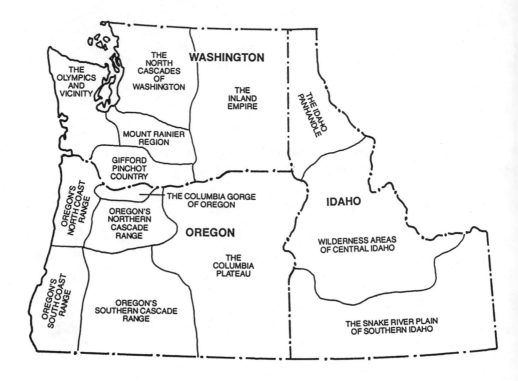

A Note About Safety

Safety is an important concern in all outdoor activities. No guidebook can alert you to every hazard or anticipate the limitations of every reader. Therefore, the descriptions of roads, trails, routes, and natural features in this book are not representations that a particular place or excursion will be safe for your party. When you visit any of the waterfalls described in this book, you assume responsibility for your own safety. Under normal conditions, such excursions require the usual attention to traffic, road and trail conditions, weather, terrain, the capabilities of your party, and other factors. Keeping informed on current conditions and exercising common sense are the keys to a safe, enjoyable outing.

The Mountaineers

Contents

Preface 9

Acknowledgments 10

Introduction 11
    Accessibility Symbols 12
    Starred Rating System 13
    Waterfall Forms 13
    The Maps 15

The North Cascades of Washington 17
   1   North Bend Area 18
   2   Snoqualmie Pass 20
   3   Leavenworth Area 21
   4   Lake Wenatchee 21
   5   Stevens Pass 22
   6   Index 23
   7   Gold Bar 24
   8   Roesiger Lake 25
   9   Granite Falls 26
 10   Robe Valley 26
 11   Twin Falls Lake 28
 12   Arlington Area 29
 13   Boulder Creek 29
 14   Sauk River Drainage 29
 15   Suiattle River Drainage 30
 16   Sauk Valley 31
 17   Mount Baker 32
 18   Nooksack River 33
 19   Ross Lake National Recreation Area 34
 20   Methow Valley 35
 21   Chewuch River Drainage 36
 22   Foggy Dew Creek 37
 23   Lake Chelan 38
 24   North Cascades National Park 39
 25   Entiat Valley 40

The Olympics and Vicinity 43
   1   Orcas Island 44
   2   Elwha 46
   3   Mount Carrie Area 46
   4   Lake Crescent 48
   5   Soleduck 48

6 Beaver Creek 49
7 Clallam Bay Area 50
8 Cape Flattery 50
9 Olympic Coast 52
10 Enchanted Valley 52
11 Quilcene Area 53
12 Dosewallips 53
13 Brinnon 54
14 Kamilche 55
15 Olympia 55
16 Rainbow Falls State Park 57

Mount Rainier Region 59
1 Carbon River Drainage 60
2 Mowich Lake Area 62
3 St. Andrews Creek 62
4 Nisqually Drainage 64
5 Paradise 67
6 Stevens Canyon 68
7 Silver Falls Area 70
8 Chinook Creek Drainage 72
9 Backpackers' Falls 73
10 Camp Sheppard 75
11 Dewey Lake 75
12 Rainier Valley 75
13 Naches Area 77
14 Rimrock Lake Area 78
15 Lower Ohanapecosh Drainage 80
16 Johnson Creek Drainage 83
17 Silverbrook Area 83

Gifford Pinchot Country 85
1 Cowlitz River 85
2 Iron Creek Access 86
3 North Fork Drainage 88
4 Kalama River Road 89
5 Lake Merwin 90
6 Kalama Falls 90
7 Eagle Cliff Area 91
8 Lewis River 93
9 East Fork Lewis River 95
10 Dougan Camp 95
11 Beacon Rock State Park 96
12 Rock Creek Drainage 97
13 Carson Area 98
14 Wind River Road 99
15 Dog Creek 100
16 Mount Adams Ranger District 100
17 Mount Adams Wilderness 102
18 Glenwood Area 103

The Inland Empire 105
1   Spokane 107
2   Spokane Indian Reservation 107
3   Boundary Dam 109
4   Park Rapids 109
5   Colville Area 109
6   Kettle Falls 111
7   Northport 111
8   Franklin D. Roosevelt Lake 113
9   Sherman Creek 114
10 Conconully 115
11 Coulee City 116
12 Rock Creek Coulee 117
13 Upper Palouse Canyon 117
14 Lower Palouse Canyon 118

The Columbia Gorge of Oregon 119
1   Bridal Veil Area 119
2   Multnomah Falls Area 121
3   Oneonta and Horsetail Drainages 124
4   John B. Yeon State Park 125
5   Tanner Creek Drainage 126
6   Eagle Creek Drainage 128
7   Cascade Locks Area 129
8   Wyeth 131
9   Starvation Creek State Park 131
10 Hood River Area 133
11 Mosier Area 134
12 The Dalles Area 134

Oregon's North Coast Range 137
1   Scappoose 137
2   Beaver Creek 137
3   Olney 139
4   Jewell 140
5   Nehalem River Road 140
6   Tillamook Area 141
7   Dolph 142
8   Cherry Grove 143
9   Falls City 144

Oregon's South Coast Range 145
1   Alsea Area 145
2   Smith River 147
3   Mapleton Ranger District 147
4   Lorane Area 149
5   Millicoma River Drainage 149
6   Fairview Area 149
7   East Fork Coquille 150
8   Siskiyou National Forest 151

  9 Rogue River 152

Oregon's Northern Cascade Range 155
  1 Mount Hood Wilderness 155
  2 Zigzag River Drainage 157
  3 Salmon-Huckleberry Wilderness 157
  4 Bennett Pass 158
  5 Northeast Mount Hood 159
  6 Eagle Creek 161
  7 Bagby Hot Springs Area 162
  8 Silver Falls State Park 163
  9 Mehama 165
  10 North Fork Drainage 165
  11 Niagara Park 166
  12 Marion Forks Area 167
  13 McKenzie River 168
  14 House Rock 169
  15 Cascadia 169
  16 McDowell Falls Area 170

Oregon's Southern Cascade Range 173
  1 Three Sisters Wilderness 173
  2 Cascade Lakes Highway 175
  3 Big Fall Creek 176
  4 Salmon Creek Drainage 176
  5 Salt Creek Drainage 177
  6 Row River Drainage 179
  7 Little River Drainage 181
  8 Cavitt Creek 182
  9 Idleyld Park Area 183
  10 Steamboat 183
  11 Toketee 184
  12 Northeastern Umpqua 185
  13 Falls of the Upper Rogue 186
  14 South Umpqua 187
  15 Azalea Area 188
  16 Mill Creek Scenic Area 189
  17 Sky Lakes Wilderness 190
  18 Crater Lake National Park 190
  19 Butte Falls 191

The Columbia Plateau 193
  1 Redmond 193
  2 Tumalo Creek 195
  3 Lava Butte Geological Area 195
  4 La Pine Area 196
  5 Newberry Crater 197
  6 Wallowa Lake Area 199
  7 Hurricane Creek Drainage 200
  8 Ochoco East 201

9   Strawberry Mountains Wilderness 201
10   Adel 202

The Idaho Panhandle 203
1   Priest River Drainage 203
2   Priest Lake 204
3   Pend Oreille 205
4   Colburn Area 207
5   Pack River Drainage 207
6   Bonners Ferry 209
7   Moyie River 209
8   Boundary Line 209
9   Mullan 210
10   St. Joe Drainage 211
11   Elk Creek Falls Recreation Area 211

Wilderness Areas of Central Idaho 215
1   Selway River 215
2   Lochsa Drainage 217
3   Warm Springs Creek 218
4   Riggins 218
5   Lost Valley 220
6   Garden Valley 220
7   South Fork Boise River 221
8   Middle Fork Salmon River 222
9   Sawtooths West 224
10   Baron Creek 224
11   Stanley Lake Creek 225
12   Sawtooths East 226
13   Hunter Summit 226
14   Ketchum Area 227
15   Salmon National Forest 227
16   Salmon River 229

The Snake River Plain of Southern Idaho 231
1   Jump Creek Canyon 231
2   Hot Springs 232
3   Deadman Canyon 233
4   Hagerman Area 233
5   Snake Plains Aquifer 234
6   Snake River Canyon West 236
7   Snake River Canyon East 236
8   Lava Hot Springs 239
9   City of Idaho Falls 240
10   Swan Valley 240
11   Upper Palisade Lake 240
12   Henrys Fork 241
13   Yellowstone 242

Index 243

▲   *Fall Creek Falls in the Snake Plain*

Preface

Water, in its many forms, provides some of the earth's most beautiful landscapes. Rivers, lakes, and coasts all offer images of scenic beauty, but undoubtedly waterfalls are the most impressive of hydrologic features. People have always been drawn to falls as places of wonder, relaxation, and inspiration.

As a youth, my first experience of this sparkling water formation was the popular Tahquamenon Falls on Michigan's Upper Peninsula. The shimmering waters of this block-type waterfall naturally tint to a burnt orange during its descent. Our family so enjoyed this waterfall that we began including stops at other falls in our itinerary on vacations "up north." However, we had difficulty finding waterfalls other than those marked by "point of interest" symbols on the state highway map. Even these were not always easy to find.

As an adult, my interest in waterfalls peaked while I was living in northern Idaho. The Pacific Northwest was a new region to be explored, and on many trips I discovered waterfalls. After visiting a few, I wanted to see more. Unfortunately I discovered that no text had been written on the subject. At that point an idea was kindled. The first edition of this recreational guidebook was the result.

Several years have passed since its publication. Since then, additional waterfalls have been found ...forest road designations have changed ... the first book sold out. Now, thanks to The Mountaineers, this new edition is available. Whether you're a novice or an old waterfall buff, I hope you enjoy using this updated guide on your adventures.

Acknowledgments

Many sources contributed directly or indirectly to this guidebook. I would like to recognize them here.

In compiling an inventory of waterfalls prior to field investigations, I scanned the 7½-minute and 15-minute series of topographic maps printed by the U.S. Geological Survey. U.S. Forest Service maps provided a secondary reference. I originally reviewed these map collections at the University of Idaho library, and subsequently examined recently published maps residing at the University of Oklahoma library. Over 130 additional descents were found on the new maps! Other falls were discovered from book sources, including Harvey Manning's *Footsore: Walks and Hikes Around Puget Sound* series; S.R. Bluestein's *Hiking Trails of Southern Idaho;* and E.M. Sterling's *Trips and Trails* series. A few waterfalls were encountered during field travels. Rangers and local residents mentioned some, and I fortuitously stumbled upon others.

The most enjoyable part of preparing this book was, of course, seeking out the falls of the Pacific Northwest. The personnel at ranger stations of the National Park Service and U.S. Forest Service were very helpful in providing road and travel information. I also want to thank the following individuals for their assistance with this edition: Matt Siron of Glenns Ferry, Idaho; Bob Stengel of Gaines, Michigan; Scott and Diane Ackerman of Kennewick, Washington; and John Nelson of Cascade Locks, Oregon. The maps in this book were designed by the author. Craig Torbenson of Norman, Oklahoma, assisted with the cartographic production. Most of the photographs were taken and prepared by the author.

Geologic, cultural, and historical information was primarily obtained through library research, although some facts were gathered in the field. Geologic sources included *Cascadia: The Geologic Evolution of the Pacific Northwest,* by Bates McKee; *Geology of Oregon,* by E.M. Baldwin; *Humid Landforms,* by Ian Douglas; *Guide to the Geology and Lore of the Wild Reach of the Rogue River,* by William Purclom; *Catastrophic Flooding: The Origin of the Channeled Scabland,* edited by Victor R. Baker; and *Geologic Map of Mount Rainier National Park,* by R.S. Fiske, C.A. Hopson, and A.C. Waters. An exhaustive array of cultural and historical trivia was found in *Oregon Geographic Names,* by L.A. McArthur; *The Idaho Encyclopedia,* a Federal Writers' Project; and *Origin of Washington Place Names,* by Edmond Meany.

Introduction

Welcome to the waterfalls of the Pacific Northwest! This book has been written as a field guide to lead you to falls of all shapes and sizes. Whether you want an afternoon trip or an extensive vacation, a short walk or a backpacking trek, this guidebook will tell you where to find the waterfalls. Extraordinary adventures await you!

But first, a warning. The grandeur of waterfalls is accompanied by an element of risk. Accidents can occur at even the most developed locations, particularly when youngsters are left unsupervised or people forget their sanity and unduly place themselves in dangerous situations. The keys to safe and sane travel to and about waterfalls are:

1) Do not stray from fenced observation points or trails in steep areas.
2) Remain aware of your surroundings when taking pictures, and don't startle others when they are concentrating on photography.
3) Stay away from sloping, unvegetated surfaces.
4) Remember each party member's limitations concerning steep climbs, long trails, or undeveloped areas. Turn back whenever you feel insecure about the route ahead.
5) If you must travel alone, be sure someone knows your travel plans.

Hundreds of waterfalls are described in this guidebook. They are grouped into 14 geographic regions for easy use. Each region is divided into subsections describing various waterfalls, accompanied by maps showing their locations.

Many of the falls described here have no official names, so for convenience I have called them by the names of their streams or of nearby landmarks. Physical, cultural, historical, and geological information is included when known. Symbols accompanying each description show the relative accessibility, a subjective rating, and the general shape or form of the falls. Public campgrounds are shown on many of the maps within the book. Also, it is permissible to pitch camp at almost any location on National Forest land as long as you carry an ax, shovel, and bucket for fire control.

Some falls in this book are located on private property. The traveler must exercise added responsibility in these areas. A land-owner may decide *not* to allow access, even though it was previously acceptable. "No Trespassing" signs must be heeded.

Because the rivers and streams of the Pacific Northwest tend to fluctuate dramatically and regularly each year, the majesty and accessibility of their waterfalls also vary seasonally. As a general rule, cataracts at low elevations should be visited from autumn through spring. Waterfalls at high elevations are usually limited to summer, due to snowpack during the rest of the year. For more specific information, you may wish to check with local officials about discharge levels before planning a trip.

Camping, hiking, and backpacking are not described in this book, since a great variety of books are available on these subjects. But when hiking, you should at least carry the "Ten Essentials" — sunglasses, knife, matches, firestarter, first-aid kit, flashlight, compass, a map, extra clothing, and extra food. Use a day pack or rucksack. And remember, *please don't litter.* Pick up after careless individuals who have come before you. The cleaner you leave our environment, the more beautiful and enjoyable it will be.

ACCESSIBILITY SYMBOLS

 Located within 0.25 mile of a road accessible by passenger vehicle. If not visible from the road, a well-developed trail leads to the falls.

 Located within 0.25 mile of a road recommended for four-wheel-drive vehicles. If not visible from the road, a well-developed trail leads to the falls.

 Located more than 0.25 mile from a road accessible by passenger vehicle. Developed trails provide good access for day hikers.

 Located many miles from a road accessible by passenger vehicle. Developed trails provide access for backpackers with supplies for overnight or multiple-night camping.

 Located in an undeveloped area. These are accessible from unmaintained pathways or by walking up drainages. See text for details on individual falls. A strong pair of hiking boots is recommended. *Not* recommended for young children; may be risky for nervous adults or those with physical limitations.

 Located adjacent to a lake, reservoir, or secluded river; primary access by some type of watercraft.

Some falls may have more than one symbol in order to further define accessibility. Examples:

 or

Accessible for ambitious day hikers, but backpacking is recommended for leisurely jaunts.

and
Accessible by hiking more than 0.5 mile from a road recommended for four-wheel-drive vehicles.

STARRED RATING SYSTEM

This is a subjective rating determined by the form and height of a waterfall, and by the scenery surrounding it. When viewing several descents in a short time, it is best to see the less spectacular ones first, then progress to the better falls.

Exceptional. Awe inspiring.

Very Good. Many of these would seem exceptional if not compared to the higher-rated falls.

Good. Scenic attractions for all.

Pretty. Nice background for a picnic.

Uninspiring. Probably not interesting except to waterfall collectors.

No Rating. Known to me only from maps or from reports by people who have visited the falls.

WATERFALL FORMS

Most falls have elements of more than one form; the symbol shows the most representative element of each waterfall.

Plunge. Descends vertically from a stream, losing contact with the bedrock surface.

Horsetail. Descends vertically from a stream, maintaining some contact with the bedrock surface.

Fan. Similar to the horsetail form, except that the breadth of spray increases downward.

Punchbowl. Descends from a constricted breadth of a stream into a pool below.

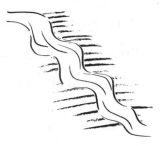

Cascade. Follows along a series of rock steps or along a dipping bedrock surface.

Block. Descends from a wide breadth of a stream.

Tiered. Descends from a distinct series of two or three falls, all visible from a single vantage point (double or triple).

Segmented. Descends as the stream diverges into two or three parts (twin or triplet).

THE MAPS

When used correctly, the maps in this book will lead you to falls, with a minimum of confusion. To locate a particular waterfall, first note the number of the subsection in which it occurs. Then, to find the general vicinity of the waterfall, locate that number on the regional map at the beginning of the appropriate chapter. Finally, you can pinpoint the location of the falls by using the appropriate detailed subsection map. Use a state highway map as an aid in route selection; directions to each fall are included with its description.

For the sake of consistency, and to reduce map-reading problems, each map has north oriented upward. Check the accuracy of your odometer, and make allowances if it is off. For a rough gauge of hiking distances, remember that an average person takes a half hour to hike 1 mile. The map key below shows the symbols used throughout the book.

As a further assistance to readers, USGS maps are listed for most of the waterfalls in this book. Some waterfalls occur in areas mapped with the newer, larger-scale USGS 7½-minute series; others in areas for which only the older, smaller-scale 15-minute maps exist. This information is included with most of the waterfall entries. Where no map is listed, either the falls are not indicated on the map or the 7½-minute map has yet to be published. As new maps appear, they will be listed in future printings.

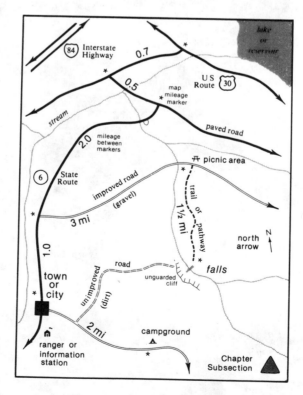

The North Cascades
of Washington

*T*he Cascade Range extends from British Columbia through Washington and Oregon to northern California. A progression of spectacular volcanic peaks towers above the range from north to south, with Mount Baker, Mount Rainier, and Mount Adams in Washington; Mount Hood, Three Sisters, and Mount McLaughlin in Oregon; and Mount Shasta in California. Since the Cascades encompass a large part of the Pacific Northwest and contain many waterfalls, the range has been divided into six chapters in this book.

The North Cascades include the central portion of Washington, starting at Interstate 90, which crosses Snoqualmie Pass, and covering the mountains north to the Canadian border. This region features three large national forests, three wilderness areas, two national recreation areas, and North Cascades National Park. Of the 95 falls mapped within the region, 56 are described in this chapter.

Aside from two volcanoes, Mount Baker and Glacier Peak, most of the mountains of the North Cascades are older than those of the range's southern extension. The North Cascades form a rugged and complex arrangement of various nonvolcanic materials. Large masses of granite are distributed within the region. Other rock forms found in the area include gneiss and schists. These rock types vary from 50 million to 500 million years in age, but their arrangement in the general mountainous terrain as seen today is due to uplifting over the past 10 million years.

Intensive glaciation accounts for the great relief from the region's peaks to its valleys. Four major periods of glacial activity occurred from 10,000 years to 2 million years ago. The heads of glaciers eroded into the mountains, sharpening their peaks, and extended to lower elevations, deepening and widening valleys.

The abundance of waterfalls in the North Cascades is largely due to the glacial scouring of the range's bedrock surfaces. Many descents plummet into *glacial troughs*, or valleys. *Wallace Falls* and *Rainbow Falls* (the one near Lake Chelan) are stunning examples. Others skip and bounce off rock walls into the troughs, for instance, *Bridal Veil Falls*, *Gate Creek Falls*, and *Preston Falls*.

Sometimes cataracts are associated with a rounded depression previously carved by the upper portion of a glacier. Water may pour into this *cirque* from ridgetops, or tumble from its outlet into a trough. *Falls of Horseshoe Basin* and *Twin Falls* (at Twin Falls Lake) are classic descents of this type.

◀ *Canyon Falls*

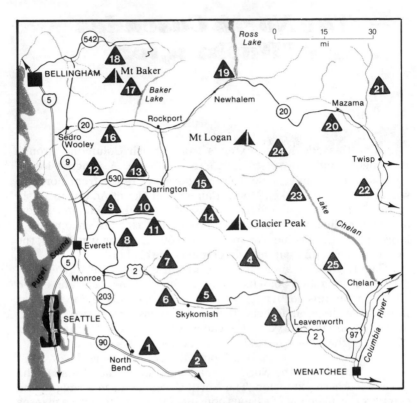

Glaciers may erode unevenly when carving out their *U*-shaped troughs. The streams that presently occupy the valley floors are called *misfit streams* and have falls where sharp drops occur. These descents are generally less dramatic than the types previously mentioned. Representative falls of this form include *Sunset Falls* and *Teepee Falls.*

1. NORTH BEND AREA

You should not be surprised, particularly in developed areas, to see hydroelectric facilities in association with waterfalls. A great amount of force is required to turn turbines for generating kilowatts of electricity. Because water can serve as that force, and its power is maximized where it is free-falling, falls sites can be desirable sources of energy. Water lines may be built into or beside the vertical escarpment and stream flow diverted to them. The scenic quality of the cataracts need not be lost, however, if enough water is allowed to continue its natural course. Such is the case, thankfully, for the following three entries.

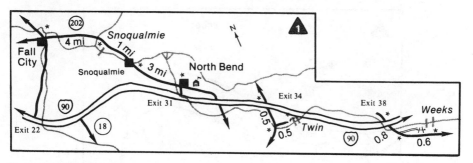

Snoqualmie Falls

Type: plunge; map: USGS Snoqualmie 7½'

This 268-foot plunge is one of Washington's most visited attractions. Puget Sound Power and Light Company preserves the integrity of the falls while diverting enough of the Snoqualmie River to provide power for 16,000 homes. The waterfall is located next to S.R. 202 between Fall City and Snoqualmie. There are several vantage points from the gorge rim. Snoqualmie Falls River Trail offers views from below the falls, requiring a steep 0.5-mile hike.

Twin Falls

Type: tiered; map: USGS Bandera 15'

When I last surveyed this entry, only a view of the 75- to 100-foot lower portion of this double waterfall was possible. Also known as *Upper Snoqualmie Falls*, both cataracts should be accessible by mid-1989 as trail improvements are made.

To reach Twin Falls State Park, leave Interstate 90 at Edgewick Road (Exit 34) and follow 468th Avenue SE for 0.5 mile. Turn left (east) at SE 159th Street and drive to its end. When I last visited, the 0.75-mile trail ended just before the falls came into view. If this is still the case, climb the ridge to your left, descend its other side, and ford the South Fork Snoqualmie River to its east bank, facing the base of the lower waterfall.

Weeks Falls

Type: cascade

A series of cascades descend 30 to 40 feet along South Fork Snoqualmie River. Depart Interstate 90 at the Forest Fire Training Center (Exit 38) and drive eastward for 0.8 mile to the obscurely signed entrance to Ollalie State Park. Continue 0.4 mile to an overlook of the falls. The Washington State Parks Commission is planning on constructing a trail from here to Twin Falls.

More cascades can be found by driving past the park entrance for 0.6 mile to the hydroelectric facility. When leaving the area, east-bounders must first go west on I-90, then use Exit 34 as a U-turn.

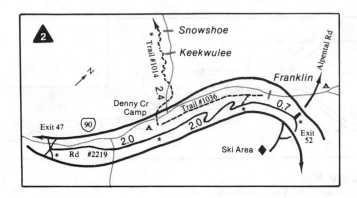

2. SNOQUALMIE PASS

This area's main campground has the unfavorable distinction of being between lanes of Interstate 90! Actually it's not as bad as it sounds, but the soft murmur of speeding traffic detracts from the natural setting. The campground, named Denny Creek, is the point of departure to the surrounding falls. Leave I-90 at Snoqualmie Pass Recreation Area (Exits 47 and 52) and follow Denny Creek Road #58 for 2 to 3 miles to the camp. Trailheads for the following falls are located 0.25 mile east of the camp.

Keekwulee Falls

Type: tiered; map: USGS Snoqualmie Pass 7½'

Begin hiking at Denny Creek Trailhead #1014. Cross South Fork Snoqualmie River once and Denny Creek twice, the second time at 1.5 miles. The trail ascends steeply 0.5 mile farther to the falls. Keekwulee is a Chinook word meaning "falling down."

Snowshoe Falls

Type: horsetail; map: USGS Snoqualmie Pass 7½'

Begin hiking at Denny Creek Trailhead #1014. Reach Keekwulee Falls after 2 miles. Continue hiking for almost 0.5 mile past Keekwulee Falls to this descent from Denny Creek. Snowshoe Falls and Keekwulee Falls were named in 1916 by The Mountaineers.

Franklin Falls

Type: plunge; map: USGS Snoqualmie 7½'

Start hiking at Franklin Falls Trailhead #1036, 0.25 mile east of the campground. After a leisurely 1.5-mile jaunt, reach a 70-foot falls on South Fork Snoqualmie River. An alternative route to the falls is via the historic Snoqualmie Pass Wagon Road. This route intersects Denny Creek Road #2219 about 2 miles east of the camp and leads to the falls in less than 300 yards.

▲ *Franklin Falls*

3. LEAVENWORTH AREA

Downtown Leavenworth is a place of Old World character. The traditional storefronts and the surrounding alpine setting are reminiscent of Bavaria. Enjoy seasonal activities such as the Mai Fest, Autumn Leaf Festival, and Christmas Lighting.

Drury Falls

Type: horsetail; map: USGS Leavenworth 15'

Fall Creek drops over the cliffs of Tumwater Canyon into the Wenatchee River. For views of the cataract from across the river, drive 6 miles northwest of Leavenworth along U.S. 2. The site is 1 mile southwest of Swiftwater Picnic Area.

4. LAKE WENATCHEE

Lake Wenatchee is a popular vacation area for family camping, with several campsites on the eastern shore. Drive 14 miles northwest of Leavenworth along U.S. 2 to S.R. 207, then 5 miles north to the eastern end of the lake. All the area's falls are located a short distance upriver from the lake's western extreme.

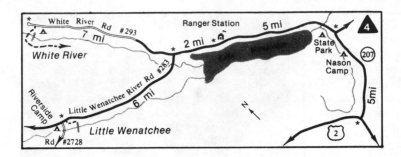

Little Wenatchee Falls
Type: cascade

Turn off S.R. 207 onto Little Wenatchee River Road #283. In 6 miles Road #283 meets with Rainy Creek Road #2728. Park at the junction and backtrack about 150 feet to an undesignated trail. A short walk farther, Little Wenatchee River tumbles over a series of rock steps.

White River Falls
Type: punchbowl; map: USGS Wenatchee Lake 15'

Although this 60- to 100-foot cataract is near a roadway, you must hike to find a good view. Drive to the end of White River Road #293 and park. Follow Panther Creek Trail #1502 across White River, then downstream. In 1 mile, a spur trail to the left leads to good views of the falls. At White River Falls Campground, adults can climb on chunks of bedrock for obstructed overviews of the descent. Be careful! This is definitely not a place for fooling around.

5. STEVENS PASS

Many waterfalls beckon from the roadside as you drive west on U.S. 2 over the 4,061-foot elevation of Stevens Pass.

Deception Falls
Type: cascade; map: USGS Scenic 7½'

Deception Creek steeply cascades 30 to 60 feet. Drive on U.S. 2 to Deception Falls Picnic Area, 8 miles west of Stevens Pass and 10 miles east of Skykomish. There is a parking area across the highway from the falls.

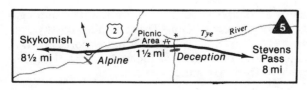

Alpine Falls
Type: segmented; map: USGS Scenic 7½'

A very short trail leads to the top of this 30- to 50-foot descent. Drive west on U.S. 2 about 8.5 miles east of Skykomish and 9.5 miles west of Stevens Pass. Park at the turnout just past the bridge crossing Tye River. Determined bushwhackers can find good views of Alpine Falls by hiking down the slope to the river from the far end of the turnout.

6. INDEX

Eagle Falls
Type: cascade; map: USGS Index 15'

Drive U.S. 2 about 9 miles west of Skykomish, or 4 miles east of Index to the parking turnout closest to mile marker 39. A path immediately east of the marker leads to a noisy 25- to 40-foot cascade along South Fork Skykomish River. National Forest maps incorrectly show this descent at the site of Canyon Falls; Eagle Falls is actually farther upstream.

Canyon Falls
Type: punchbowl; map: USGS Index 15'

The geology of this waterfall is very interesting. Granite, which is common in the North Cascades region, decomposes grain by grain when united with water. As a stream flows over granitic outcrops, its boulders are chemically smoothed and hollowed by the water, often in unusual shapes. South Fork Skykomish River has physically eroded and widened a fracture in the granite to form Canyon Falls, dramatically illustrating how running water can modify a landscape both chemically and physically.

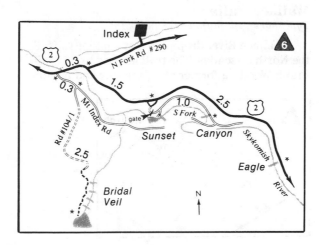

Turn off U.S. 2 between mile markers 36 and 37, about 1.5 miles east of Index and 2.5 miles west of Eagle Falls. Follow the private road about 0.2 mile and park where a gate blocks the way. The falls are about 1 mile down the drive. Bear left at the fork at the start of the walk. Close-up views are possible, but be careful. Stay away from the slippery, moss-covered boulders and bare rocks that slope toward the river.

Sunset Falls
Type: cascade; map: USGS Index 15'

The South Fork Skykomish River slides 60 to 100 feet in impressive fashion. Follow the directions to Canyon Falls (above), but take the right fork at the beginning of the walk. The descent is less than 0.25 mile away. For views from the other side of the river, drive along Mount Index Road, which is described in the Bridal Veil Falls entry (below).

Bridal Veil Falls
Type: tiered; map: USGS Index 15'

Water pours off Mount Index in four parts, each descending 100 to 200 feet along Bridal Veil Creek. Leave U.S. 2 at Mount Index Road, immediately south of the bridge over South Fork Skykomish River. Turn right (south) in 0.3 mile on Road #104/1. Only high-clearance vehicles can follow the entire 1.5-mile length of the road. Most automobiles park after 1 mile. A hiking trail begins at the road's end and ascends moderately to the first of the cataracts in 1 mile. The falls are also visible from the main highway, appearing as silvery white threads.

7. GOLD BAR

Wallace Falls
Type: horsetail; map: USGS Index 15'

Wallace River drops 250 feet, making the falls one of the tallest in the North Cascades. The trail leading to it is called Woody Trail after Frank Woody, a former state senator and lifelong outdoorsman.

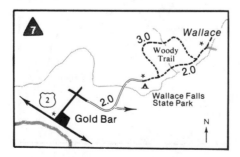

Wallace Falls State Park, opened in 1977, is a popular camping and hiking attraction along the U.S. 2 corridor. Leave the highway at Gold Bar and follow the signs 2 miles to the park. The trailhead to the cataract begins past the campsite area. It soon diverges, the right fork ascending moderately, while the left goes up at a gentler rate. The trails converge after 1 mile on the steeper path or 2 miles on the gradual path. There is a picnic area and a first view of the falls a short distance farther, and a favorite viewpoint 0.5 mile beyond. The trail continues up above the falls to a vista of the Skykomish Valley.

8. ROESIGER LAKE
Explorer Falls
Type: horsetail

Drive 13 miles north from Monroe on Woods Creek Road to cottage-lined Roesiger Lake. Or reach the lake by driving about 8 miles south from Granite Falls on Lake Roesiger Road. Turn east on

▲ *Wallace Falls*

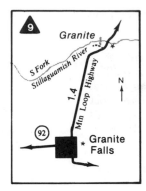

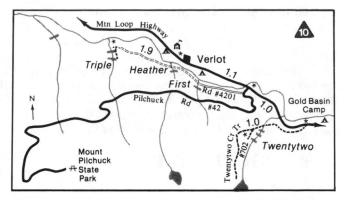

the gravel Monroe Camp Road from Lake Roesiger Road. Ignore spur roads as you leave and reenter wooded tracts. After 3.5 miles, park at a gravel pit on the right side of the road. Hike upstream a few hundred feet to an exposed view of an unnamed tributary of Woods Creek dropping 50 to 70 feet from a cliff. The falls are perfect for taking an invigorating shower.

9. GRANITE FALLS

Granite Falls
Type: cascade; map: USGS Granite Falls 15'

The community of Granite Falls is named after these cascades, located 1.5 miles north of town on the Mountain Loop Highway, the extension of S.R. 92. Water froths along South Fork Stillaguamish River in a series of descents totaling 30 to 40 feet. A short trail leads to the falls from a parking area on the south side of a bridge crossing the river. A 580-foot fishway connects the top and bottom parts of the river via a 240-foot tunnel, allowing salmon to bypass the cascades and proceed upstream to spawn.

10. ROBE VALLEY

Waterfalls abound in this area, where creeks flow from Mount Pilchuck into the South Fork of the Stillaguamish River. Follow the Mountain Loop Highway 10 miles northeast from Granite Falls to the Verlot Ranger Station and townsite. After the main road crosses the South Fork Stillaguamish about 1 mile east of the ranger station, make two successive right turns — the first on Pilchuck State Park Road #42, the second on gravel Monte Cristo Grade Road #4201.

First Falls
Type: horsetail

The 30- to 40-foot cataract drops along an unnamed creek 0.4 mile beyond the turnoff from Pilchuck Road. This waterfall has no official name, so I've named it for being the first falls encountered along Road #4201.

Heather Creek Falls

Type: cascade

Water tumbles 60 to 100 feet along Heather Creek. Drive on Road #4201 for 0.6 mile past First Falls (above) to a small pond. Hike along its far (west) bank to a series of cascades, the pond's source of water.

Triple Creek Falls

Type: fan

Drive along Road #4201 to its end 0.9 mile past Heather Creek Falls. Walk along a well-worn path for 200 yards to this 15- to 25-foot drop. A 40-foot upper falls are accessible by climbing (no trail) a few hundred feet upstream.

Twentytwo Creek Falls

Type: tiered

A series of three falls is accessible from trails within Lake Twentytwo Research Natural Area. Drive along Mountain Loop Highway 2 miles past the Verlot Ranger Station to Twentytwo Creek Trailhead #702. The lowest falls are encountered after 0.5 mile of easy walking and 0.5 mile of moderately strenuous hiking. A short distance farther, follow short spur trails to view the two other falls.

▲ *Twentytwo Creek Falls*

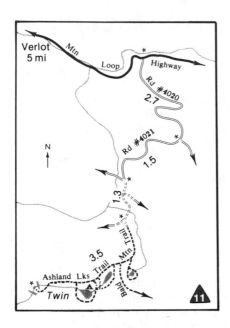

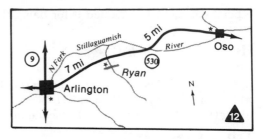

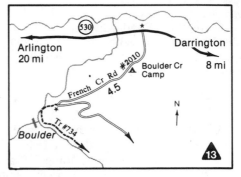

11. TWIN FALLS LAKE

Twin Falls
Type: tiered

Spend the day hiking to a unique double falls whose waters pause between descents in minuscule Twin Falls Lake. Wilson Creek drops 125 feet into the pool, then tumbles another 400 feet from the outlet. The trail system on this state-owned land was built by the Department of Natural Resources.

Drive about 5 miles east of the Verlot Ranger Station along the Mountain Loop Highway Road #4020, labeled Bear Lake Trail and Bald Mountain Trail. In 2.75 miles turn right (east) at the junction of Road #4021. Drive to the next fork in 1.5 miles and turn left at the Bald Mountain Trail sign. Ignore the many short spurs along the final 1.25 miles. Turn right at the Y in 0.25 mile, then left again in another 0.75 mile. The Bald Mountain Trailhead is located at the end of this steep 0.25-mile road.

Hike 0.75 mile along Bald Mountain Trail to Beaver Plant Lake. Soon after, take the right fork on Ashland Lakes Trail. Pass both Upper and Lower Ashland Lakes in 2 miles. There are campsites at both lakes. Twin Falls Lake and its falls are 1.5 miles beyond Lower Ashland Lake.

12. ARLINGTON AREA

Ryan Falls
Type: horsetail

This waterfall is located on private property, but can be seen from the main highway. Water slides 50 to 75 feet down a hillside along an unnamed creek. Take S.R. 530 almost 7 miles northeast from Arlington. The falls, just west of mile marker 28, are at their best during late autumn, according to the landowner.

13. BOULDER CREEK

Boulder Falls
Type: plunge; map: USGS Granite Falls 15'

An unnamed creek curtains 80 feet over a cliff into Boulder Creek. Take S.R. 530 to French Creek Road #2010, located 8 miles west of Darrington, or 20 miles east of Arlington, and turn south. After 4.5 miles, the gravel road takes a sharp turn. The Boulder Creek Trail #734 sign is at the apex of the bend. The falls are an easy 1-mile walk ahead across the river from the trail. This waterfall is incorrectly marked on National Forest and USGS topographic maps.

14. SAUK RIVER DRAINAGE

Asbestos Creek Falls
Type: cascade

From Darrington follow Sauk River Road #20 south 2.5 miles to Clear Creek Road #2060 and turn right. Drive another 2.5 miles to where Asbestos Creek flows beneath the gravel road. The steep cascades are a few hundred feet upstream.

North Fork Falls
Type: punchbowl; map: USGS Sloan Peak 7½'

Water thunders 60 to 80 feet along North Fork Sauk River. From Darrington take Sauk River Road #20 south for 15.5 miles to North Fork Road #49. Turn left and drive 1.2 miles to the sign for Trail #660. Hike 0.25 mile to an overlook of the falls. North Fork Road #49 can also be reached from Verlot; drive east 27 miles along Mountain Loop Highway, which begins as S.R. 92, and turn right.

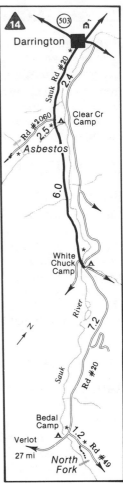

▲   *North Fork Falls*

15. SUIATTLE RIVER DRAINAGE

Suiattle Falls
Type: tiered

This double cascade falls a total of 70 to 100 feet along an unnamed creek from Suiattle Mountain. Take the Darrington-Rockport Road 6.5 miles north of Darrington or 12 miles south of Rockport to the bridge crossing the Sauk River. About 0.25 mile east of the bridge, turn east on Suiattle River Road #26. Drive 2.75 miles to a turnout on the right side of the road. Walk to the drainage just crossed and scramble 100 feet upstream to the falls. The waterfall has no official name, so I have called it by the name of the nearby mountain and river.

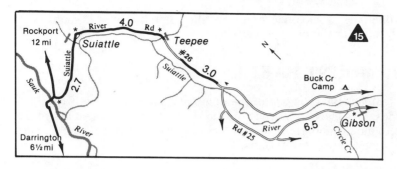

Teepee Falls

Type: cascade; map: USGS Prairie Mountain 7½'

Follow the directions to Suiattle Falls (above) and continue along Suiattle River Road #26 for 4 more miles. Teepee Falls is a 50- to 60-foot series of cascades located directly under the bridge spanning the chasm of Big Creek.

Gibson Falls

Type: fan; map: USGS Huckleberry Mountain 7½'

A narrow fan of water glistens in a dimly lit recess. Follow the directions to Teepee Falls (above) and continue 3 miles more to the Suiattle River, next to the junction of Road #25. The falls are hidden along an unnamed creek 6.5 miles up Road #25. A dip in the bridge over Circle Creek is a good reference point. Drive 0.1 mile past this point to the next drainage and park. Follow the creek upstream 200 feet to the base of the falls.

16. SAUK VALLEY

Marietta Falls

Type: tiered

This 100- to 125-foot double waterfall plunges at the end of its final descent. Take S.R. 20 to Sauk Valley Road, 1 mile west of Concrete, and turn south. After crossing the Skagit River, bear right (west). Marietta Creek is a total of 8 miles from the junction of Sauk Valley Road and S.R. 20.

Park at the undesignated area immediately west of the bridge. The falls is 0.25 mile upstream. The hike is enjoyable, but requires

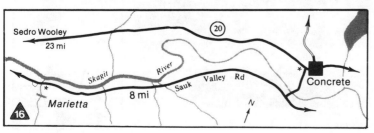

fording the creek once or twice and climbing over a small rock outcrop near the base of the falls.

17. MOUNT BAKER

Mount Baker is one of the dominant features of the North Cascades. This glacier-covered volcano rises thousands of feet above the surrounding mountains. Meltwaters from its northeast-facing glaciers feed the following waterfalls.

Rainbow Falls
Type: plunge; map: USGS Mt Shuksan 15'

At Concrete, turn north from the North Cascades Highway, S.R. 20, onto Baker Lake Road #11. (Eastbounders can take a short-cut to

▲ *Nooksack Falls*

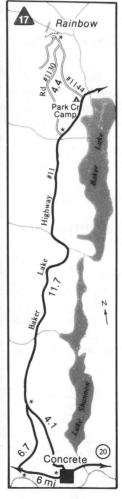

Road #11 by using the signed turnoff 6 miles west of Concrete.) After 16 or 18.5 miles, depending upon the route taken, turn left (north) on Road #1130. There are views of Mount Baker and Mount Shuksan before the turn. Follow Road #1130 for 4.4 miles to the signed parking for the falls. A few steps away is a cross-canyon vista of Rainbow Creek pouring 150 feet into a gorge. Most of the cataract is visible from the overlook, with the bottom portion hidden by vegetation and the canyon escarpment.

18. NOOKSACK RIVER

Nooksack Falls

Type: segmented; map: USGS Mt Baker 15'

To reach this explosive 170-foot waterfall, drive 34 miles east of Bellingham along S.R. 542 to the hamlet of Glacier and continue 7 miles east to Wells Creek Road #33. Turn right here and drive 0.5 mile to where Nooksack Falls and its adjacent cousin, **Lower Wells Creek Falls,** descend into the river. Do not cross the bridge over Nooksack River or you will miss the cataracts. While the owner, Puget Sound Power and Light, has constructed an observation platform, only partial views are possible. The most dramatic view of this raging torrent would be from the bottom of the gorge, but there is currently no access.

Wells Creek Falls

Type: plunge

A beautiful 80- to 100-foot plunge, except the roadside view is somewhat distant and obscured. Follow the directions to Nooksack Falls (above) and continue 4.6 miles more on Wells Creek Road #33 to the falls, with a view of Mount Baker along the way. Better vantages of the falls require walking and scrambling along the creek, so plan on getting wet (only waterproof gear should be carried along). Curiously, this waterfall was not previously named, even though inaccessible **Mazama Falls** occurs a few miles upstream.

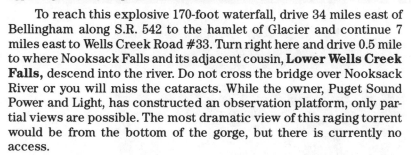

19. ROSS LAKE NATIONAL RECREATION AREA

North Cascades National Park is bisected by Ross Lake National Recreation Area and its three reservoirs — Gorge Lake, Diablo Lake,

▲ *Gorge Creek Falls*

and Ross Lake. Reach this rugged portion of Washington via the North Cascades Highway (S.R. 20), normally open June through October.

Ladder Creek Falls
Type: tiered; map: USGS Diablo Dam 7½'

This series of falls is unique because Seattle City Light illuminates them at night with colored lights. Take S.R. 20 to the eastern part of Newhalem and park near the Gorge Powerhouse. Walk across the footbridge spanning Skagit River and follow the trail through a landscaped rock garden. The major falls, totaling 80 to 120 feet, highlight the short walk along with many miniature cataracts also to be seen.

Gorge Creek Falls
Type: tiered

Gorge Creek streams down 120 to 150 feet in three portions. Take S.R. 20 to the eastern part of Newhalem and continue 2.6 miles eastward from the Gorge Powerhouse to a parking area on the near (west) side of Gorge Creek Bridge. There are views from the bridge walkway, with two smaller falls adjacent to the featured one.

Ketchum Creek Falls
Type: horsetail

Take S.R. 20 to the eastern part of Newhalem and continue east 3.6 miles to this 80- to 100-foot cataract. Park at the undesignated turnout on the far (east) side of the creek.

John Pierce Falls
Type: horsetail; map: USGS Ross Dam 7½'

Water slides 40 to 50 feet toward Diablo Lake. Drive east on S.R. 20 for 3.5 miles from Colonial Creek Camp, or west for 0.5 mile past the junction for Ross Dam, to an undesignated turnout on the northeast side of the highway. Although the drainage extends 400 to 450 feet further down, it is usually dry, its runoff absorbed by the rocky substrate. Also known as *Pierce Falls* and *Horsetail Falls*.

Skymo Creek Falls
Type: horsetail

Skymo Creek rushes into Ross Lake about halfway up the reservoir. To reach Ross Dam and Ross Lake Resort, take a tugboat from Diablo Lake or hike 1 mile from the North Cascades Highway as shown on the map. Rent a boat at the resort. Unfortunately, there are no launching facilities for private craft. The falls are on the west shore of the lake across from aptly named Tenmile Island.

20. METHOW VALLEY

Mazama represents the eastern outpost for travel along the North Cascades Highway (S.R. 20). For westbound travelers, it has the last

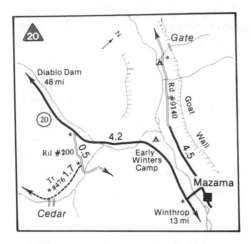

facilities for 75 miles. The two falls located in the area are both within Okanogan National Forest, as are the entries under the Chewuch River Drainage and Foggy Dew Creek subsections of this chapter.

Cedar Creek Falls
Type: tiered; map: USGS Mazama 15'

The creek has cut deeply into granite bedrock to form this series of 20- to 30-foot cataracts. Drive 4.2 miles west of Mazama along S.R. 20 and turn left (south) on Sandy Butte– Cedar Creek Road #200. Follow this gravel route for 0.5 mile and park near the marked Cedar Creek Trail #476 leading to the right. The trail ascends moderately 1.7 miles to the falls.

Gate Creek Falls
Type: cascade; map: USGS Mazama 15'

This 100-foot drop skips down a portion of Goat Wall, a glaciated cliff rising 2,000 feet above the Methow Valley floor. Drive to an informal campsite located along West Fork Methow Road #9140, 4.5 miles north of S.R. 20. Find the creek on the far side of the camp and climb a rigorous 0.25 mile upstream along a steep *talus* (rocky) slope. Scramble up this jumble to see the stream's descent from Goat Wall. The falls aren't very impressive, but the valley view is nice. Recommended only for those who like climbing rocks.

21. CHEWUCH RIVER DRAINAGE

Falls Creek Falls
Type: horsetail; map: USGS Doe Mtn 15'

A refreshing 35- to 50-foot drop along Falls Creek. Turn north off S.R. 20 on Chewuch Road #51, located just west of the frontier-style town of Winthrop. Drive 11.5 miles to Falls Creek Campground. An access trail along the south side of the creek leads quickly to water pouring from faulted (fractured) bedrock.

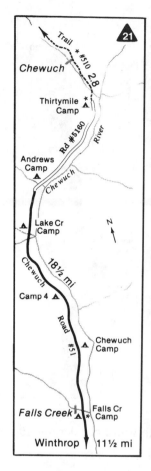

▲   *Falls Creek Falls*

Chewuch Falls
Map: USGS Coleman Peak 7½'

Chewuch River descends 30 feet over granite benches. Drive a short distance past Thirtymile Campground to the end of Chewuch Road, labeled #5160 along the northern portion of road, and park. Hike 2.8 miles along Thirtymile Trail #510 to the falls. At one time the falls' name was spelled, phonetically, *Chewack Falls.*

22. FOGGY DEW CREEK

Foggy Dew Falls
Type: horsetail; map: USGS Martin Peak 7½'

Take S.R. 153 to Gold Creek Road #4340, about halfway between the towns of Twisp and Pateros, and turn west. Go 5 miles and turn left (south) on Foggy Dew Creek Road #200. The trailhead is 4 miles farther, at the end of the road. A moderate 2.5-mile hike along Foggy

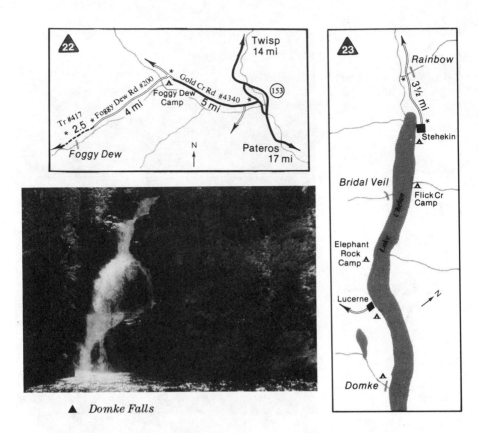

▲ *Domke Falls*

Dew Trail #417 brings you to the falls, where water accelerates 100 feet through a narrow chute.

23. LAKE CHELAN

Lake Chelan is a classic example of a large *paternoster lake*. It is the result of a *terminal moraine* formed by the accumulation of rock debris deposited at the end of a glacier. The glacier carved out the Chelan Valley 10,000 to 12,000 years ago. The moraine acts as a natural dam for meltwater entering the valley from the adjacent snow-laden mountains. The lake is 51 miles long and attains a depth of over 1,500 feet. It is one of the largest alpine lakes in the continental United States.

Rainbow Falls
Type: tiered; map: USGS Stehekin 7½'

Rainbow Creek drops 470 feet with a main plunge of 312 feet. Board Lake Chelan Boat Company's *Lady of the Lake,* or pilot your own craft from Chelan to the secluded village of Stehekin. Once in Stehekin, bus service is available to shuttle visitors 3.5 miles to the falls.

Bridal Veil Falls
Type: horsetail; map: USGS Stehekin 7½'

This 50- to 75-foot waterfall is distantly visible to the west from the tour boat on the return trip from Stehekin to Lucerne. Bridal Veil Falls earns a higher rating if you have a private boat to approach it more closely.

Domke Falls
Type: fan; map: USGS Lucerne 15'

Water rushes 30 to 50 feet into Lake Chelan from Domke Creek. The tour boat passes near the falls, located to the west, on the return trip from Lucerne to Chelan. The falls and the creek are named for the first settler in the vicinity.

24. NORTH CASCADES NATIONAL PARK

While the majority of national parks within the continental United States have developed routes for motorized travel, North Cascades National Park remains overwhelmingly wilderness in character. The remote Stehekin River Road, one of only two gravel roads entering the park, allows access to five falls in the park's southeast sector. Take the Lake Chelan Boat Company's *Lady of the Lake* from Chelan to Stehekin. A shuttle service transports hikers and backpackers to various campsites and trailheads along the road.

Amazingly, there are no symbols for falls on the USGS topographic maps of the national park. Perhaps the remoteness of the North Cascades explains this omission. I would not be surprised if the area actually has hundreds of waterfalls.

Carwash Falls
Type: horsetail

McGregor Creek falls 40 to 60 feet before splashing next to Stehekin River Road. If you get wet 2 miles past High Bridge, you have obviously not missed this aptly named waterfall.

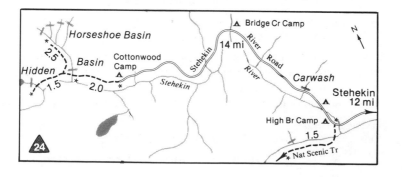

Basin Creek Falls
Type: plunge

Take a shuttle bus to its farthest destination at Cottonwood Camp. Hike 1.2 miles west from the camp to a distant view of and 125- to 175-foot drop of Basin Creek. Best vantage is 50 yards downstream from Basin Creek swinging bridge.

Falls of Horseshoe Basin
Type: segmented

An entire series of waterfalls pours off the surrounding mountain ridges into Horseshoe Basin. This is a good example of a *cirque*, a bowl-shaped depression eroded by the upper portion of a former alpine glacier.

From Basin Creek Falls, a 2-mile hike (see directions above), continue hiking for 0.5 mile to a fork in the trail. Bear right and follow switchbacks steeply upward, meeting Basin Creek in less than 0.5 mile. The basin and falls are 1.5 miles farther.

Doubtful Creek Falls
Type: tiered

The outlet of Doubtful Lake pours down a mountainside as a series of 20- to 50-foot cataracts. Hike 1.7 miles on the main trail to the fork to Horseshoe Basin (see directions above), then continue on the left fork 1 mile to the crossing of Doubtful Creek. Waterfalls directly above and below the ford.

Hidden Falls
Type: cascade

Water cascades 250 to 300 feet from the meltwaters of Yawning Glacier. Hike to Doubtful Creek (see directions above) and look across the valley at the falls with Pelton Peak as a backdrop.

25. ENTIAT VALLEY

Apple orchards are common along the fertile plain of the lower Entiat Valley. Farther upstream the valley becomes less gentle and the orchards give way to coniferous forest. The upper valley has three scenic, though not overwhelming, waterfalls.

Preston Falls
Type: horsetail; map: USGS Brief 7½'

Preston Creek slides 75 to 100 feet down the mountainside. To reach it, turn west off U.S. 97 onto Entiat River Road #371 less than 1 mile south of Entiat. Reach Ardenvoir in 8.5 miles and the falls 13.5 miles farther, approximately 1.25 miles past Entiat Valley Ski Area.

Silver Falls
Type: block; map: USGS Silver Falls 7½'

Take U.S. 97 to Entiat River Road #371 and turn west. Drive 31 miles along Road #371, which becomes Wenatchee National Forest Road #51. There is a good, but distant roadside view of the cataract from Silver Falls Service Station. Silver Falls National Recreation Trail ascends 0.5 mile to the base of the cliff from which Silver Creek drops 100 to 140 feet. The trail is dedicated to J. Kenneth and Opal F. Blair, stewards of public lands during the 1950s and 1960s.

Entiat Falls

Type: block; map: USGS Silver Falls 7½'

The Entiat River breaks over a rock ledge and thunders 30 feet to boulders below. The waterfall is most impressive during spring high water periods. Drive 3 miles northwest of Silver Falls (see directions above) to Entiat Falls Viewpoint. Entiat is an Indian word meaning "rapid water."

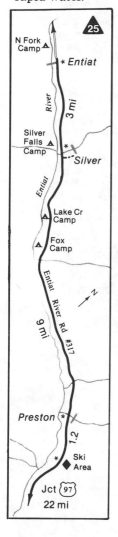

▲ *Silver Falls*

The Olympics and Vicinity

*T*he Olympic Peninsula is dominated by the mountains that rise 6,000 to 8,000 feet above its coastal margins. This abrupt relief causes moist air masses moving into the area to produce some of the highest annual precipitation in the continental United States. Normal figures reach 140 inches of rain on the Pacific Coast and 40 feet of snow in the high mountains. Most precipitation occurs from November to April.

Many small glaciers lie on the northern flanks of the highest mountains. Meltwater from the glaciers as well as from snowfields feeds the region's rivers and streams during the drier summer season. As a result, the larger watersheds throughout the Olympics drain liberally year-round. An abundance of water flowing over a mountainous landscape dissected by glaciation has created most of the 46 waterfalls that have been mapped throughout the peninsula. This chapter describes 30 of the falls.

The Olympic Mountains are quite youthful geologically. The range was formed by forced uplift of a contact zone between two large *crustal plates* of the earth's exterior. The collision of these plates began about 70 million years ago and has continued the mountain-building process to the present. During the four Ice Age episodes between 2 million and 10,000 years ago, alpine glaciers stretched to lower elevations than today, carving large *U-shaped valleys*. Major rivers presently rush along the base of these glacial troughs, sometimes descending over rocks that erode at unequal rates. More common are the falls created when tributary streams pour over the steep sides of glacial troughs on their way to the valley floors.

Gigantic continental glaciers played an important role in shaping Puget Sound and the Strait of Juan de Fuca. The Laurentide Ice Sheet covered almost all of Canada and the northern tier of the eastern United States about 10,000 years ago. A lobe of this massive glacial system extended into western Washington and gouged out large expanses of the former "Puget Lowland." As the glacier retreated, ocean water inundated the land area that had been eroded below sea level. The familiar water bodies we know today are the result. Vashon, Bainbridge, Whidbey, and Camano islands to the east and the San Juan Islands to the north represent erosional remnants of the preglacial landscape. They were not denudated, or eroded away, by the Puget Lobe.

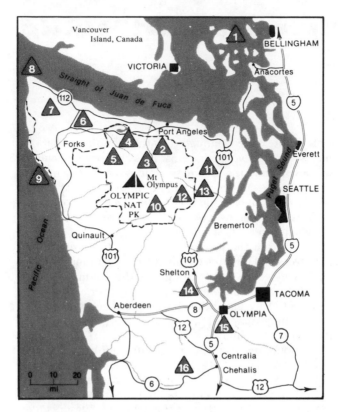

Coastal waterfalls are also distributed around the Olympic Peninsula. Along the northwestern portion of the coast, small streams tumble over marine cliffs carved by the wave action of the sea. Although most of these falls are visible only from watercraft, a few are accessible by trail.

1. ORCAS ISLAND

The San Juan Islands are one of the most beautiful archipelagos in the world. Orcas Island, the largest of the chain's 172 islands, has four miniature waterfalls. Board a Washington state ferry at Anacortes. After an enjoyable hour and a half spent churning across Puget Sound, get off at Orcas Landing. Follow Horseshoe Highway 12.75 miles north, passing the hamlets of Westsound, Crow Valley, and Eastsound before arriving at Moran State Park. Drive 1.25 miles within the park to a turnout at a marked trailhead. The waterfalls drop into Cascade Creek as you hike the Cascade Creek Trail.

Rustic Falls
Type: fan; map: USGS Mt Constitution 7½'

This small 5- to 10-foot cataract is usually the first of the falls seen along Cascade Creek Trail. Follow the short spur trail from the

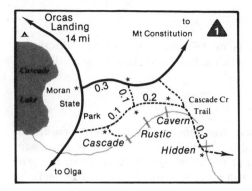

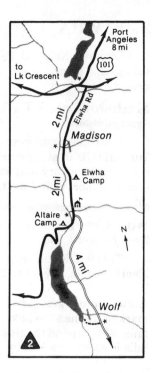

road into the small canyon. Cascade Creek and Rustic Falls are in 0.1 mile.

Cavern Falls
Type: cascade; map: USGS Mt Constitution 7½'

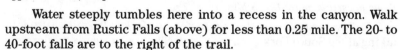

Water steeply tumbles here into a recess in the canyon. Walk upstream from Rustic Falls (above) for less than 0.25 mile. The 20- to 40-foot falls are to the right of the trail.

Hidden Falls
Type: horsetail; map: USGS Mt Constitution 7½'

This 15- to 20-foot drop is "hidden" only if you are not observant. Continue walking upstream along Cascade Creek Trail. Cross the creek twice. The second crossing is above the top of the falls, 0.6 miles from the trailhead.

Cascade Falls
Type: fan; map: USGS Mt Constitution 7½'

This is the largest waterfall on Orcas Island. Its form is actually fan-shaped; the name is derived from the creek. Follow the access trail from the road into a small canyon with a streamside trail. A short spur trail leads toward the base of the falls.

2. ELWHA

Olympic National Park is best known for its lush rain-forest valleys and snow-topped mountains, but its beautiful waterfalls also deserve attention.

Madison Creek Falls

Type: horsetail

Most motorists never see this obscure 40- to 50-foot cataract. Turn off U.S. 101 at the marked Elwha Valley entrance. Drive 2 miles to the park boundary and stop at an undesignated turnout to the left (east). A short walk from the road into a wooded tract brings the falls into view.

Wolf Creek Falls

Type: horsetail; map: USGS Hurricane Hill 7½'

This is a double falls, but only the 30- to 40-foot lower descent is clearly visible. The 50- to 70-foot upper portion is hidden by the gorge. Drive 2 miles beyond the park boundary, turning left past the ranger station onto a gravel road. In 4 miles, park along the turnout at the marked trailhead to Lake Mills. Follow the steep trail to its end in 0.4 mile. Walk around the ridge to the right to Wolf Creek. The base of the falls is easily reached by going upstream less than 100 feet.

3. MOUNT CARRIE AREA

To reach the trail system leading to the following falls, stay on the paved Elwha Road to its end. The north shore of Lake Mills is 2 miles past the ranger station. Boulder Creek Camp and Boulder Creek Trailhead are 7.5 miles farther.

Lower Boulder Creek Falls

Type: horsetail; map: USGS Mt Carrie 7½'

Follow the trail past the campsites to a fork in 0.6 mile. Turn left, hiking along South Fork Boulder Creek. The trail ascends moderately for 0.6 mile, then intersects a short spur trail leading to the falls. Water cascades 25 to 35 feet into Boulder Creek Gorge.

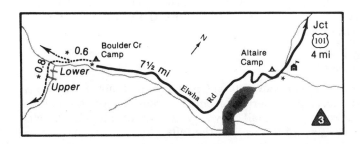

▲ *Lower Boulder Creek Falls*

Upper Boulder Creek Falls
Type: tiered; map: USGS Mt Carrie 7½'

Take the Boulder Creek Trail 1.2 miles to Lower Boulder Creek Falls (see directions above). Continue along the trail for 0.25 mile past the lower descent to a second marked spur trail. The short path leads between a set of falls. Upstream are 15- to 25-foot cascades, while downstream the top of a 75- to 100-foot plunge is visible.

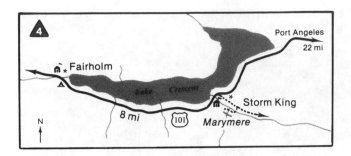

4. LAKE CRESCENT

Marymere Falls
Type: tiered; map: USGS Lake Crescent 7½'

Falls Creek plunges and horsetails 90 feet over a rock wall. Drive 14 miles west from Elwha Valley on U.S. 101 or 8 miles east from Fairholm. Storm King Visitor Center and Ranger Station, across the highway from Lake Crescent, is the starting point for the Marymere Falls Nature Trail, which leads 0.75 mile to the falls. Take a self-guided tour or accompany a scheduled group.

5. SOLEDUCK

There are two waterfalls along the Soleduck River drainage. Drive 1.75 miles west of Fairholm on U.S. 101 to Soleduck Road, which leads to Soleduck Hot Springs resort in 12 miles and the road's end 1.5 miles farther. The Soleduck Trail starts here.

Soleduck Falls
Type: segmented; map: USGS Bogachiel Peak 7½'

The Soleduck River turns at a right angle, where its waters rush 40 to 60 feet downward. Hike 1 mile from the Soleduck Trailhead at the end of the paved road, then turn right (south). The falls can be seen from the footbridge crossing the river. Soleduck is an English variant of the Indian phrase "Sol Duc," meaning "magic waters."

Bridge Creek Falls
Map: USGS Mt Carrie 7½'

Obtain a backcountry permit at Soleduck Ranger Station and proceed along Soleduck Trail, passing the junction to Soleduck Falls in 1 mile. Travel 4 miles farther to a second fork. Bear right, heading toward Soleduck Park and High Divide. The trail crosses the river in 1 mile and follows Bridge Creek. The cataract is less than 0.25 mile away. Campfires are prohibited in this area of the park. A portable stove is a necessity if you plan to cook.

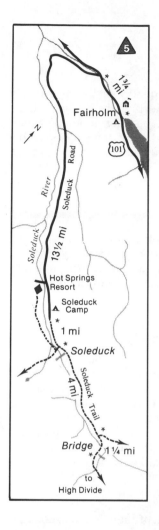

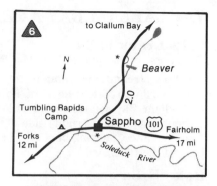

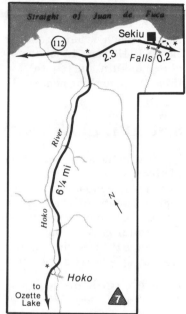

6. BEAVER CREEK

Beaver Falls

Type: segmented; map: USGS Lake Pleasant 7½'

Beaver Creek tumbles 30 to 40 feet in three sections across an 80-foot-wide rock escarpment. Turn off U.S. 101 at Sappho 12 miles north of Forks and 17 miles west of Fairholm. Follow the northbound secondary road 2 miles to an undesignated turnout 0.1 mile past Beaver Creek bridge. A short, unimproved path leads to the base of the cataract.

7. CLALLAM BAY AREA

Falls Creek Falls
Type: horsetail; map: USGS Clallam Bay 7½'

Low streamflows reduce the scenic quality of this previously unnamed 25- to 35-foot descent. Follow S.R. 112 to the seaside village of Clallam Bay. Continue 1.6 miles west, parking at an unsigned turnout on the north (right) side of the road. Walk down a jeep trail a short distance, passing beneath the highway and progressing to the base of the falls.

Hoko Falls
Type: punchbowl; map: USGS Hoko Falls 7½'

The calm waters of Hoko River momentarily rush 5 to 10 feet at a narrow reach where erosion-resistant rock constricts the stream. Take S.R. 112 west 4.1 miles past Clallam Bay, passing the resort town of Seiko. Turn left (south) for Ozette Lake and drive 6.25 miles to Hoko River, parking near the bridge. Fishermen's paths lead down to the base of the falls.

8. CAPE FLATTERY

One of the most rugged sections of the Washington coast is Cape Flattery, where the Strait of Juan de Fuca merges with the Pacific Ocean. While most visitors take to the sea for fishing excursions, the scenic beauty of the cape's coast, accented by several minor waterfalls, also merits an afternoon boatride. Charter or launch your own craft from Neah Bay, located about 5 miles east of the cape. Early summer is the best time of the year to view the falls; the streamflows are usually adequate and the weather conditions seaworthy.

Beach Creek Falls
Type: horsetail; map: USGS Cape Flattery 7½'

A 30- to 40-foot waterfall into the Strait of Juan de Fuca. Located within a small cove 3.6 miles west of Neah Bay. I've named the falls after its stream.

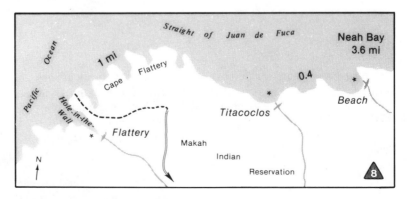

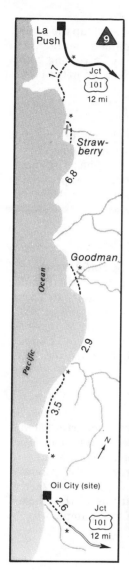

▲ *Beach Creek Falls*

Titacoclos Falls
Type: horsetail; map: USGS Cape Flattery 7½'

This 100- to 120-foot drop is located 4 miles west of Neah Bay. It tends to be seasonal, seldom flowing from mid- to late summer.

Flattery Creek Falls
Type: horsetail; map: USGS Cape Flattery 7½'

Water slides 45 to 60 feet into a crevasse at the head of Hole-in-the-Wall Cove. Accessible only by small-craft boaters experienced in navigating rocky embayments. Proceed to Cape Flattery and enter

Hole-in-the-Wall (see map). After dropping anchor, walk up the drainage a short distance to view this previously unnamed cataract. An ankle-deep wade may be required part of the way. Intriguing 20th-century ruins of some sort of building are also to be seen in the cove.

9. OLYMPIC COAST

Access to the following pair of waterfalls is unique in that the hiker or backpacker must be aware of tide conditions. Some of the beaches are inundated by the Pacific at high tide, thus one must know when and where access is restricted by the ocean. Appropriate information for coastal hiking can be obtained at the Mora or Kalaloch ranger stations of Olympic National Park.

Strawberry Bay Falls
Type: horsetail; map: USGS Toleak Point 7½'

An unnamed creek pours 100 to 120 feet into the surf. Depart U.S. 101 1.5 miles north of Forks, heading toward LaPush and the Pacific Coast. After 8 miles, turn left (south) and continue 4 miles to Third Beach Trailhead. Hike 1.3 miles to the ocean, then 0.4 mile south to the nearest beachside view of the falls. Closer vantages are possible from wave-cut rocks, but for safety's sake must be restricted to time periods when the tide is receding. I've named the falls after the adjacent cove.

Goodman Falls
Map: USGS Toleak Point 7½'

This previously unnamed falls is fairly remote, occurring along Falls Creek just above Goodman Creek. It is located next to one of the headland, or nonbeach, trails of Olympic National Park's southern coast. From Third Beach Trailhead (see Strawberry Bay Falls, above) walk 1.3 miles to the beach, then 7.2 miles south. Or, take a northerly 9-mile jaunt from Oil City site (get directions at one of the ranger stations). Don't forget to bring a tide table and a trail pamphlet!

10. ENCHANTED VALLEY

This entry is for all the waterfall enthusiasts who also like to backpack. Enjoy! Enchanted Valley, in the southern part of Olympic National Park, is accessible only to backpackers. The most popular

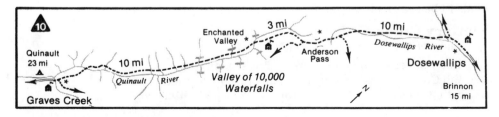

access route to the trail is 23 miles east of Quinault, off U.S. 101, near the ranger station. For an alternate point of departure from Dosewallips Camp, see the map for the "Dosewallips" subsection (below).

Valley of 10,000 Waterfalls

Many visitors and long-time residents of the Olympic Peninsula prefer the name "Valley of 10,000 Waterfalls" to the more common "Enchanted Valley." Although the number of falls may be exaggerated in the name, you will be hard-pressed to keep track of the scores of waterfalls seen during a single day's journey in this valley. Practically every tributary encountered along Enchanted Valley Trail breaks into a waterfall as it enters the Quinault River's glacially carved valley. Varied vegetation completes the serene scenery of the gorge.

Secure a backcountry permit at the Graves Creek or Dosewallips ranger stations. A ranger station in the Enchanted Valley is open during the summer if you need information or assistance.

11. QUILCENE AREA

Falls View Falls
Type: horsetail

Turn off U.S. 101 at Falls View Camp, 4 miles south of Quilcene and 9 miles north of Brinnon. A short trail at the south end of the campground leads to a fenced vista high above the canyon floor. An unnamed creek drops 80 to 120 feet into Big Quilcene River. The flow is best during the wet season from autumn to spring. It may disappear entirely during droughts. The cataract is also known as *Campground Falls.*

12. DOSEWALLIPS

The eastern portion of Olympic National Park is an ideal spot for those who wish to avoid crowds. The lack of paved access roads discourages many travelers. Turn off U.S. 101 at the sign for the Dosewallips Recreation Area, 1 mile north of Brinnon.

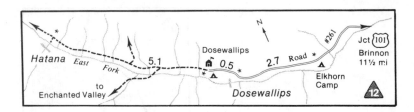

Dosewallips Falls
Type: cascade

Water pours 100 to 125 feet over and around boulders along Dosewallips River. Drive 14.2 miles west from the Dosewallips Recreation Area turnoff from U.S. 101 to the signed turnout at the base of the cataract, 0.75 mile beyond the park boundary.

Hatana Falls
Map: USGS Mt Angeles 15'

Start at the ranger station at the Dosewallips River Trailhead. Don't forget to obtain a backpacker's permit. After 5.1 miles, a primitive marked spur trail leads to a view of Hidden Creek falling from the other side of the canyon into Dosewallips River.

13. BRINNON

Rocky Brook Falls
Type: horsetail

Drive 1 mile north of Brinnon on U.S. 101, then turn left (west) at Road #261, signed Dosewallips Recreation Area. Proceed west for 3 miles and park at the undesignated turnout on the west side of Rocky Brook bridge. A well-worn trail quickly leads to the base of the falls. Water thunders 100 to 125 feet over a massive scarp. I've named this waterfall after its stream.

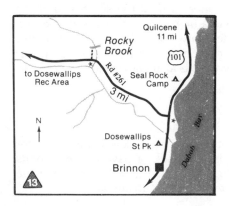

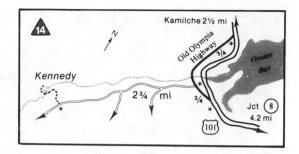

14. KAMILCHE

Kennedy Falls
Type: tiered; map: USGS Kamilche Valley 15'

Turn off U.S. 101 onto Old Olympia Highway 2.5 miles south of the Kamilche/S.R. 108 exit and 4.25 miles northwest of the junction of U.S. 101 and S.R. 8. Drive 0.75 mile to the dirt road south of Kennedy Creek. Turn west and stay on the primary route for 2.75 miles, turning right (toward the creek) at all major forks. Park at a jeep trail and hike down the trail for 0.5 mile to the emerald-tinted gorge of Kennedy Creek.

The best views of the falls are from the north side of the valley. Walk a short distance upstream to an easy ford above the upper descent, then progress downstream to open, unfenced vistas. The upper portion of this small, but pleasantly tiered waterfall drops 5 to 10 feet into a pool. A little lower the creek pours 20 to 30 feet into a tight gorge.

15. OLYMPIA

Leave Interstate 5 at Exit 103. The Olympia Brewery and visitor parking are one block east of the freeway. Paths lead through the landscaped setting of Tumwater Falls Park past four cataracts for a leisurely 30-minute stroll. Afterwards, take an interesting tour

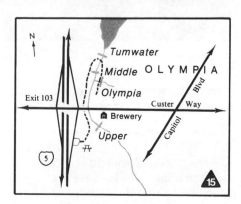

▲   *Tumwater Falls*

through the brewery and enjoy a complimentary glass of beer or soda
in the hospitality room.

Upper Tumwater Falls
Type: block

The form of this 10- to 20-foot drop is defined by previous
alterations made to harness water power. The waterfall is near the
picnic area along the Deschutes River.

Olympia Falls
Type: tiered

Purified water is returned to Deschutes River from the brewery as a nice display dropping a total of 40 to 60 feet. From the upper falls, walk downstream a short distance past the bridge over the river. The trail eventually crosses the river and passes between the upper and lower portions of this waterfall.

Middle Tumwater Falls
Type: cascade

Water tumbles 15 to 25 feet along the Deschutes River a short distance downstream from Olympia Falls.

Tumwater Falls
Type: punchbowl; map: USGS Tumwater 7½'

This 40-foot waterfall has been made famous by its likeness on the label of the brewery's products. Walk to a vista overlooking the falls. A footbridge crosses above the descent.

The waterfall was originally named *Puget Sound Falls* in 1829 and retitled *Shute's River Falls* in 1841. Michael Troutman Simmons led a party of American settlers to the vicinity in 1845. He coined the word Tumwater based on a Chinook word. The Indians called running water "tumtum" because they felt its sound was like the throb of a heart.

16. RAINBOW FALLS STATE PARK

Rainbow Falls
Type: punchbowl; map: USGS Adna 15'

A large pool at the base of this 5- to 10-foot waterfall serves as a popular swimming hole. The falls of the Chehalis River are at the entrance to Rainbow Falls State Park, next to S.R. 6, about 3 miles east of Doty or 12 miles west of Adna. Interpretive trails guide the visitor through the park's stands of virgin timber.

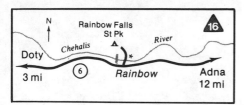

Mount Rainier Region

The Mount Rainier region of Washington is among the most scenic in North America. The mountain itself, called Takhoma by the Yakima Indians, is the area's centerpiece, but there are many other beautiful natural features. Mount Rainier National Park, my favorite park, has 123 recognized waterfalls within and near its boundaries. Of these, 68 are described in the following pages.

This is a land of fire and ice. The oldest rocks predate Mount Rainier itself. Between 30 million and 60 million years ago, the region was part of a large, low-lying coastal zone scattered with terrestrial and subterranean volcanoes. These ancient volcanoes deposited thick accumulations of lava, which played an important part in the formation and composition of the Cascade Range. Ten million to 30 million years later, continued volcanic activity brought molten material toward the earth's surface, but most of the *magma* cooled before it could pour from the vents as lava. The bedrock formed from the magma became surface material when it was thrust upward by internal earth forces or was exposed by the erosion of its overburden.

Therefore, the landscape on the periphery of modern Mount Rainier comprises different types of rocks that streams erode at unequal rates. *Silver Falls* occurs where Ohanapecosh River intersects resistant vertical layers of basalt before continuing along relatively weak *volcanic breccia*, formed when lava intermingled with sandstone and siltstone. Another example is *Lower Stevens Falls*, where magma was injected into an older rock complex. The resulting bedrock proved to be more resistant than neighboring material.

Mount Rainier formed 1 million to 5 million years ago and is composed of interlayering andesitic lava and volcanic ash from repeated eruptions. One large lava flow blocks the northward course of Maple Creek, diverting the stream eastward. Coincidentally, a vertical break in the local topography, called a *fault*, was positioned along the stream's redefined route. *Maple Falls* currently descends from the fault.

The abundance of waterfalls in the region is due not to the processes described above, but to the large-scale landscape modifications achieved by glaciers. A total of 27 named glaciers surround Mount Rainier today; 10,000 years ago these awesome spectacles, the earth's greatest erosive agents, extended to much lower elevations.

A topographic feature common to areas of high relief is a *step*, formed where an alpine glacier gouges its valley floor unevenly. *Clear*

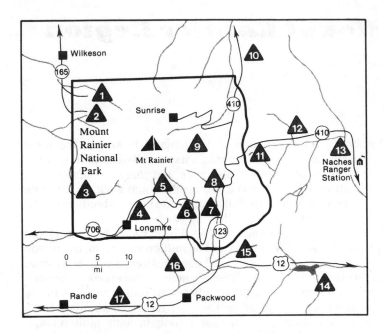

Creek Falls and *Sylvia Falls* are along breaks probably formed in this manner. Waterfalls from *hanging valleys* are also common around Mount Rainier. These are formed because small, tributary glaciers cannot erode their valleys as deeply as can the large, main glaciers. Therefore, a smaller glacial valley will be high above a main glacial valley floor where they meet. *Comet Falls* and *Spray Falls* are dramatic examples of this type.

1. CARBON RIVER DRAINAGE

Vacationers visiting the region for the first time usually overlook this portion of Mount Rainier National Park, favoring instead better-known locations like Sunrise and Paradise. Since the northwestern part of the park is frequented mostly by locals, it has been called "Our Own Little Corner of the Mountain." But wherever you are from, you will be warmly welcomed.

Drive to the city of Buckley on S.R. 410 or S.R. 162, then turn south along S.R. 162/165 through the historic mining towns of Wilkeson and Carbonado. Follow paved S.R. 162 to the park entrance along the Carbon River, 12 miles past Carbonado. The road turns to gravel at the entrance.

Ranger Falls
Type: tiered; map: USGS Mowich Lake 7½'

These falls tumble a total of 100 to 125 feet along Ranger Creek. Their form is eye-catching because the lower portion splits into twin falls. Drive S.R. 162 3 miles past the park entrance to Green Lake Trailhead. The trail ascends moderately for about 1 mile to a marked spur leading to the falls.

Chenuis Falls

Type: cascade; map: USGS Mowich Lake 7½'

Water slides 70 to 100 feet across rock layers along Chenuis Creek. Drive S.R. 162 3.5 miles past the park entrance to a parking turnout adjacent to Carbon River. The falls are only 0.2 mile away. A log bridge provides access across the river.

Ipsut Falls

Type: tiered; map: USGS Mowich Lake 7½'

This double falls along Ipsut Creek totals 40 to 60 feet. Drive S.R. 162 just past Ipsut Camp to the trailhead at the end of the road. Hike right (south) on Wonderland Trail a little way from the trailhead, and follow it for a short distance to a designated spur trail leading to the falls. Please stay on the trail since the creek serves as the water supply for the camp.

Carbon Falls

Type: tiered; map: USGS Mowich Lake 7½'

Hike 2.2 miles from Ipsut Camp along Wonderland Trail where it follows Carbon River. Soon after you leave the forested area and catch sight of the slopes across the river, the waterfall comes into view — first the lower falls, then the upper portion. This waterfall is best viewed during the afternoon. Its rating decreases during the low water periods of late summer. Also, **Alice Falls** is located along an adjacent drainage, but is well hidden by the surrounding vegetation.

Lower Cataract Falls

Type: cascade

These 50- to 75-foot falls along Cataract Creek are best viewed from the footbridge 2.7 miles past Ipsut Camp, on Wonderland Trail along the way toward Carbon Glacier.

Cataract Falls

Type: segmented; map: USGS Mowich Lake 7½'

Follow the directions for Lower Cataract Falls (above) and follow the right (west) fork at the trail junction. (The left fork goes to the toe of Carbon Glacier, which extends to a lower elevation than any other glacier in the continental United States.) Hike 1.1 miles (3.8 miles from the trailhead) to a designated spur trail leading to the 50- to 75-foot falls. In 1988, a major blowdown of trees blocked access to the spur trail and the descent. Before embarking, check with a ranger on the current status of the route.

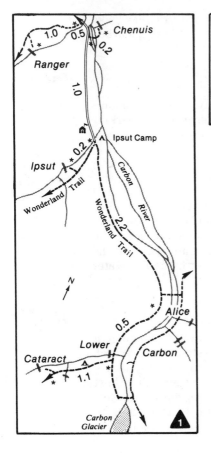

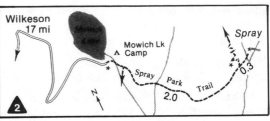

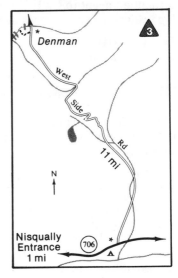

2. MOWICH LAKE AREA

Drive to the city of Buckley via S.R. 410 or 162 and turn south on S.R. 162/165 to Wilkeson and Carbonado. Three miles past Carbonado, turn right on the gravel extension of S.R. 165. This road has imposing views of Mount Rainier. It ends at Mowich Lake in 16 miles.

Spray Falls
Type: fan; map: USGS Mowich Lake 7½'

This enormous display descends 300 to 350 feet and is 50 to 80 feet wide. Reach it by a leisurely hike of 2.3 miles. Follow the Wonderland Trail southeast from Mowich Lake for 0.4 mile, then turn left on Spray Park Trail and follow it for 1.6 miles. Finally, turn right at Spray Falls Trail. An exciting view of the falls is 0.3 mile farther.

3. ST. ANDREWS CREEK

Enter Mount Rainier National Park at the Nisqually entrance and continue about 1 mile on the eastward extension of S.R. 706 to West

▲ *Spray Falls*

Side Road. This gravel road may eventually be discontinued for vehicular use. If so, the waterfall will be accessible only to backpackers.

Denman Falls
Map: USGS Mt Wow 7½'

 NR

Drive 11 miles to St. Andrews Creek, parking on the near side of the bridge. To the left is a trail that leads downstream to an observation point above the 122-foot falls. Further downstream are **Larrupin Falls** and **Ethania Falls.** Unfortunately, they are not accessible.

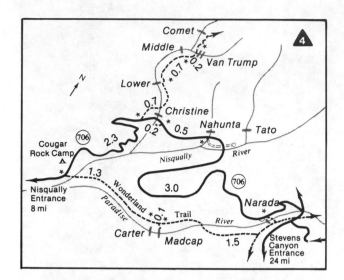

4. NISQUALLY DRAINAGE

The south-central part of Mount Rainier National Park has a wealth of waterfalls. The area is bounded on the west by Cougar Rock Campground and on the east by the entrance to the Paradise area.

Carter Falls
Type: horsetail; map: USGS Mt Rainier West 7½'

Drive S.R. 706 to Cougar Rock Campground 8 miles east of the Nisqually entrance, 30 miles west of the Stevens Canyon entrance. Head east on Wonderland Trail across the highway from Cougar Rock Camp. A sign directs you toward the falls, but first cross Nisqually River with its two footbridges. Hike 1.3 miles up the moderate trail to the falls. This 50- to 80-foot waterfall is named for Harry Carter, who built much of the early Paradise Trail.

Madcap Falls
Type: cascade; map: USGS Mt Rainier West 7½'

Hike 1.3 miles to Carter Falls (see directions above). A short distance past Carter Falls an unlabeled spur trail leads 0.1 mile to these 20- to 30-foot cascades along the Paradise River. USGS topographic maps label this feature about 0.25 mile farther upstream, but darned if I could see anything there resembling falls.

Narada Falls
Type: horsetail; map: USGS Mt Rainier East 7½'

These popular falls descend 168 feet or 241 feet, depending on whether the plunge at the end of the horsetail is included. A parking area near the falls is located on S.R. 706 about 1 mile west of the entrance to the Paradise area, or you can continue hiking 1.5 miles along the Wonderland Trail from Carter Falls (above). A branch of the

▲ *Narada Falls*

Theosophical Society of Tacoma named the falls after their guru, Narada, in 1893.

Middle Van Trump Falls

Type: plunge; map: USGS Mt Rainier West 7½'

Van Trump Creek has many series of falls. Four major falls are described in this and the next two entries. Drive 2.3 miles east of Cougar Rock Campground to the Comet Falls Trailhead. The trail is steep but safe, ascending 1,400 feet in 1.6 miles. It is usually devoid of snow after mid-July. The roar of **Lower Van Trump Falls** can be heard after less than 0.75 mile, but the shape of the canyon hides the descent from view. The middle falls is 0.75 mile farther. Its 40- to 50-foot drop can be seen easily from a few feet off the trail.

Van Trump Falls

Type: tiered; map: USGS Mt Rainier West 7½'

Don't give up hiking yet! The next waterfall, a double falls totaling 60 to 90 feet, is only 0.2 mile from Middle Van Trump Falls (above),

▲   *Comet Falls*

or 1.8 miles from the trailhead. And you're less than 100 yards away from the best of them all....

Comet Falls

Type: plunge; map: USGS Mt Rainier West 7½'

You've made it! Before you is a spectacular 320-foot plunge, only 1.9 miles from the trailhead. This is a classic example of a waterfall descending from a hanging valley. If you are a glutton for punishment, the trail continues for almost 1 mile toward the top of the falls.

Christine Falls

Type: plunge; map: USGS Mt Rainier West 7½'

Drive S.R. 706 east less than 0.25 mile past Comet Falls Trailhead to the turnout on the east side of the Van Trump Creek bridge. Stairs lead down from the bridge to a picturesque view of these 40- to 60-foot falls.

Nahunta Falls
Type: cascade; map: USGS Mt Rainier West 7½'

These falls steeply cascade 150 to 175 feet along an unnamed tributary to Nisqually River. Park at the old gravel spur 0.5 mile east of Van Trump Creek bridge on S.R. 706 and look up the side of the slope. During low discharge periods of late summer, this waterfall deserves a lesser rating.

Tato Falls
Type: horsetail; map: USGS Mt Rainier West 7½'

Park at the old gravel spur road 0.5 mile east of Van Trump Creek bridge on S.R. 706. Walk along the gravel spur 0.3 mile to its end. The 40- to 60-foot waterfall is best seen from a moderate distance away. Surrounding vegetation obscures closer views. The falls are on an unnamed tributary of Nisqually River.

5. PARADISE

At 5,800 feet of elevation, Paradise is the highest point to which you can drive on Mount Rainier's southern face. Travel 15 miles east from the Nisqually entrance or 24 miles west from the Stevens Canyon entrance along the park's eastward extension of S.R. 706. The contemporary-looking visitor's center and the traditionally rustic Paradise Inn are located about 1.5 miles off the main road and are accessible via the Paradise Loop Road.

Myrtle Falls
Type: fan

The Skyline Trail begins at Paradise Inn. Walk an easy 0.3 mile to Edith Creek. A stairway descends to a superb vista overlooking the 60- to 80-foot falls with Mount Rainier in the background.

Paradise Falls
Type: block; map: USGS Mt Rainier East 7½'

The Skyline Trail begins at Paradise Inn. Just past Edith Creek, take the southern loop of Skyline Trail, passing its junction with

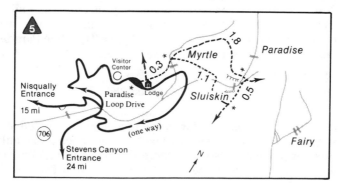

Lakes Trail in 1.4 miles. Far away to the right in Stevens Basin, **Fairy Falls** can be faintly heard and even seen with an afternoon sun. See the "Stevens Canyon" subsection (below) for a description. In 0.5 mile more, Skyline Trail passes Paradise Glacier Trailhead, Stevens–Van Trump historic monument, and then a footbridge crossing the headwaters of Paradise River. Look upstream from the bridge to the distant 30- to 50-foot drop of Paradise Falls.

Sluiskin Falls

Type: fan; map: USGS Mt Rainier East 7½'

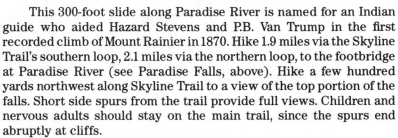

This 300-foot slide along Paradise River is named for an Indian guide who aided Hazard Stevens and P.B. Van Trump in the first recorded climb of Mount Rainier in 1870. Hike 1.9 miles via the Skyline Trail's southern loop, 2.1 miles via the northern loop, to the footbridge at Paradise River (see Paradise Falls, above). Hike a few hundred yards northwest along Skyline Trail to a view of the top portion of the falls. Short side spurs from the trail provide full views. Children and nervous adults should stay on the main trail, since the spurs end abruptly at cliffs.

6. STEVENS CANYON

It is no exaggeration to say that the National Park Service's eastward extension of S.R. 706 is one of the most scenic roads ever engineered. The Stevens Canyon stretch is not as convoluted as other sections of the route, but its construction was just as daring an undertaking. The view across the canyon from Wonderland Trail confirms that judgment. The fine line of the highway can be seen cut into the side of Stevens Ridge over 400 feet above the canyon floor.

Fairy Falls and Upper Stevens Falls

Type: horsetail; map: USGS Mt Rainier East 7½'

The large falls from Stevens Basin are not highly regarded because there are no close views of them. Drive to the turnout at The Bench, located about 5.5 miles east from Paradise or 6 miles west from Box Canyon. Look up the valley toward Stevens Basin, which is below and to the right (east) of Mount Rainier. Two silvery white threads drop from the basin. Upper Stevens Falls descends 200 to 400 feet, while Fairy Falls plummets 700 feet in two major drops. Fairy Falls can also be viewed from the Skyline Trail. See Paradise Falls in the "Paradise" subsection (above) for details.

Martha Falls

Type: fan; map: USGS Mt Rainier East 7½'

Water spills 125 to 150 feet along Unicorn Creek. The waterfall can be viewed from S.R. 706 at the recently constructed Martha Falls wayside, located 2 miles northeast of The Bench and 4 miles west of Box Canyon. It can also be accessed by hikers using Wonderland Trail, which intersects with the road 0.8 mile north of The Bench. Starting

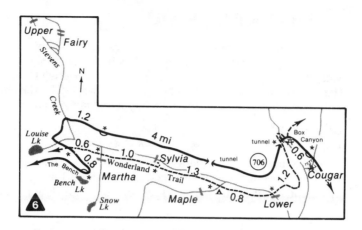

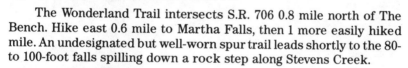

on the east side of the road, the trail winds moderately down 0.6 mile
east to a footbridge overlooking the falls.

Sylvia Falls

Type: fan; map: USGS Mt Rainier East 7½'

The Wonderland Trail intersects S.R. 706 0.8 mile north of The
Bench. Hike east 0.6 mile to Martha Falls, then 1 more easily hiked
mile. An undesignated but well-worn spur trail leads shortly to the 80-
to 100-foot falls spilling down a rock step along Stevens Creek.

Lower Stevens Falls

Type: cascade; map: USGS Mt Rainier East 7½'

Water cascades 30 to 40 feet over granite bedrock along Stevens
Creek. Hike south on Wonderland Trail 1.2 miles from Box Canyon, or
continue 2.1 miles past Sylvia Falls (see directions above), for a total
of 3.7 miles, to the footbridge above the falls.

Maple Falls

Map: USGS Mt Rainier East 7½'

NR

Hike along the Wonderland Trail to Maple Creek Camp, located
0.8 mile past Lower Stevens Falls and 1.3 miles east of Sylvia Falls.
Start at the footbridge below the camp and head upstream for about
0.5 mile. I did not survey this waterfall because the thick bushes
prevented me from approaching it and I lacked waterproof legwear to
wade through the stream.

Cougar Falls

Type: plunge; map: USGS Mt Rainier East 7½'

This impressive 100- to 125-foot plunge is accessible to adults
only. Drive S.R. 706 0.6 mile southeast from Box Canyon to the
undesignated turnout immediately northwest of the Nickel Creek
bridge. Walk down the primitive trail to good direct views of the falls
in 0.1 to 0.2 mile. *Warning:* Stay away from the bare rock surfaces
near the creek. They slope sharply into a steep canyon!

7. SILVER FALLS AREA

This popular area near the southeast entrance of Mount Rainier National Park boasts hot springs and giant forest stands in addition to waterfalls. Walk a short distance from Ohanapecosh Campground to the natural setting of the hot springs. Feel dwarfed by the Grove of the Patriarchs between the Stevens Canyon entrance and Olallie Creek.

Silver Falls
Type: punchbowl; map: USGS Chinook Pass 7½'

Rushing water thunders 30 to 40 feet into a pool. Drive 0.3 mile south of Stevens Canyon entrance along S.R. 123. Find the East Side Trailhead to the right (west), which shortly leads down to the bottom

▲ *Silver Falls*

of the gorge and the falls along the Ohanapecosh River. Two trails from Ohanapecosh Campground also provide a leisurely 1-mile stroll to the falls. There are at least three smaller waterfalls immediately upstream and one downstream from the main falls. Warning: Limit your views to those available from the trail and designated vantages. The tumultuous river has claimed the lives of many who failed to heed the posted warnings.

Olallie Creek Falls
Type: cascade; map: USGS Chinook Pass 7½'

Hike north along the East Side Trail from the parking area near Stevens Canyon entrance or from Silver Falls. One mile north of the highway, the East Side Trail crosses Olallie Creek. The 30- to 50-foot cascades are upstream from the footbridge. I've called this unnamed waterfall after the creek.

Fall Creek Falls
Type: horsetail

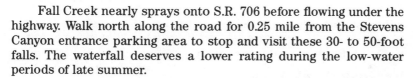
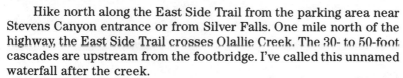

Fall Creek nearly sprays onto S.R. 706 before flowing under the highway. Walk north along the road for 0.25 mile from the Stevens Canyon entrance parking area to stop and visit these 30- to 50-foot falls. The waterfall deserves a lower rating during the low-water periods of late summer.

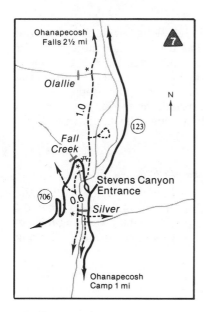
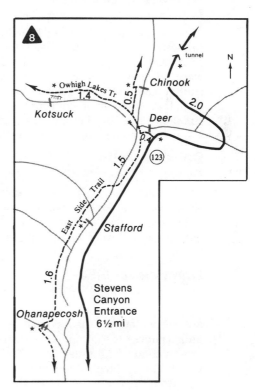

8. CHINOOK CREEK DRAINAGE

This pleasant collection of waterfalls lies along a sparsely used, but easily accessible trail system within Mount Rainier National Park. Drive to the Owyhigh Lakes Trailhead next to S.R. 123, located 6.5 miles north of the Stevens Canyon entrance and 4.5 miles south of Cayuse Pass. Alternatively, hikers can continue north past Olallie Creek, (see Olallie Creek Falls, above) along the East Side Trail.

Deer Creek Falls
Type: cascade; map: USGS Chinook Pass 7½'

Wind down Owyhigh Lakes Trail to Deer Creek in less than 0.25 mile. Look upstream into the steeply cascading 60- to 80-foot falls. I've named this waterfall after the stream.

Chinook Creek Falls
Type: cascade; map: USGS Chinook Pass 7½'

Trees in the foreground partially block the view of these sharp 75- to 100-foot cascades. Hike along the East Side Trail for about 0.5 mile past the trail's north junction with Owyhigh Lakes Trail, a total of 0.9 mile from S.R. 123. The falls are seen just before the trail switches back uphill. I've named this waterfall after its stream.

Kotsuck Creek Falls
Type: segmented; map: USGS Chinook Pass 7½'

Hike a total of 1.8 miles from S.R. 123 along Owyhigh Lakes Trail to views over the top of these falls. The trail ascends moderately for 1.4 miles past its junction with the East Side Trail. The 125- to 150-foot waterfall actually deserves a four-star rating, but the view from the trail is inadequate. To get a better one, retrace your steps down the trail, then carefully make your way through the woods to the canyon rim facing the falls. Perhaps the Park Service will someday construct a spur trail providing a viewpoint for all.

Stafford Falls
Type: punchbowl; map: USGS Chinook Pass 7½'

Water plummets 30 to 40 feet into a large pool below. Follow the East Side Trail south from its junction at Owyhigh Lakes Trail, 0.4 mile from the trailhead at S.R. 123. An easy 1.5 miles later, an undesignated but well-worn spur trail leads to this descent along Chinook Creek.

Ohanapecosh Falls
Type: tiered; map: USGS Chinook Pass 7½'

This double punchbowl waterfall drops 50 to 75 feet along the grayish waters of Ohanapecosh River. Continue south past Stafford Falls (above) for 1.6 miles to where the East Side Trail crosses the river a total of 3.5 miles from S.R. 123, or 2.5 miles north of Olallie Creek Falls (above). The best view is south of the footbridge, a few feet from the trail. I've named the falls after the river.

▲ *Ohanapecosh Falls*

9. BACKPACKERS' FALLS

The extensive trail system within Mount Rainier National Park provides access to many of Mount Rainier's remote areas. Because the backcountry falls described here are widely scattered, it was not practical to include maps showing their locations. Instead, obtain the USGS map for Mount Rainier National Park, or use the appropriate large-scale USGS maps listed with the falls. Also, remember to secure a backpacking permit at a park ranger station.

Marie Falls and Mary Belle Falls
Map: USGS Mt Rainier East 7½'

There are at least five waterfalls within the basin of Nickel Creek, of which two have been officially named. Hike north from Box Canyon along the Wonderland Trail for 5.5 to 6 miles. Bird's-eye views of the falls are to the west (left), well past the heavily timbered region along the Cowlitz Divide ridge.

Wauhaukaupauken Falls
Map: USGS Mt Rainier East 7½'

Hike north from Box Canyon for 7.25 miles on the Wonderland Trail. The falls are 100 feet below the shelter along Ohanapecosh River. The name, obviously of Indian origin, is reputed to be larger than the waterfall!

Falls of Ohanapecosh Park
Map: USGS Mt Rainier East 7½'

At least six falls drop into the Boulder Creek drainage at Ohanapecosh Park. Climb steadily up switchbacks on the Wonderland Trail from Wauhaukaupauken Falls (see directions above). A series of falls streaming from the adjacent cliffs come into view to the northeast about 1 mile past timberline.

Huckleberry Creek Falls
Map: USGS Mt Rainier East 7½'

Hike 3 to 4 miles north of Sunrise to the base of these falls as shown on the topographic map.

Garda Falls
Map: USGS Sunrise 7½'

Hike 6 to 7 miles west of Sunrise along the Wonderland Trail. The falls are immediately upstream from where the trail crosses Granite Creek.

Affi Falls
Map: USGS Sunrise 7½'

Hike 5 miles northwest of Sunrise, first on Wonderland Trail, then on the Northern Loop Trail. The trail passes near the top of the falls where Lodi Creek descends down a glacial valley to West Fork White River.

Van Horn Falls
Map: USGS Sunrise 7½'

Hike 4 to 5 miles past Affi Falls along the Northern Loop Trail to the footbridge crossing West Fork White River. Look along the west side of the valley to see this series of three waterfalls from Van Horn Creek.

10. CAMP SHEPPARD

Camp Sheppard is a Boy Scouts of America site, but visitors are welcome to use the trail system. In fact, the Boy Scouts blazed the pathways for that purpose. The entrance to the camp is along S.R. 410, about 11 miles south of Greenwater and 5 miles north of Mount Rainier National Park. Use of the accompanying map is essential.

Snoquera Falls
Type: plunge; map: USGS Sun Top 7½'

The impressiveness of this 200- to 300-foot waterfall decreases from spring to autumn. Follow Moss Lake Nature Trail from the parking area to the east side of the small lake. Take the designated Snoquera Falls Loop Trail #1167 to the falls in 1.5 miles. Alternatively, hike from the north end of Trail #1167 via White River Trail #1199.

Dalles Falls
Type: tiered

Each portion of this double waterfall can be viewed separately. Continue hiking along White River Trail #1199 to its north end, where Dalles Creek Trail #1198 is met. This trail ascends steeply but safely through switchbacks to the top of The Dalles Gorge. In 0.25 mile a short spur trail leads to the lower falls. In 0.5 mile more, the upper falls can be seen from the main trail. Both falls are reduced to trickles during the low-water periods of late summer.

Skookum Falls
Type: tiered; map: USGS Greenwater 15'

Take the Moss Lake Nature Trail from the parking lot to the west side of the lake. Cross the highway, then the footbridge over White River to Snoquera Flats Trail #1194. Hike 2.25 miles to where this descent of Skookum Creek can be seen from the trail. Motorists can gain a cross-valley view of the falls by driving to an unsigned turnout along S.R. 410, 1.4 miles north of Camp Sheppard.

11. DEWEY LAKE

Dewey Lake Falls
Type: block; map: USGS Bumping Lake 15'

The outlet from Dewey Lake trickles down a 25- to 35-foot escarpment. Departing from Chinook Pass, follow Pacific Crest Trail #958 eastward 2.3 miles to Dewey Lake Trail #968 and turn left. Hike past the north end of the lake to the falls in 0.7 mile. The falls were previously unnamed.

12. RAINIER VALLEY

For an excellent example of a *glacial trough* shaped by the enormous erosive powers of an alpine glacier, look down from

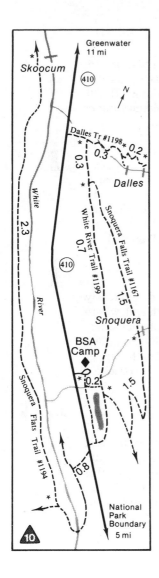

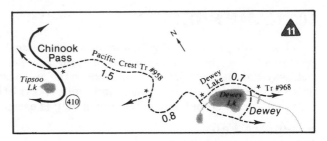

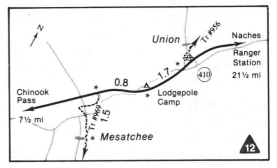

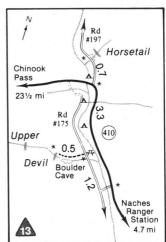

Chinook Pass and admire the characteristic steep-sided, U-shaped form of Rainier Valley. The glacier has long since disappeared, and the Rainier Fork now flows along the valley bottom. The pass was also formed by glacial activity. It is geomorphically known as a *col*, a notch eroded in a ridge by glaciers on either side.

Mesatchee Creek Falls
Type: horsetail; map: USGS Bumping Lake 15'

Drive 7 miles east from Chinook Pass on S.R. 410 and turn south at Wenatchee National Forest Road #1710. Park at the trailhead of Mesatchee Creek Trail #969, several hundred feet from the turnoff,

▲   *Union Creek Falls*

and begin hiking. After crossing Morse Creek and American River, the trail steepens considerably. The 100-foot falls can be seen from the trail after 1.5 miles.

Union Creek Falls

Type: horsetail; map: USGS Bumping Lake 15'

Turn into the parking and picnic area at Union Creek Trail #956, located 10 miles east of Chinook Pass. Follow the trail about 0.25 mile to a well-traveled but unmarked spur leading to the 40- to 60-foot falls.

13. NACHES AREA

Drive to the junction of S.R. 410 and Little Naches Road #197, located 23.5 miles east of Chinook Pass and 38 miles northwest of Yakima.

Horsetail Falls

Type: horsetail; map: USGS Cliffdell 7½'

This is a pretty falls during early spring and late autumn, but it becomes a trickle during the summer. Drive about 0.75 mile north along Little Naches Road #19, then turn right (east) onto a short turnout. Water from an unnamed tributary descends 40 to 50 feet from cliffs into Little Naches River.

Devil Creek Falls
Type: tiered; map: USGS Cliffdell 7½'

The unique geology of this area is not to be missed. Continue south on S.R. 410 for 3.3 miles beyond the Little Naches Road #19 junction. Cross the bridge over the Naches River and turn right (north) on Naches River Road #1704. Park in 1.2 miles at Boulder Cave Picnic Area.

Hike an easy 0.5 mile along the canyon rim, then drop down to the base of these 20- to 30-foot falls. The falls alone would deserve a lower rating, but the bizarre landscape makes it all so interesting. The waterfall is viewed from within a recess shaped like an amphitheater. Immediately downstream is Boulder Cave. At one time a landslide blocked the stream's course, but Devil Creek eventually eroded a tunnel through the debris. A flashlight is required to explore the cavern. A larger **Upper Falls** is 0.4 mile upstream, but there is no developed access.

14. RIMROCK LAKE AREA

U.S. 12 traverses through the Rimrock Lake area, a part of Wenatchee National Forest. The Tieton Ranger Station is a primary reference point for the following falls. It is located on U.S. 12 34 miles west from Yakima or 17 miles east from White Pass.

Clear Lake Falls
Type: cascade

Water tumbles 40 to 60 feet as the outlet from Clear Lake proceeds to Rimrock Lake. Turn south off U.S. 12 onto Tieton Road #12, 10 miles west of the ranger station. Drive 0.8 mile to Clear Lake Road #740 and turn south. The cascades are 0.4 mile away and are divided by a bridge spanning the drainage.

South Fork Falls
Type: block

A 0.25-mile pathway ends at a misty vista directly in front of this 30- to 40-foot drop along South Fork Tieton River. Drive 0.5 mile west of the ranger station, then turn south on Tieton Road #12. After 4.5 miles, turn left (south) on South Fork Road #1000. Continue for 11.25 miles (1.3 miles past the bridge over Bear Creek) to an undesignated turnout and its moderately steep trail to the river.

Clear Creek Falls
Type: plunge

Drive 2.5 miles east of White Pass along U.S. 12 to the marked parking area. Follow the trail there a short way along the canyon rim to a grand view of this spectacular 300-foot plunge along Clear Creek.

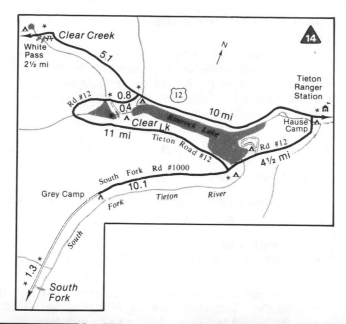

▲ *South Fork Falls*

Upper Clear Creek Falls
Type: fan

Every waterfall collector should see this unusual configuration. One side of the 60- to 80-foot falls horsetails, while the other side veils downward into a pool adjacent to the main portion of the creek. A trail a few yards from the west end of the Clear Creek Falls parking area (above) leads to the waterfall.

15. LOWER OHANAPECOSH DRAINAGE

Vacationers tend to zip past the northeast portion of Gifford Pinchot National Forest on their way to Mount Rainier during the summer and White Pass during the winter. Slow down. Better yet, stop and explore. The fine scenery includes, of course, waterfalls.

 ## Lava Creek Falls
Type: horsetail; map: USGS Packwood 15'

Drive on U.S. 12 to an obscurely marked turnout 7.6 miles west of White Pass and 4.8 miles east of the junction with S.R. 123. A vista overlooks the Clear Fork Cowlitz River canyon. Braids of water stream 200 to 250 feet down the facing canyon wall.

 ## Grant Purcell Falls
Type: cascade; map: USGS Packwood 15'

Enter La Wis Wis Campground, on the west side of U.S. 12, 0.5 mile south of its junction with S.R. 123. Park at the C-Loop Tent Site Area. A sign directs you to the trail leading shortly to Purcell Creek, which slides 75 to 100 feet across bedrock.

 ## Upper Falls
Type: cascade

Turn north on Summit Creek Road #4510 from U.S. 12, 1.3 miles east of the U.S. 12/S.R. 123 junction. Drive 2 miles farther, and park at the unmarked turnout on the north edge of the road. Follow the well-worn trail about 40 yards to Summit Creek and a view of rushing water skipping 25 to 35 feet across rock slabs.

  ## Thunder Falls
Type: fan; map: USGS Packwood 15'

Although a path leads to an excellent view of this 80-foot waterfall, the way is steep and recommended only for nimble hikers. Follow the directions to Upper Falls (above) and continue almost 0.25 mile to the base of Thunder Falls.

  ## Fish Ladder Falls
Map: USGS Packwood 15'

This entry has not been explored by a confirmed source, therefore I recommend it for experienced and determined cross-country hikers only. Start at the bridge crossing at Summit Creek Camp

▲   *Thunder Falls*

(shown on map) and bushwhack along the stream for 1.5 to 2 miles. *Do not* attempt an access farther upstream where Summit Creek Road #4510 runs adjacent to the falls. The creek is far below and the canyon walls are dangerously steep. The waterfall reportedly drops 150 feet along Summit Creek.

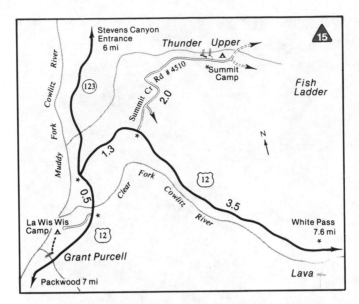

Stevens Canyon
Entrance
6 mi

Thunder Upper

123

Summit Cr Rd # 4510

*Summit
Camp

2.0

*Fish
Ladder*

N

1.3

*

Clear Fork

Cowlitz

River

12

3.5

0.5

*

La Wis Wis
Camp

12

White Pass
7.6 mi
*

Grant Purcell

Lava

Packwood 7 mi

15

Muddy Fork

Cowlitz River

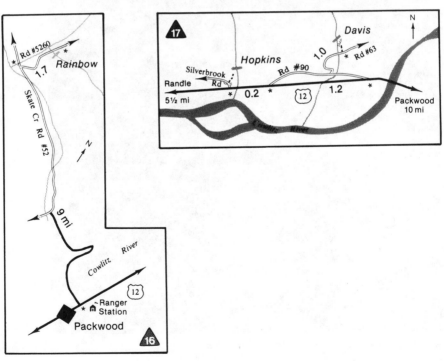

Rd #5260

*

1.7 *Rainbow*

Skate Cr Rd #52

N

9 mi

Cowlitz River

12

Ranger
Station
*

Packwood

16

17

Davis

1.0

Rd #63

Hopkins

Silverbrook
Rd

Rd #90

Randle

5½ mi

*   0.2

12   1.2

*

Packwood
10 mi

N

Cowlitz River

16. JOHNSON CREEK DRAINAGE

Rainbow Falls
Type: plunge

This 100-foot drop from an unnamed tributary to Johnson Creek is reduced to a trickle in late summer. Leave U.S. 12 at Skate Creek Road #52, across from the Packwood Ranger Station. Turn right (northeast) onto Dixon Mountain Road #5260 in 9 miles — just after Road #52 crosses Skate Creek for the second time. Drive 1.7 miles farther and park along the road. Scramble 100 yards up the small draw to the base of the falls.

17. SILVERBROOK AREA

Davis Creek Falls
Type: horsetail; map: USGS Randle 15'

Drive 5.7 miles east of Randle or 10 miles west of Packwood on U.S. 12, and turn north on County Road #90, which later turns to Davis Creek Road #63. In 1 mile, a bridge crosses 146 feet above the creek and its impressive gorge. Park across the bridge and find an unmarked trailhead about 20 yards north from the span. The trail is extremely short, ending at the rim of the gorge with a view upstream toward the 30- to 50-foot falls.

Hopkins Creek Falls
Type: horsetail; map: USGS Randle 15'

Turn off U.S. 12 onto Silverbrook Road 5.5 miles east of Randle or 11.2 miles west of Packwood. Park across the road from the first driveway to the right (east). The unmarked trailhead is obscured by vegetation. Search at the intersection of the road and the driveway. Once the trailhead is found, its well-worn path leads easily and quickly to the base of the 50- to 75-foot falls. I've called the falls by the name of the stream.

Gifford Pinchot Country

Gifford Pinchot National Forest is named after the pioneer of professional forestry in the United States. Pinchot was the first chief of the U.S. Forest Service, serving under presidents McKinley, Roosevelt, and Taft from 1898 to 1910. During his tenure, the entire forest service system and administrative structure were developed. Pinchot's leadership in the conservation movement of this period was important in developing a policy of preserving and managing our nation's public lands.

There are 84 waterfalls mapped within Gifford Pinchot country. In addition, Wayne Parsons has informed me that over 150 falls have been inventoried within Gifford Pinchot National Forest; most of which are not accessible. A total of 44 cataracts are described in this chapter.

With the establishment of Mount St. Helens National Volcanic Monument, the region is more popular with tourists than ever before. The influx can reach a point, however, where one will have to endure a gridlock of traffic to reach the prime viewpoints of the volcano. This has been a major problem in places such as Yosemite National Park, where everyone is trying to get to the same destination at the same time. Fortunately, many other existing and developable recreational opportunities are in proximity to Mount St. Helens (including, you guessed it, waterfalls). As time progresses, the National Park Service and Forest Service will need to publicize these ancillary sites in order to spread the visitors around.

1. COWLITZ RIVER

Cowlitz Falls
Type: cascade; map: USGS Cowlitz Falls 7½'

Leave U.S. 12 at Savio Road 2.5 miles west of Randle and 13 miles east of Morton. Then turn south on Kiona Road and drive 2.5 miles to Falls Road. Turn right (west) and drive 6 miles farther to a point where many spur roads join Falls Road. Continue south on a spur, then bear left (east) on a dirt road above the Cowlitz River. Park along a wide stretch of road about 0.9 mile from the maze of route intersections. Walk down the short, steep slope to the river. The 5- to 10-foot descent is visible from the rocky bank.

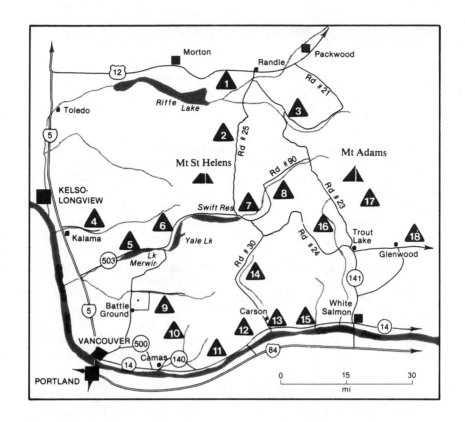

2. IRON CREEK ACCESS

Iron Creek Falls
Type: punchbowl

Turn south off U.S. 12 about 1.25 miles west of Randle Ranger Station onto Randle–Lewis River Road #25. Drive about 9 miles to Cispus River and continue 11 additional miles along Road #25. The route rises above the stream near the 25- to 35-foot falls. It is located 0.4 mile past the junction with Big Creek Road #2517 and 0.4 mile before Spirit Lake–Iron Creek Road #99. Park at the unsigned turnouts before or after the cataract. Some people gain the best views either by scrambling down the moderately steep slope or by walking and wading upstream from Iron Creek's crossing with Road #7708 (shown on map).

Last Hope Falls
Type: horsetail

A cross-valley view of water cascading 70 feet from an unnamed tributary into the headwaters of Green River. Located outside the National Volcanic Monument, but within the area devastated by the eruption of Mount St. Helens. From Cispus River, take Road #25 to

Road #26, turn west, go 12.3 miles to Road #2612, and turn right. Vantages of the falls are at the 2.5-mile conclusion of the gravel road. Polar Star Mine is nearby, on your side of the valley. Look, but don't enter!

Harmony Falls

Type: fan; map: USGS Spirit Lake East 7½'

This waterfall, which formerly fell 50 feet into Spirit Lake, was significantly altered by the catastrophic eruption of Mount St. Helens on May 18, 1980. Drive to Harmony Viewpoint, situated within the National Volcanic Monument along Road #99, 4.2 miles south of the route's junction with Road #26. The current 40- to 60-foot cataract is located at the end of Harmony Falls Trail, a moderately steep hike of 1 lengthy mile. Like the previous entry, the appearance of the falls will continue to change as its watershed matures along with successional changes in the accompanying vegetative cover.

▲   *Harmony Falls*

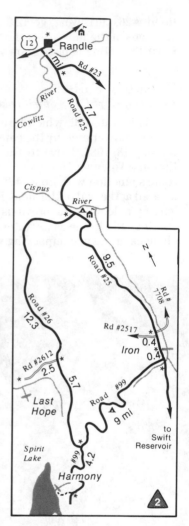

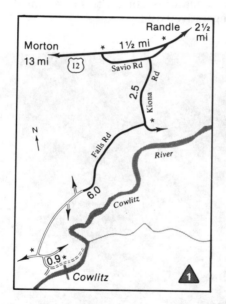

3. NORTH FORK DRAINAGE

There are several falls near North Fork Cispus River, but their flows decrease as summer progresses. Turn south off U.S. 12 onto Randle–Lewis River Road #25 about 1.25 miles west of Randle Ranger Station; after 1 mile, turn left (east) on Randle–Trout Lake Road #23. Drive 10.5 miles, then bear left on North Fork Cispus Road #22. After 5.8 miles, turn right on Timonium Road #78.

Initial Falls

Type: horsetail

The first cataract is encountered after driving 2.7 miles along Timonium Road #78. This particular entry was previously unnamed and descends from an unnamed stream.

Yozoo Creek Falls
Type: fan

Water veils 25 to 40 feet from Yozoo Creek, 3.4 miles along Road #78 (0.7 mile past Initial Falls).

Grouse Creek Falls
Type: cascade

Proceed 4.3 miles along Road #78 (0.9 mile from Yozoo Creek Falls) to this 40- to 50-foot slide along Grouse Creek.

4. KALAMA RIVER ROAD

Marietta Falls
Type: plunge; map: USGS Kalama 7½'

Marietta Creek plunges and tumbles 75 to 100 feet into Kalama River. Exit Interstate 5 on Kalama River Road 0.5 mile north of Kalama and drive 4 miles to the falls. Unfortunately, the only possible view is from the car window, since there are no parking turnouts. For better views, bring an inner tube or canoe and float down the main river. Launch your craft 0.4 mile upstream from the falls.

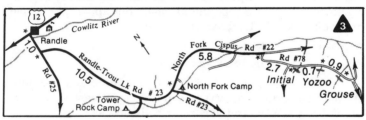

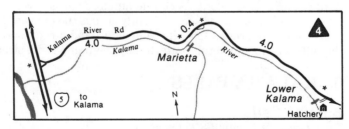

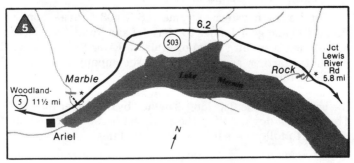

Lower Kalama River Falls
Type: cascade; map: USGS Pigeon Springs 15'

This 15- to 25-foot cascade is uninspiring, except when fish are swimming up it. Exit I-5 on Kalama River Road, 0.5 mile north of Kalama, and drive 8.4 miles to the marked turnoff to Kalama Falls Salmon Hatchery (4.4 miles past Marietta Falls, above). The view is over the top of the falls at the end of the road.

5. LAKE MERWIN

Lake Merwin is the first of three reservoirs along Lewis River. The other two are Yale Lake and Swift Reservoir. The valley sides are steep, with two waterfalls accessible in the area. Turn off Interstate 5 at Woodland and drive east on S.R. 503.

Marble Creek Falls
Type: horsetail; map: USGS Ariel 7½'

Take S.R. 503 east 11.4 miles past Woodland to the Marble Creek bridge. Park at the turnout on the east side. Walk upstream through the lush meadow, then along a short footpath through a wooded tract. The 40- to 60-foot drop is less than 0.2 mile from the road. A lower falls is shown on a USGS topographic map, but apparently a rise in the reservoir's surface level has covered it.

Rock Creek Falls
Type: horsetail; map: USGS Amboy 7½'

Drive S.R. 503 east 17.6 miles past Woodland (6.2 miles past Marble Creek Falls, above), and park on the east side of the Rock Creek bridge. When traffic is clear, walk across the interesting steel-girded span over the gorge. A couple hundred yards farther the 75- to 100-foot horsetail can be seen distantly across the canyon. The creek makes an incongruous 180-degree bend around a rock outcrop near the falls. I have called this waterfall by the name of its stream.

6. KALAMA FALLS

Kalama Falls
Type: punchbowl; map: USGS Cougar 7½'

At the northeastern extreme of S.R. 503, turn east on Lewis River Road #90 and go 4.4 miles to Merrill Lake Road #81. Drive north 6.3 miles, then turn left (west) on Kalama River Road #7500. Continue 1.75 miles farther, as shown on the accompanying map. Park at any available turnout.

A short trail leads down to the Kalama River, then upstream to the base of the falls. The land is owned by the Weyerhaeuser Company. Trees blown down during the previous harsh winter made the path difficult to follow when I reviewed the falls.

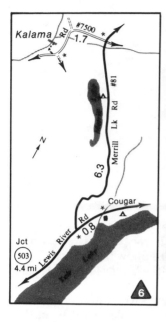

▲ *Curly Creek Falls*

7. EAGLE CLIFF AREA

Located in close proximity to Mount St. Helens National Volcanic Monument, this is one of the areas where recreational development is taking place. Three of the following four waterfalls are now mentioned in Gifford Pinchot National Forest literature and are readily accessible. Also, plans are in the works to construct a trail within the National Monument along nearby Lava Canyon, passing many falls. Check with the Pine Creek Ranger Station (information station) on the current status of this project.

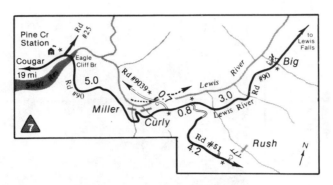

Curly Creek Falls

Type: tiered

The erosive power of the stream has formed a natural arch between tiers of this 50- to 75-foot waterfall from Curly Creek. From S.R. 503, turn east on Lewis River Road #90. Follow Lewis River Road #90 for 5 miles past the Eagle Cliff bridge (the bridge is 19 miles east of Cougar), then turn left (east) on Road #9039 and drive about 0.75 mile to a parking area on the near side of Lewis River. Walk across the bridge and follow the trail downstream for 0.3 mile to a view of the falls from across the river. Look closely: a second arch is in the process of being formed.

Miller Creek Falls

Type: plunge

Continue 0.1 mile east past Curly Creek Falls (above) to this 40- to 60-foot plunge on the opposite side of Lewis River.

Big Creek Falls

Type: plunge

Drive 8.8 miles east from Eagle Cliff bridge along Lewis River Road #90. Park on the north side of the marked crossing of Big Creek. Follow the path downstream a short distance along the south side of the gorge to a breathtaking view of water hurtling 125 feet into an obscured pool. *Be careful at the unguarded, sheer cliffs of the canyon's rim!*

Rush Creek Falls

Type: fan

This is, by far, the toughest bushwhack in this book; only adults with a penchant for physical challenge can visit this 100- to 125-foot cataract. Drive 4.2 miles south along Road #51 from Lewis River Road #90. Park at the turnout next to County Stockpile 2-7, located 0.1 mile from mile marker 3. Walk a short distance past the stockpile and through a clear-cut to the valley rim. Carefully make your way down the steep slope, cursing at the prickly Devil's club ground cover that you will inevitably encounter. It's a 0.25-mile scramble. *Warning:* Approaching the creek, be sure to choose a route downstream from the falls, as the slopes are too treacherous adjacent to and immediately below the main cataract and the minor falls at its base.

8. LEWIS RIVER

The scenic quality of the following falls within Gifford Pinchot National Forest tends to improve as one progresses downstream. Therefore, the farthest entries have been listed first.

Twin Falls
Type: tiered; map: USGS Steamboat Mtn 7½'

The view is across Lewis River to a pair of 15- to 20-foot punchbowls along Twin Falls Creek. Drive Lewis River Road #90 for 26.5 miles northeast of Eagle Cliff bridge. Go right and drive 0.3 mile down the Twin Falls Camp access road to its end at the camp and its namesake.

Straight Creek Falls
Type: cascade

Drive Lewis River Road to the parking area of Quartz Creek Trailhead #5, located 16.8 miles northeast of Eagle Cliff bridge. Hike 2 miles, passing a logged area in 1.75 miles. Walk across the log bridge over Straight Creek, then pick up your own path upstream to a pleasant series of cascades totaling 30 to 60 feet.

Upper Lewis Falls
Type: block; map: USGS Quartz Creek Butte 7½'

Upper Falls Trail turns off from Lewis River Road at a sign 0.8 mile southwest of Quartz Creek Trail #5 (see directions Straight Creek Falls, above). The path is moderately steep but only 0.25 mile long. At the end, Lewis River thunders over a 35-foot escarpment.

Copper Creek Falls
Type: punchbowl

A sharp 40- to 60-foot drop along Copper Creek. Drive Lewis River Road 1 mile southwest of Upper Falls Trail (see directions to Upper Lewis Falls, above) to parking for this trail accessing Lewis

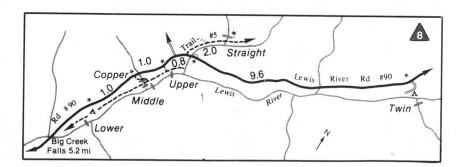

▲   *Lower Lewis Falls*

River. After walking along the path for several hundred yards, look back into the waterfall, descending beneath the just crossed footbridge.

Middle Lewis Falls
Type: block; map: USGS Quartz Creek Butte 7½'

Lewis River rushes 30 feet downward. Take the trail to Copper Creek Falls (above) and continue along the trail to its end at the falls in 0.6 mile. Nearby, **Lower Copper Creek Falls** can be seen dropping 20 to 30 feet into the river.

Lower Lewis Falls
Type: block; map: USGS Spencer Butte 7½'

A heavy volume of water crashes 35 feet in an impressive block form. Drive along Lewis River Road to Lewis River Campground, located 1 mile south of Copper Creek, 14 miles northwest of Eagle Cliff bridge, or 5.2 miles north of Big Creek. Park in the southeast portion of the campground, where a short trail leads to good vistas overlooking the falls.

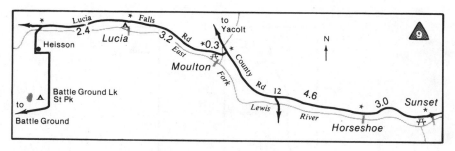

9. EAST FORK LEWIS RIVER

Four small waterfalls tumble along East Fork Lewis River. Follow the marked route 3 miles from the town of Battle Ground to Battle Ground Lake State Park. Continue 2.75 miles northbound from the state park, passing the hamlet of Heisson, to Lucia Falls Road.

Lucia Falls
Type: block; map: USGS Yacolt 7½'

The park surrounding this 15- to 25-foot waterfall is privately developed. There is an admittance fee. Drive 2.4 miles east along Lucia Falls Road from the junction. Turn at the Lucia Falls Park and Cafe.

Moulton Falls
Type: cascade; map: USGS Yacolt 7½'

Continue east 3.2 miles past Lucia Falls (above) along Lucia Falls Road. Turn at the public park to views of East Fork Lewis River sliding 15 to 25 feet.

Horseshoe Falls
Type: block; map: USGS Dole 7½'

This crescent-shaped 20- to 30-foot waterfall would earn a higher rating if closer views were possible. Follow Lucia Falls Road east to its end 0.3 mile past Moulton Falls (above). Take the right (southeast) fork, called County Road #12. This roadway rises 100 to 200 feet above the East Fork. Continue driving 4.6 miles to where the waterfall is visible from the road.

Sunset Falls
Type: block; map: USGS Gumboot Mtn 7½'

Drive 3 miles past Horseshoe Falls (above) to Sunset Picnic Area. East Fork Lewis River splashes 20 feet a short way upstream.

10. DOUGAN CAMP

Dougan Falls
Type: tiered; map: USGS Bobs Mtn 7½'

This stairstep series of block-type falls totals 30 to 50 feet along Washougal River. Water also slides 20 to 30 feet into the river from

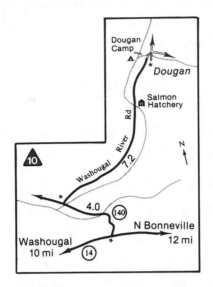

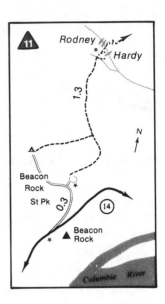

Dougan Creek. Turn north off S.R. 14 onto S.R. 140 10 miles east of Washougal and 12 miles west of North Bonneville. Drive up the hill and after 4 miles, turn right (north) onto Washougal River Road. The waterfall is 7.2 miles farther, where the road crosses the river for a second time.

11. BEACON ROCK STATE PARK

The 600-foot projection of Beacon Rock is a major landmark on the Washington side of the Columbia River Gorge. Nearby, Hamilton Mountain Trail passes two waterfalls. Beacon Rock State Park is next to S.R. 14 about 18 miles east of Washougal and 4 miles west of North Bonneville.

Hardy Falls
Type: horsetail; map: USGS Beacon Rock 7½'

Turn north off S.R. 14 onto the spur road across the highway from Beacon Rock. Drive 0.3 mile to the picnic area and the start of Hamilton Mountain Trail. After a moderate climb of about 1.25 miles, reach two short spur paths. The upper way to the far right leads to a viewpoint overlooking an 80- to 120-foot drop along Hardy Creek.

Rodney Falls
Type: tiered; map: USGS Beacon Rock 7½'

Hardy Creek plunges and cascades a total of 100 to 150 feet. Follow Hamilton Mountain Trail as to Hardy Falls (above), but take the lower spur path to a viewpoint of this entry. Continue on the main trail to a footbridge crossing at the base of the falls. Another short spur ascends to the base of its upper tier, 1.3 miles from the trailhead.

12. ROCK CREEK DRAINAGE

Rock Creek Falls
Type: block; map: USGS Bonneville Dam 7½'

Turn off S.R. 14 onto Second Street either in Stevenson, or 1 mile west of town. Turn west off Second Street onto Ryan Allen Road. In 0.2 mile, turn right on Iman Cemetery Road. Continue on this road to its end in 0.7 mile. A short, well-worn path leads to side views of Rock Creek shimmering as it drops 35 to 50 feet over a wide ledge.

▲ *Rock Creek Falls*

Steep Creek Falls
Type: horsetail; map: USGS Bonneville Dam 7½'

Go as to Rock Creek Falls (above) but instead of turning on Iman Cemetery Road, continue along Ryan Allen Road for 1 more mile. Turn left on Red Bluff Road and drive 5.5 miles to where the gravel road crosses Rock Creek. Steep Creek can be seen tumbling 30 to 40 feet into the main creek. I've named the falls after the stream.

13. CARSON AREA

The Carson area is best known for St. Martin Hot Springs, but the owners have periodically closed the waters to the public. Lesser-known Shipherd Falls, however, is always open to visitors.

Shipherd Falls
Type: tiered; map: USGS Carson 7½'

This 40- to 60-foot series of cascades along Wind River is next to a fishway, gauging station, and (locked) footbridge. Follow Hot Springs

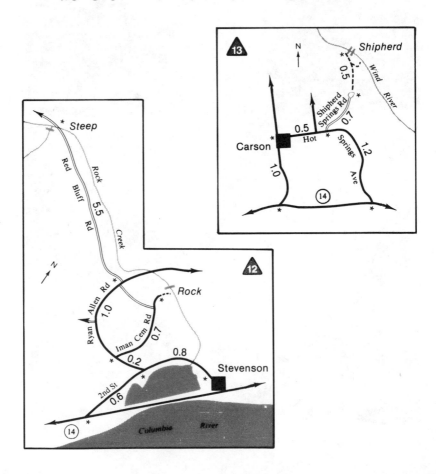

Avenue 0.5 mile east from Carson or 1.2 miles north from S.R. 14 to Shipherd Springs Road; turn north. The graveled route ends in 0.7 mile. A trail leads to views of the falls in 0.3 mile and 0.5 mile.

14. WIND RIVER ROAD

Panther Creek Falls

Type: segmented

This 50- to 75-foot waterfall is unique because it is technically *two* waterfalls dropping side by side from Panther Creek and Big Creek! Turn north onto Wind River Road #30 from S.R. 14. Pass Carson in 1 mile and after another 5.8 miles turn right (east) on Old State Road. Almost immediately, take a left (north) onto Panther Creek Road #65. Drive 7.4 miles up this road and find a safe place to park near its junction with Road #6511. Walk about 100 yards up Panther Creek Road #65 to a faint path that drops sharply down from the road (the most difficult part), then quickly leads to an undeveloped vista overlooking the falls.

Falls Creek Falls

Type: tiered; map: USGS Termination Point 7½'

This fantastic triple totaling 250 feet is so outstanding that I wonder why it has maintained such a common and dull name. Start north on Wind River Road #30 and continue 16.3 miles to Road #3062-057. Turn right and drive 2.3 miles on it to Lower Falls Creek Trail #152A.

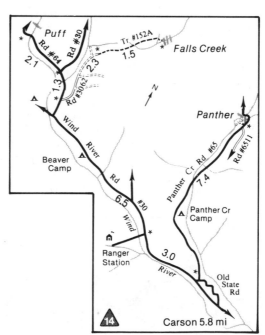

The trail crosses Falls Creek in 0.75 mile. Half a mile beyond is a steep cascade, which can be forded easily during high-water periods. The upper and middle portions of the falls soon come into view. The trail ends in front of the middle and lower falls 0.25 mile farther. Superb!

Puff Falls
Type: plunge

Dry Creek leaps 120 feet into a pool in seclusion. Turn left off Wind River Road #30 at Dry Creek Road #64, and go 2.1 miles to where the road crosses the creek. Proceeding upstream to the falls, also known as *Dry Creek Falls*, isn't overly difficult, except the 0.75-mile route is slow going and requires perseverance. The plunge pool makes a good swimming hole if you can bear the chilly water.

15. DOG CREEK

Dog Creek Falls
Type: fan; map: USGS Mt Defiance 7½'

Motorists zipping along S.R. 14 seldom notice this 15- to 25-foot waterfall. Stop at the undesignated parking area just west of mile marker 56, 6 miles east of Carson and 10 miles west of Bingen. Walk a short distance upstream to the falls.

16. MOUNT ADAMS RANGER DISTRICT

The point of departure for the pleasing waterfalls of this area is Mount Adams District Ranger Station, located 0.5 mile west of Trout Lake on S.R. 141.

Little Goose Creek Falls
Type: segmented

Peer into a canyon, looking down on a 75- to 100-foot triplet descending from Little Goose Creek. Drive about 1 mile west of the ranger station, then turn right (north) on Trout Lake Creek Road #88. After 8.3 more miles, park on the far (northwest) side of the gorge where the paved road leaves the creek. Although there is no trail, viewpoints are easily and quickly reached. *Warning:* Be careful at the canyon rim; the sheer cliffs are dangerously abrupt.

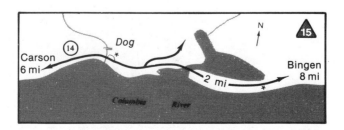

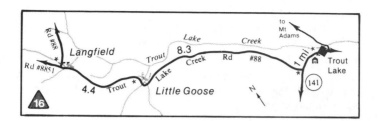

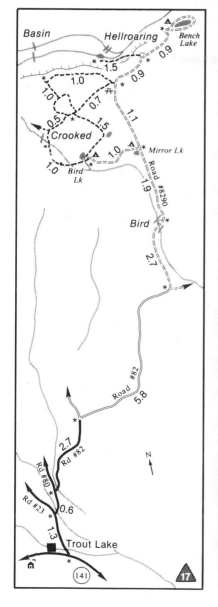

▲ *Puff Falls*

Langfield Falls
Type: fan; map: USGS Sleeping Beauty 7½'

Drive Trout Lake Creek Road #88 4.4 miles past Little Goose Creek Falls (above) to the marked turnout for Langfield Falls. A short trail leads to an excellent viewpoint of Mosquito Creek veiling 110 feet downward. The waterfall is named after a retired ranger who apparently discovered it.

17. MOUNT ADAMS WILDERNESS

These high-country waterfalls are all accessible from the Yakima Indian Reservation, adjacent to Mount Adams Wilderness Area. The best visiting period is from late summer to early autumn. The roads are rough and slow but usually navigable by passenger vehicles. Proceed north from Trout Lake along Road #23 for 1.3 miles, then bear right onto Road #80. Bear right again after 0.6 mile, this time onto Road #82. Stay on this route for 8.5 miles, then turn left (north) on Mount Adams Road #8290.

Bird Creek Falls
Type: tiered

A series of 5- to 10-foot cascades and punchbowls adjacent to the road toward Mount Adams. From junction at the southern end of Road #8290, proceed 2.7 miles to an unmarked turnout at the falls.

Crooked Creek Falls
Type: horsetail; map: USGS Mt Adams East 7½'

Water pours 35 to 50 feet from a small cliff, then steeply cascades along the stream course. Departing from either Bird Lake or Bird Creek Picnic Area, use the accompanying map to select your route through the subalpine environs to the falls. Lots of flowering plants and miniature waterfalls make the 1-mile hike absolutely charming.

Falls from Hellroaring Basin
Type: segmented; map: USGS Mt Adams East 7½'

A distant view of several 100- to 150-foot cataracts dwarfed by the specter of Mount Adams in the background. Your destination is Hellroaring Viewpoint, a moderately strenuous hike from either of two access trails (see map on page 101). The trails are 1 mile and 1.7 miles

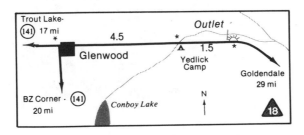

▲ *Outlet Falls*

long. Nonhikers can gain a more distant view from the Hellroaring Falls overlook (described below). I called these falls *Upper Hellroaring Falls* in the first edition of the book.

Hellroaring Falls
Map: USGS Mt Adams East 7½'

From Bird Creek Picnic Area, proceed east toward Bench Lake on Road #8290. Park at the overlook in 0.9 mile and start hiking on Hellroaring Meadows Trail #184. The trail ends at Heart Lake in 1.5 miles. The topographic map shows the falls 0.2 mile east of the lake along the adjacent stream. Due to lack of more detailed information, I recommend it for experienced cross-country enthusiasts only.

18. GLENWOOD AREA

Outlet Falls
Type: plunge; map: USGS Outlet Falls 7½'

Outlet Creek roars toward Klickitat Canyon in an exciting 120- to 150-foot plunge. Drive east to Glenwood from S.R. 141. The town is 20 miles north from BZ Corner or 17 miles east from Trout Lake. Continue 6 miles past Glenwood to the obscurely marked parking area and viewpoint. *Warning:* This canyon is unguarded, making it extremely dangerous for immature individuals.

The Inland Empire

*T*he eastern half of Washington is known locally as the Inland Empire. The name was popularized in the late 1800s, when the region ceased to be part of the frontier. Since then it has grown into a substantial producer of agricultural products, timber, minerals, and hydroelectric power. Railroads played a vital role in developing the Inland Empire and establishing Spokane as its center of commerce. The region's rail passenger service is still known as "The Empire Builder."

There are 42 falls known to occur in this region; 25 of them are described on the following pages. Waterfalls are distributed throughout the Inland Empire: in the Selkirk Mountains, Okanogan Highlands, and the Channeled Scablands.

The Selkirks are composed of old sedimentary rocks ranging from 80 million to 500 million years old. Recent folding and faulting, 1 million to 3 million years ago, was followed by glaciation, giving the range its present appearance. The Okanogan Highlands, a complex metamorphic mixture of schists and gneisses, were formed and uplifted 50 million to 75 million years ago. Glaciation and stream erosion have sharpened the peaks and valleys. Most of the falls in these mountainous terrains formed where rivers flow over heterogeneous rock material. Escarpments are shaped where water descends from resistant rock to weaker components downstream.

The *Channeled Scablands,* west and southwest of Spokane, are a uniquely eroded province of the Columbia Plateau where waterfall development has paralleled scabland formation. Toward the end of the last Ice Age, 10,000 to 13,000 years ago, Glacial Lake Missoula occupied an area in western Montana roughly half the size of Lake Michigan. This glacial lake existed due to a natural ice dam that blocked the valley's drainage at Clark Fork in northern Idaho. The ice dam broke repeatedly, each time liberating staggering volumes of water to the Columbia Plateau and portions of the Palouse Hills. These events, called the *Spokane Floods,* scoured the landscape and created waterfalls from the Columbia River and Snake River canyon rims.

Many of the cataracts are gone today, but the evidence of their magnitude is clearly visible. Famous *Dry Falls* was so powerful that its plunge pools remain, although several thousand years have passed since its waters thundered over the adjacent rock walls!

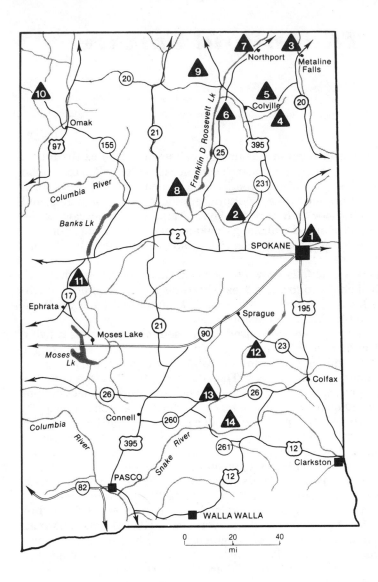

The Spokane Floods also created a descent along Trail Lake Coulee called *Summer Falls*. It became a dry cataract once the floodwaters ceased, but the torrent was resurrected by an irrigation project whose outlet follows the coulee (streambed). But alas! A new dam has reduced *Summer Falls* to a trickle. Nature giveth and taketh away, and so has man.

The Palouse River originally flowed into the Columbia River, but the Spokane Floods diverted its course into a fracture in the basaltic bedrock near the present site of Washtucna. The new river course flowed south and eventually plunged into the Snake River. The waterfall has since eroded its way 7.5 miles upstream, creating a 400-

to 800-foot-deep canyon from the Snake River to the present location of *Palouse Falls.*

1. SPOKANE

A renaissance occurred in downtown Spokane when the city hosted Expo '74, an international fair. The resulting national image boost has had a lasting effect. The former fair site is now Riverfront Park. It includes gardens, exhibits, an impressive opera house, and several falls along the Spokane River. Turn off Interstate 90 at the U.S. 2/U.S. 395/Division Street exit. Turn north at the end of the ramp and drive eight blocks north to Spokane Falls Boulevard near Riverfront Park.

Spokane Falls
Type: cascade; map: USGS Spokane NW 7½'

The Spokane River absolutely roars 60 to 100 feet downward as white water foams. An exciting gondola ride glides above the falls. When it is not operating, there is another good viewpoint near City Hall, two blocks west of Riverfront Park.

Upper Falls
Type: segmented

Walkway bridges cross just above these 15- to 30-foot falls where Canada Island splits the Spokane River. There is also a vista at a small pavilion in the northwest corner of the park.

2. SPOKANE INDIAN RESERVATION

Don't bring your rod and reel to the following waterfalls. The Spokane Indian Reservation, like all Native American lands, prohibits public fishing in its streams.

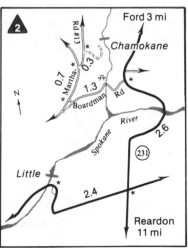

Chamokane Falls

Type: segmented; map: USGS Long Lake 7½'

Turn north off U.S. 2 at Reardan onto S.R. 231. Drive 13.5 miles to Martha-Boardman Road, located about 0.75 mile past the bridge over Spokane River. Turn left, follow the dusty road 1.3 miles and bear right (north). After 0.7 mile, turn right on an old dirt road. Watch for an old sign attached to a tree at a turnoff 0.3 mile farther. Park at this junction and walk toward the creek. The road ends in 0.5 mile at a small picnic site. Chamokane Creek tumbles 25 to 35 feet a short distance upstream.

Little Falls

Type: cascade

Spokane River pours off uniquely V-shaped Little Falls Dam, then cascades down another 20 to 30 feet. Turn north off U.S. 2 at Reardan and drive 11 miles on S.R. 231 to the marked Little Falls access road. Turn left and drive 2.4 miles to the undesignated turnout on the east side of the river. There are good views from the bridge.

▲ *Pewee Falls*

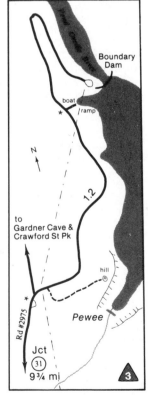

3. BOUNDARY DAM

This major descent is in the Colville National Forest in the northeastern tip of Washington. Additional attractions include Boundary Dam and Gardner Cave.

Pewee Falls
Type: horsetail; map: USGS Boundary Dam 7½'

Pewee Creek ribbons 150 to 200 feet down a vertical rock wall into Boundary Dam Reservoir. This starkly beautiful waterfall was originally named *Periwee Falls* in 1895 by a French-Canadian hunter and prospector. Turn north off S.R. 31 onto Crawford Park Road #2975, about 1 mile southwest of the town of Metaline Falls. Drive 11 miles to the boat launch site preceding the dam. Boaters can follow the shoreline south up the west side of the lake about 1.5 miles to the falls.

A hilltop vista of the falls can be reached on foot, but I recommend it for experienced cross-country hikers only. Backtrack 1.25 miles by car from the boat ramp to an undesignated parking spot west of the power lines. Walk up the road a short distance toward the reservoir to avoid a marsh, then follow the power line into the woods. After a few hundred yards, bear left (east) and climb the small knob 0.3 mile away. *Warning:* Do not attempt to get close to the waterfall, its stream, or the lakeside. Slopes in the drainage area are dangerously unstable and must be avoided.

4. PARK RAPIDS

Crystal Falls
Type: tiered; map: USGS Park Rapids 7½'

Little Pend Oreille River descends a total of 60 to 80 feet in tiered fashion. Look for the marked turnout along S.R. 20, located 14 miles east of Colville and 22 miles southwest of Tiger ghost town. The waterfall is on privately owned land with public access.

5. COLVILLE AREA

The small city of Colville developed from old Fort Colville, a U.S. Army outpost from 1859 to 1882. There are two falls nearby.

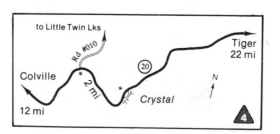

Marble Creek Falls
Type: horsetail; map: USGS Gillette Mountain 7½'

Go east from Colville on S.R. 20 and turn left (north) on County Road #700 in 1.25 miles. After 2 miles, bear right on Alladin Road. Drive 11 miles farther, watching for the obscurely marked National Forest Road #200 to the left (west). Park along this primitive route, which soon deteriorates into a well-worn path. Marble Creek descends 25 to 35 feet a short distance farther.

Douglas Falls
Type: fan; map: USGS Colville 7½'

Turn off S.R. 20 east of Colville onto County Road #700, and after 2 miles, turn again on Douglas Falls Road. Continue 3 miles to historic Douglas Falls Grange Park. An enclosed vista near the picnic area and playground gives a good view of Mill Creek veiling down 60 feet.

In 1855, R.H. Douglas harnessed the cataract for a grist mill, which he later converted into a sawmill. Failing to negotiate a lumber

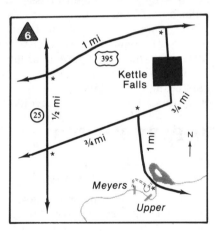

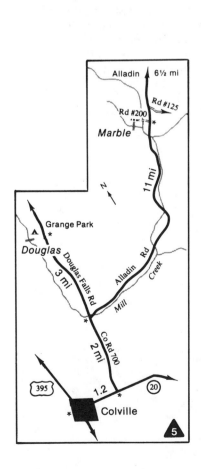

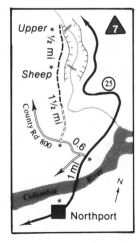

contract with Fort Colville, Douglas abandoned the project, but not his entrepreneurship. He turned his talents to the production of distilled spirits!

6. KETTLE FALLS

Kettle Falls is now only the name of a town. A cascade once tumbled nearby along the Columbia River, but the river's once mighty waters have since been pacified by Grand Coulee Dam, which created Franklin D. Roosevelt Lake. However, two other waterfalls still exist in the vicinity.

Upper Falls
Type: punchbowl

Turn off U.S. 395 and drive south through Kettle Falls. After 0.75 mile, turn left (south) on a paved road, then right on a dirt road 1 mile farther. Park at the undesignated parking area and walk to the Colville River and this small 15- to 20-foot waterfall.

Meyers Falls
Type: fan; map: USGS Kettle Falls 7½'

From Upper Falls (above), walk west down the road a short distance to where the Colville River crashes 60 to 100 feet. Please respect the landowner's privacy by not driving on the road and by making your midday visit brief. The waterfall is named for Louther Walden Meyers, a pioneer who lived here in the 1860s. A small Washington Water Power facility now operates beneath the falls.

7. NORTHPORT

Sheep Creek Falls
Type: fan; map: USGS Northport 7½'

Drive north along S.R. 25 to the village of Northport. Cross the Columbia River and turn left (west) on County Road #800. Continue approximately 0.75 mile to the first dirt road to the right (north). Park and hike along the primitive road about 1 mile to the canyon rim. Follow an old railroad grade for 0.5 mile and look down on a high-volume cataract exploding 125 to 150 feet along Sheep Creek.

Upper Falls
Type: block; map: USGS Northport 7½'

Sheep Creek roars down 40 to 60 feet 0.5 mile upstream from Sheep Creek Falls (above). The waterfall is a short distance below a collapsed railroad trestle, which marks the end of the trail, 2 miles from the trailhead.

▲   *Quillisascut Creek*
    Falls and author

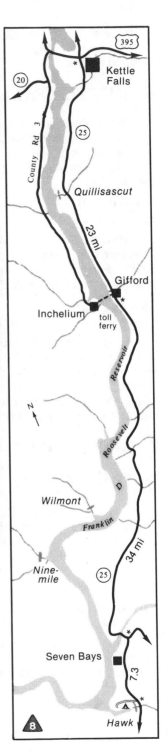

8. FRANKLIN D. ROOSEVELT LAKE

All but one of the following waterfalls are accessible only by boat. Due to the great length of the reservoir, nautical maps should be taken along to aid in lake orientation. They can be obtained at the marinas in Kettle Falls or Seven Bays, where boat rentals are also available.

Quillisascut Creek Falls
Type: fan; map: USGS Rice 7½'

Low streamflows limit the impressiveness of this 20- to 30-foot cataract. From the boat ramp and picnic area immediately north of Barnaby Island, head almost due east to a cove on the lake's eastern shore. After dropping anchor, follow the jeep trail an easy 0.25 mile to a very short path leading to the base of the falls. It has not been previously named.

▲ *Hawk Creek Falls*

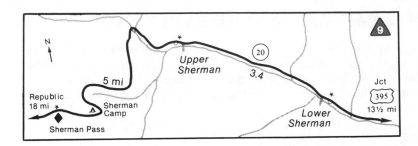

Ninemile Falls
Map: USGS Ninemile Flat 7½'

This waterfall can reportedly be seen by boat. Enter the cove that drains Ninemile and Little Ninemile creeks (erroneously labeled on some maps as Sixmile Creek, which doesn't exist). I've also been informed that **Wilmont Creek Falls** occurs 6.5 miles uplake. It cannot be seen from Wilmont Bay, but requires a short walk upstream.

Hawk Creek Falls
Type: punchbowl; map: USGS Olsen Canyon 7½'

A nice 35- to 50- foot drop next to Hawk Creek Campground. Depart S.R. 25 at the sign for Seven Bays, proceeding 7.3 miles to an access road for the lake. Turn right. Falls and camp are in 0.7 mile. Boaters may also view this previously unnamed waterfall by proceeding to the head of the embayment at Hawk Creek.

9. SHERMAN CREEK

Upper Sherman Creek Falls
Type: horsetail; map: USGS Sherman Peak 7½'

Sherman Creek drops 15 to 25 feet next to S.R. 20. Drive S.R. 20 east 5 miles from Sherman Pass to an unsigned turnout preceding the falls. Walk along the highway for a short distance to a view of the falls. This and the following entry are both located within Colville National Forest.

Lower Sherman Creek Falls
Type: horsetail; map: USGS South Huckleberry Mtn 7½'

Continue eastward from Upper Sherman Creek Falls (above) for 3.4 miles to another undesignated turnout. This 35- to 50-foot waterfall is located several hundred yards west from the vista; closer views require a scramble downslope. Both of the falls along this stream were previously unnamed.

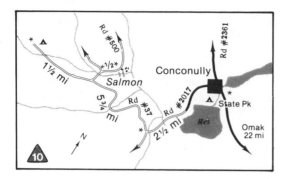

10. CONCONULLY

Conconully is a small resort town 22 miles northwest of Omak in north-central Washington. One notable series of falls is accessible in this area, located within Okanogan National Forest.

Salmon Falls

Type: tiered; map: USGS Tiffany Mtn 15'

West Fork Salmon Creek drops 300 feet over a reach of 0.25 mile, and features among its many waterfalls four primary falls each 20 to 40 feet high. Drive west from Conconully on Road #2017, which turns into Forest Road #37 in about 2.5 miles. After a total of 8.3 miles, turn right on Road #500. Continue 0.5 mile to a jeep trail on the right (south). Walk down this dirt road for 0.25 mile to several routes leading to the various descents. Be careful! The paths tend to be steep and crumbly.

▲ *Salmon Falls*

11. COULEE CITY

Dry Falls
Map: USGS Coulee City 7½'

The largest waterfall ever known once plunged 400 feet over cliffs in five sweeping horseshoes totaling 3.5 miles in width! The discharge was 40 times mightier than Niagara Falls. Follow U.S. 2 west from Coulee City, turning south on S.R. 17. Stop at the scenic turnout and viewpoint 2 miles farther.

Summer Falls
Type: punchbowl; map: USGS Coulee City 7½'

Formerly an outlet for Banks Lake Reservoir, water once thundered 70 to 100 feet from Trail Lake Coulee. Unfortunately, the falls have been reduced dramatically, with most of their discharge di-

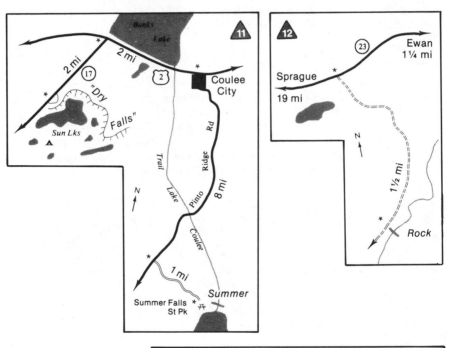

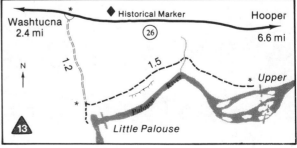

▲   *Rock Creek Falls*

verted to another hydroelectric facility. Drive 8 miles south of Coulee City along Pinto Ridge Road. Turn left (east) at the marked access road to Summer Falls State Park. The picnic area and the waterfall are in 1 mile. There is a memorial at the state park for three teenagers who, in 1978, drowned due to the whirlpool action and forceful undertow in the basin beneath the once-powerful falls.

12. ROCK CREEK COULEE

Rock Creek Falls
Type: block; map: USGS Texas Lake 7½'

This cooling 10- to 15- foot drop in a sagebrush setting is located on private land. Fortunately, as the posted signs indicate, permission to hike can be obtained from the adjacent landowner. Drive along S.R. 23 about 1.25 miles west from Ewan. Find a dusty backroad to the left (south). Walk along this route for 1.5 miles to the stream and the falls.

13. UPPER PALOUSE CANYON

Do cattle rustlers still work in this area? The rangeland between the highway and the canyon is leased for grazing, so it is best to avoid suspicion by informing a county patrolman in Washtucna of your hiking plans.

Little Palouse Falls
Type: block; map: USGS Palouse Falls 7½'

At a 90-degree turn in the Palouse River, the stream widens to 200 feet and drops 15 feet as a solid sheet into a large circular basin. The river was diverted into a rock fracture here during the Spokane Floods. Drive along S.R. 26 east from Washtucna for 2.4 miles, or drive 6.6 miles west from Hooper. Park just west of the historical marker. Follow a dirt road 1.2 miles south until it deteriorates into a trail above the falls. This route is a small portion of the historic Mullan Road, which extended 624 miles between Fort Benton, Montana, and Walla Walla, Washington. Immigrants poured westward over it during the 1860s and 1870s.

Upper Palouse Falls
Type: segmented; map: USGS Palouse Falls 7½'

The river separates into five different channels, each of which falls 22 feet. The descents are 1.5 miles upstream from Little Palouse Falls (above), 2.7 miles from the trailhead. Hike along the canyon rim. The entry gets a low rating only because the view is poor from the north side of the river.

14. LOWER PALOUSE CANYON

Palouse Falls
Type: plunge; map: USGS Palouse Falls 7½'

Palouse River hurtles 185 feet into Lower Palouse Canyon in a thundering display. (The formation of the falls is described in the introduction to this chapter.) Turn south off S.R. 260 onto S.R. 261 and drive 9 miles southeast to the marked access road to Palouse Falls State Park. To reach the falls from the south, turn west onto S.R. 261 from U.S. 12 about 15 miles north of Dayton.

The Wilkes Expedition of 1841 called this descent *Aputapat Falls.* Unfortunately, the name was later abandoned. In 1875 W.P. Breeding erected a flour mill at the falls. He envisioned a vibrant Palouse City at the site, but it never came to be.

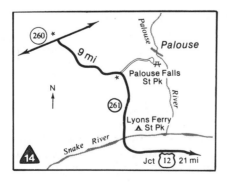

The Columbia Gorge
of Oregon

*T*he Oregon side of the Columbia Gorge is a haven for waterfall lovers. Although it is the smallest of the 14 regions in this book, it has the greatest density of waterfalls. There are 77 recognized falls in this area of 420 square miles. Descriptions of 49 are given in this chapter. The others cannot be viewed either because no trails lead to them or because they are in watersheds restricted to travel.

The majority of the falls along the Oregon side of the gorge were formed by the geological events that shaped the region. Two major lava flows occurred throughout much of the Pacific Northwest, one over 30 million years ago and the other about 15 million years ago. Although the mighty Columbia River was sometimes partially obstructed during these time periods, it always managed to erode through and resume its course to the Pacific Ocean.

As the layers of lava cooled, they mainly formed a rock type called basalt. The Cascade Mountains were formed by the uplifting of this bedrock material by internal earth forces. Most rivers were diverted by the creation of the Cascades because basalt is relatively resistant to erosion by running water. But the Columbia River was powerful enough to erode through the rising bedrock to shape the Columbia Gorge. The small streams that flow into the Columbia from the adjacent upland cannot effectively erode the basalt, so their courses are interrupted by the sharp, vertical breaks of the gorge and are seen as spectacular waterfalls.

These great waterfalls are limited to the south side of the gorge because landslides have modified the steepness of relief on the Washington side. Because the entire region's bedrock material is tilted slightly southward, when they are water saturated, the upper basaltic layers on the north side of the river slide into the gorge. Therefore, waterfalls on the Washington side are smaller and fewer in number than those in Oregon. The falls on the north side are described in the Gifford Pinchot Country chapter.

1. BRIDAL VEIL AREA

The Columbia Gorge Scenic Highway is accessible from Interstate 84 (formerly Interstate 80) for eastbounders at Troutdale (Exit 17), Lewis and Clark State Park (Exit 18), Corbett (Exit 22), or Bridal Veil (Exit 28). Westbounders get off at Dodson (Exit 35) or Warrendale (Exit 37).

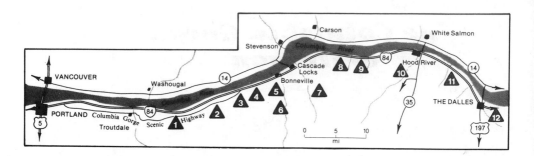

Latourell Falls

Type: plunge; map: USGS Bridal Veil 7½'

This 249-foot waterfall along Latourell Creek is within Guy W. Talbot State Park, 3.4 miles west on the Scenic Highway from Exit 28 off I-84. It is a short walk from the picnic area adjacent to the Scenic Highway to the viewpoint. The waterfall was named in August 1887, after Joseph Latourell, a prominent settler in the locality.

Upper Latourell Falls

Type: plunge

The trail to Latourell Falls (above) continues moderately for 0.8 mile to the upper falls, where Latourell Creek drops 75 to 100 feet. It is possible to walk behind the falling water. The park land was donated to the state of Oregon in 1929 by Mr. and Mrs. Guy W. Talbot.

Sheppards Dell Falls

Type: tiered

Two cataracts can be seen upstream from the bridge crossing at Sheppards Dell State Park, 2 miles west on the Scenic Highway from Exit 28 off I-84. The lower fall is of the horsetail form and drops 40 to 60 feet. The 35- to 50-foot plunge of the upper portion is not as clearly visible. I've named the entry after the site.

Bridal Veil Falls

Type: tiered; map: USGS Bridal Veil 7½'

Bridal Veil Creek drops abruptly twice, the upper portion 60 to 100 feet and the lower portion 40 to 60 feet. Drive to a parking area located about 1.5 miles east of Latourell Falls (above), or 1 mile west from the Scenic Highway's junction at Exit 28 of Interstate 84. A short trail winds down to the base of the cataract. Along the pathway, look across the Columbia River to distant views of some seasonal falls on the Washington side of the Gorge.

Coopey Falls

Type: horsetail; map: USGS Bridal Veil 7½'

This waterfall drops 150 to 175 feet along Coopey Creek. For a view from above the falls, hike 0.6 mile up Angels Rest Trail #415 from the trailhead just east off Exit 28 of I-84, on the right side of the Scenic

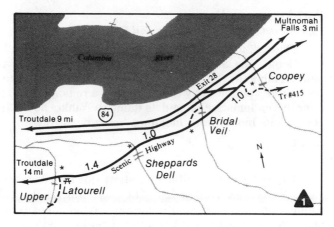

Highway. The descent is named for Charles Coopey, who owned the adjacent land. There is a convent near the base of the falls.

2. MULTNOMAH FALLS AREA

The following falls are accessible from the Columbia Gorge Scenic Highway, described in the "Bridal Veil Area" subsection of this chapter. In addition, the Multnomah Falls Rest Area (Exit 31) has a walkway to the vicinity.

Mist Falls

Type: plunge; map: USGS Bridal Veil 7½'

Water spirals down hundreds of feet from small Mist Creek. The falls can be viewed from the Scenic Highway 3.0 miles east of Bridal Veil and 0.8 mile west of Multnomah Falls, near mile marker 19.

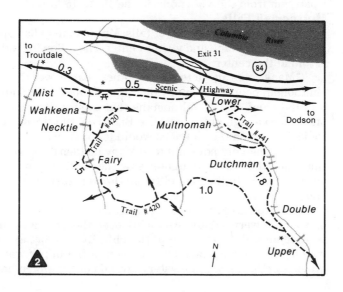

Wahkeena Falls
Type: tiered; map: USGS Bridal Veil 7½'

This 242-foot descent along Wahkeena Creek can be seen from the picnic area adjacent to the Scenic Highway 0.5 mile west of Multnomah Falls (below). It was once known as *Gordan Falls*, but a committee appointed by the Mazamas, a regional association of outdoor recreationists, changed its name to Wahkeena in 1915. The name is a Yakima Indian word meaning "most beautiful."

Necktie Falls
Type: horsetail

This entry is accessible by a short side trail from the moderately steep Wahkeena Trail #420. The side trail is 0.8 mile from the trailhead at Wahkeena Falls picnic ground (above). The waterfall drops 30 to 50 feet along Wahkeena Creek.

Fairy Falls
Type: fan

Wahkeena Trail #420 crosses in front of the base of this 20- to 30-foot falls at Wahkeena Creek, 1.1 miles from the trailhead, or about 0.3 mile past the side trail to Necktie Falls (above).

Multnomah Falls
Type: plunge; map: USGS Multnomah Falls 7½'

The most famous waterfall of the Columbia Gorge is the fourth highest in the United States. The main portion of the falls plunges 542 feet, while **Lower Multnomah Falls** drops 69 feet. Larch Mountain Trail #441 starts on the left-hand side of the lodge and ascends steeply from the lower falls to the top of Multnomah Falls. At the 1-mile mark, a side trail leads to a viewpoint over Multnomah Falls. Upstream from the viewpoint is the 10- to 15-foot descent of **Little Multnomah Falls.**

Near the base of the lower falls, Multnomah Falls Lodge houses a gift shop, restaurant, and visitor center. The following Indian folk tale is told at the center:

"Many years ago, a terrible sickness came over the village of the Multnomah people and many died. An old medicine man of the tribe told the chief of the Multnomahs that a pure and innocent maiden must go to a high cliff above the Big River and throw herself on the rocks below and the sickness would leave at once.

"The chief did not want to ask any maiden to make the sacrifice. But when the chief's daughter saw the sickness on the face of her lover, she went to the high cliff and threw herself on the rocks below and the sickness went away.

"As a token of the maiden's welcome by the Great Spirit, a stream of water, silvery white, streamed over the cliff and broke into a floating mist along the face of the cliff. Even today, as you carefully watch, the maiden's face can be seen in the upper waterfall as the breeze gently rustles the watery strands of her silken hair."

▲ *Multnomah Falls*

Dutchman Falls
Type: block

At this series of three falls along Multnomah Creek, the lower and upper falls drop 10 to 15 feet, while the middle section tumbles 15 to 20 feet. The falls can be seen from Larch Mountain Trail #441 (see directions to Multnomah Falls, above), 1.3 miles from the trailhead or between 0.2 and 0.3 mile from the side trail to Multnomah Falls viewpoint.

Double Falls
Type: plunge

Continue along Larch Mountain Trail #441 for 0.3 to 0.4 mile past Dutchman Falls (see directions above), a total of 1.6 or so miles from the trailhead, to full views of the 50- to 75-foot lower falls and a view down from the top of the 100- to 125-foot upper falls.

Upper Multnomah Falls
Type: cascade

This 15- to 20-foot drop can be viewed from Larch Mountain Trail #441 about 0.2 mile past Double Falls (see directions above), a total of 1.9 miles from the trailhead, near the junction with Wahkeena Trail #420.

3. ONEONTA AND HORSETAIL DRAINAGES

The cool, moist north-facing slopes and sheltered drainages of the Oregon side of the Columbia Gorge provide an environment for lush, diverse vegetation. This setting is described at Oneonta Gorge Botanical Area, 2 miles east of Multnomah Falls along the Columbia Gorge Scenic Highway. The "Bridal Veil Area" subsection of this chapter describes accesses to the Scenic Highway.

Oneonta Falls
Type: horsetail; map: USGS Multnomah Falls 7½'

This descent drops 50 to 75 feet along Oneonta Creek. Hike up moderately strenuous Oneonta Trail #424 for 0.9 mile to its junction with Horsetail Falls Trail #438. Follow Trail #438 for a few hundred yards to the footbridge overlooking the falls. **Lower Oneonta Falls** can be heard but not seen from the trail. Reach the falls when the water is low by hiking upstream along Oneonta Gorge from the Botanical Area just off the Scenic Highway.

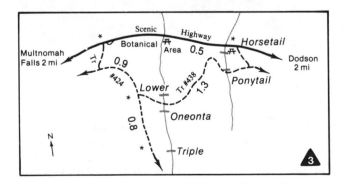

Triple Falls
Type: segmented; map: USGS Multnomah Falls 7½'

Walk along Oneonta Trail #424 for 1.7 miles from the trailhead (0.8 mile past the junction with Horsetail Falls Trail #438) to Triple Falls. The cataract plunges 100 to 135 feet along Oneonta Creek. It is of triplet form, not triple as the name implies.

Horsetail Falls
Type: horsetail; map: USGS Multnomah Falls 7½'

This 176-foot waterfall along Horsetail Creek can be viewed from a turnout from the Scenic Highway, 2.5 miles east of Multnomah Falls. It is a classic example of the horsetail form.

Ponytail Falls
Type: horsetail

These falls descend 100 to 125 feet along Horsetail Creek. They are 0.4 mile from the Scenic Highway along Horsetail Falls Trail #438, which starts at Horsetail Falls (above). The trail goes behind the base of the falls. They are also referred to as *Upper Horsetail Falls*.

4. JOHN B. YEON STATE PARK

The state park is adjacent to the east end of the Columbia Gorge Scenic Highway, just before it returns to Interstate 84.

Elowah Falls
Type: plunge; map: USGS Bonneville Dam 7½'

McCord Creek plunges 289 feet within John B. Yeon State Park. Begin on Gorge Trail #400, turning left at the first trail junction. A second junction occurs 0.2 mile from the parking area. For an aerial view of the falls, turn right on Elowah Falls Trail and take this moderately steep route 0.8 mile. To reach the base of the falls, stay on Trail #400 for 0.4 mile. A committee of the Mazamas, an outdoor recreation association, named the falls in 1915.

Upper McCord Creek Falls
Type: segmented

Continue 0.2 mile past the upper viewpoint of Elowah Falls (see directions above) to these 100- to 125-foot falls at the end of Elowah Falls Trail.

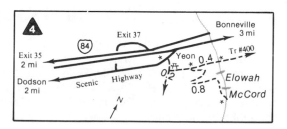

▲   *Elowah Falls*

5. TANNER CREEK DRAINAGE

When I last visited this area in August 1988, its 0.5-mile trail had been upgraded to a condition that makes for a marvelous stroll. Turn off Interstate 84 at Bonneville Dam (Exit 40) and proceed south several hundred yards to the parking area for Tanner Creek Trail, which starts out as a dirt road. *Note:* Gorge Trail #400 does *not* pass the following waterfalls.

Munra Falls

Type: fan

An unnamed creek drops 35 to 50 feet into Tanner Creek. It's only about a 0.25-mile walk from the trailhead to where the dirt road turns into a footpath. I've named the falls after nearby Munra Point.

Wahclella Falls

Type: tiered; map: USGS Tanner Butte 7½'

The upper portion of this thunderous waterfall plunges 15 to 25 feet before veiling downward 50 to 70 feet into a pool. Go 0.5 mile from the Tanner Creek Trailhead (0.25 mile from Munra Falls, above) to the trail's end at the cataract, also known as *Tanner Falls*. Wahclella, the name of a nearby Indian locality, was named in 1915 by a committee of the Mazamas, an outdoor recreation association. **East Fork Falls** can also be seen streaming above the descent from a vantage on the west side of Tanner Creek.

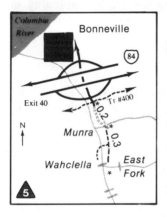

▲   *Wahclella Falls*

6. EAGLE CREEK DRAINAGE

Eastbound travelers can turn off Interstate 84 at Eagle Creek Park (Exit 41), but westbound travelers must make a U-turn at Bonneville Dam (Exit 40) to reach Exit 41. Make a similar turn at Cascade Locks (Exit 44) to get back westbound on the freeway. From the park, Eagle Creek Trail #440 ascends moderately 1,400 feet during its 6-mile length.

Ruckel Creek Falls

Type: cascade

Before embarking up Eagle Creek, waterfall collectors may first wish to visit this 30- to 50-foot slide along Ruckel Creek. It's a 0.25-mile walk east from Eagle Creek Campground on Gorge Trail #400. The trailhead is located just a short way along the access road to the campsites. The falls, which deserve a higher rating during high streamflows, are situated beneath a footbridge that is in actuality an antiquated span of an abandoned portion of the old Columbia River Highway.

Wauna Falls

Type: cascade; map: USGS Bonneville Dam 7½'

This is the first of many falls along Eagle Creek Trail #440. Wauna Falls is on the first major tributary to Eagle Creek, about 1.1 miles from the trailhead. I've called these unnamed falls by the name of nearby Wauna Point.

Metlako Falls

Type: plunge; map: USGS Bonneville Dam 7½'

This waterfall drops 100 to 150 feet along Eagle Creek. The viewpoint is 1.5 miles from the trailhead of Eagle Creek Trail #440. The waterfall was named for the legendary Indian goddess of salmon by a committee of the Mazamas, an outdoor recreation group, in 1915.

Punch Bowl Falls

Type: punchbowl; map: USGS Tanner Butte 7½'

Hike 2.1 miles from the trailhead of Eagle Creek Trail #440 (0.6 mile past Metlako Falls viewpoint) to a short side trail leading to the falls. Although it descends only 10 to 15 feet, the waterfall is exquisite, a classic example of the punchbowl form.

Loowit Falls

Type: horsetail; map: USGS Tanner Butte 7½'

This waterfall can be viewed across Eagle Creek toward Loowit Creek 3.2 miles from the Eagle Creek Trailhead (about 1.1 miles past the Punch Bowl Falls viewpoint). High Bridge crosses Eagle Creek a short distance farther and, soon after, the 10- to 20-foot base of **Benson Falls** is visible from the trail.

Skoonichuk Falls
Type: tiered; map: USGS Tanner Butte 7½'

This waterfall is along Eagle Creek Trail #440, 3.6 miles from the trailhead, about 0.4 mile upstream from High Bridge. Tenas Camp is nearby and **Tenas Falls** are on a tributary 0.2 mile farther.

Wy'east Falls
Type: plunge; map: USGS Wahtum Lake 7½'

Hike Eagle Creek Trail 3.6 miles from the trailhead to Tenas Camp, then 1 mile to Wy'east Camp, then 0.3 mile farther to the junction of Eagle-Benson Trail #434. Wy'east Falls is a short walk down Trail #434. **Blue Grouse Falls** is on Eagle Creek Trail #440 about 1.2 miles past Wy'east Camp and 0.6 mile past Blue Grouse Camp. I've called both of these unnamed waterfalls after their nearby camps.

Tunnel Falls
Type: plunge; map: USGS Wahtum Lake 7½'

Eagle Creek Trail #440 goes behind Tunnel Falls at East Fork Eagle Creek, 0.7 mile past Blue Grouse Camp. **Eagle Creek Falls** should be visible from Eagle Creek Trail #440 about 0.2 mile past Tunnel Falls. I felt I should call one of the previously unnamed falls within the drainage area by the name of the stream.

7. CASCADE LOCKS AREA

Dry Creek Falls
Type: plunge; map: USGS Carson 7½'

This cataract and the following waterfall are accessible via Pacific Crest National Scenic Trail #2000. The trail's northern entry into Oregon is at Bridge of the Gods, located off Interstate 84 at Cascade Locks (Exit 44). Alternate trailheads are at the Columbia Gorge Work Center and Herman Camp, situated off I-84 near Forest Lane–Herman Creek (Exit 47).

From Bridge of the Gods, hike 2 miles along Trail #2000 to Dry Creek. For those beginning from the Work Center or Herman Camp, take the appropriate spur trail to Trail #2000 and go 2.3 miles westward to Dry Creek. Once at the drainage, follow a dirt road 0.25 mile upstream to the 50- to 70-foot descent. *Note:* Dry Creek is part of the watershed for the city of Cascade Locks. Please obey the signs posted near the falls.

Pacific Crest Falls
Type: horsetail; map: USGS Carson 7½'

An obscured view of water pouring 25 to 40 feet from an un-named stream near Pacific Crest Trail #2000. Hike Trail #2000 for 2 miles to Dry Creek, then another 1.9 miles east (0.4 mile from the

▲ *Dry Creek Falls*

junction of Trail #2000 and Herman Bridge Trail #406-E). Look a fair distance upstream to see the waterfall, which I've named after the trail.

  ## Falls Creek Falls
Map: USGS Carson 7½'

Situated next to Herman Creek Trail #406, this previously unnamed entry is located 0.8 mile southeast of Herman Camp.

Slide Creek Falls
Map: USGS Carson 7½'

Visible from Herman Creek Trail #406, this waterfall is 3.7 miles from the trailhead (2.9 miles past Falls Creek Falls, above). I've named it after the creek.

8. WYETH

Gorton Creek Falls
Type: horsetail

A 120- to 140-foot drop along Gorton Creek. Depart Interstate 84 at Wyeth (Exit 51) and drive 0.4 mile to the parking area for Wyeth Trail #411, located at the south end of Wyeth Campground. After walking a few hundred yards, proceed straight along the dirt road; don't take either of the two marked trails. After 0.25 mile the road deteriorates into a path, crossing the creek once. In another 0.25 mile, after walking and climbing over a few large boulders, is the base of the falls. Some vantages reveal a 20- to 30-foot upper tier.

9. STARVATION CREEK STATE PARK

Turn off Interstate 84 at the eastbound-only exit for Starvation Creek State Park and Rest Area (no camping). Westbounders must make a U-turn at Wyeth (Exit 51) to enter, then make a similar turn at Viento Park (Exit 56) when leaving. All of the following waterfalls can be glimpsed from Interstate 84.

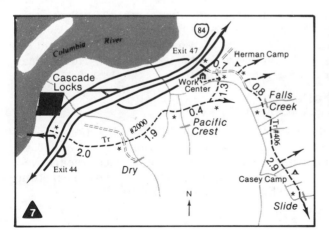
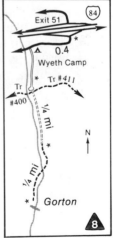

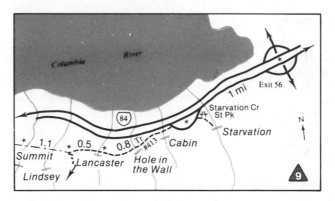

  ### Starvation Creek Falls
Type: horsetail; map: USGS Mt Defiance 7½'

This 186-foot waterfall along Starvation Creek is a short walk southeast from the picnic area. The name comes from an event in December 1884. Two trains of the recently completed railroad were snowbound nearby. The stranded passengers called the area "Starve-out," although no one perished during the incident.

 ### Cabin Creek Falls
Type: horsetail; map: USGS Mt Defiance 7½'

Starting from Starvation Creek State Park, hike 0.3 mile west along Mount Defiance Trail #413 to this 175- to 200-foot falls.

 ### Hole in the Wall Falls
Type: cascade; map: USGS Mt Defiance 7½'

Walk 0.3 mile to Cabin Creek Falls, then another 0.3 mile west on Mount Defiance Trail #413. The 75- to 100-foot plunge once sprayed onto the highway, so the course of Warren Creek was diverted by blasting a tunnel through the adjacent basaltic cliff. The original waterfall was known as *Warren Falls*.

Lancaster Falls
Type: plunge; map: USGS Mt Defiance 7½'

Walk 0.2 mile past Hole in the Wall Falls (see directions above) for a total of 0.8 mile along Mount Defiance Trail #413 to this 200- to 250-foot waterfall which falls seasonally along Wonder Creek. It was named in 1970 after Samuel C. Lancaster, who designed the beautiful Columbia River Scenic Highway prior to World War I.

  ### Lindsey Creek Falls
Map: USGS Mt Defiance 7½'

Hike the 0.8 mile to Lancaster Falls (see directions above), then go about 0.5 mile past Lancaster Falls. However, instead of following the switchbacks up Mount Defiance Trail #413, bushwhack along the power line for about 0.3 mile to Lindsey Creek. The waterfall is upstream about 0.25 mile.

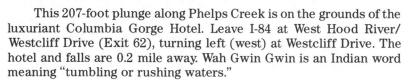

▲ *Punchbowl Falls*

Summit Creek Falls
Map: USGS Mt Defiance 7½'

Follow the directions to Lindsey Creek Falls (above), and continue along the power line about 0.8 mile past Lindsey Creek to Summit Creek for a total hike of about 2.4 miles. The waterfall is upstream about 100 yards.

10. HOOD RIVER AREA

Drivers along Interstate 84 use Exits 62 and 64. The area can also be reached from the Mount Hood area via S.R. 35.

Wah Gwin Gwin Falls
Type: plunge; map: USGS Hood River 7½'

This 207-foot plunge along Phelps Creek is on the grounds of the luxuriant Columbia Gorge Hotel. Leave I-84 at West Hood River/ Westcliff Drive (Exit 62), turning left (west) at Westcliff Drive. The hotel and falls are 0.2 mile away. Wah Gwin Gwin is an Indian word meaning "tumbling or rushing waters."

Punchbowl Falls
Type: punchbowl; map: USGS Dee 7½'

Hood River drops 10 to 15 feet into a large pool flanked by sheer cliffs of columnar basalt. Drive to the lumber processing facility at Dee, located along S.R. 281. Turn right on Punchbowl Road and

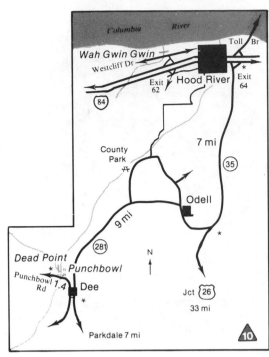
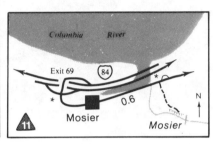

continue 1.4 miles to an unsigned parking area on the near (east) side of the river. Take a short walk down the dirt road to pathways leading to unguarded vistas at the rim of the small canyon.

Dead Point Creek Falls
Type: tiered; map: USGS Dee 7½'

Look across Hood River to view this 40- to 50-foot double falls. It is located immediately downstream from Punchbowl Falls (above); use the same viewpoints. The topographic map erroneously labels this previously unnamed cataract as Punchbowl Falls.

11. MOSIER AREA

Mosier Creek Falls
Type: horsetail; map: USGS White Salmon 7½'

Turn off I-84 at Mosier (Exit 69) and drive 0.6 mile east, passing Mosier. A short, easy trail on the right (east) side of Mosier Creek bridge leads to the 125- to 150-foot drop. I've called the waterfall by the name of its stream.

12. THE DALLES AREA

Turn off Interstate 84 at The Dalles East/U.S. 197 (Exit 87). Drive south 0.2 mile, then turn right (west) and go 0.2 mile to Southeast Frontage Road.

Cushing Falls
Type: punchbowl; map: USGS Petersburg 7½'

Drive 1 mile east along Southeast Frontage Road, then turn left and continue for 0.4 mile. Cross the bridge and turn right on an unimproved road. The 10- to 15-foot waterfall is a short, easy walk up Fifteenmile Creek.

Petersburg Falls
Type: cascade; map: USGS Petersburg 7½'

Continue for 2.5 miles past Cushing Falls (above) on Southeast Frontage Road, then turn left and drive 0.4 mile on Fifteenmile Road. Park just before the bridge. The 5- to 10-foot cascades are a short walk away. I've called this unnamed waterfall by a place name in the area.

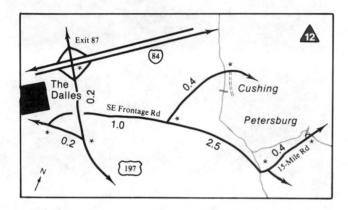

Oregon's North Coast Range

The Coast Range extends from the northwest lobe of Oregon southward to California. For convenience, the region has been divided into two chapters, entitled North Coast Range and South Coast Range. This chapter describes waterfalls found in association with the moist, montane environment stretching from the Columbia River, between Portland and Astoria, to an arbitrarily chosen southern limit along U.S. 20, which connects Newport and Corvallis.

During my travels along the coast, I found startling evidence that the Pacific Northwest has an enormous number of unmapped waterfalls. The northern Coast Range contains fewer mapped falls than most of the other regions of the northwest. The U.S. Geological Survey topographic maps list 49, of which 14 are described in the following pages. But realistically, many more falls occur in the area. Cal Baker of Hebo Ranger District in Siuslaw National Forest has surveyed and recorded 99 drops exceeding five feet — just in one district! Much of Idaho, Oregon, and Washington is more rugged and wild than the Coast Range, so if a similar proportion of falls are unlisted, the entire Northwest probably has over 10,000 falls in addition to the 925 currently mapped. It would require an encyclopedia-sized document to describe every waterfall!

1. SCAPPOOSE

Bonnie Falls
Type: segmented; map: USGS Chapman 7½'

North Scappoose Creek tumbles 15 to 25 feet over a basalt escarpment. Turn off U.S. 30 at the north end of Scappoose and drive 4.3 miles northwest along Scappoose–Vernonia Road. A small parking turnout immediately precedes the falls. A fish ladder has been built next to them.

2. BEAVER CREEK

Motorists driving along U.S. 30 formerly passed two waterfalls between Rainier and Clatskanie, but the route was altered over a decade ago. Now few travelers see these falls unless they turn off the main route to look for them. Drive 6.5 miles west from Rainier on U.S.

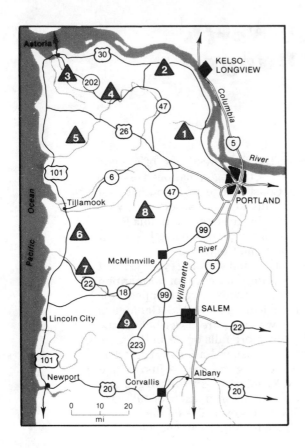

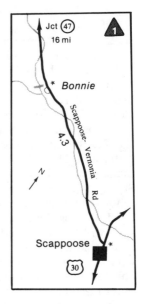

30 to the marked Delena turnoff 1.2 miles west of the turnoff to Vernonia.

Upper Falls
Type: cascade

To reach this 10- to 15-foot cataract along Beaver Creek, turn west off U.S. 30 onto Old Highway 30/Delena Road and drive 1.8 miles to the falls.

Beaver Falls
Type: block; map: USGS Delena 7½'

Continue 1.6 miles west from Upper Falls (see directions above) to an undesignated parking area to the left (south). Walk down the short dirt road to a path leading shortly to side views of water pouring 60 to 80 feet from Beaver Creek. *Be careful.* There are no guardrails around the viewpoint at the top of the waterfall.

▲ *Youngs River Falls*

3. OLNEY

Youngs River Falls
Type: fan; map: USGS Olney 7½'

Drive 10 miles southeast from Astoria on S.R. 202, or 20 miles northwest from Jewell. At Olney, turn south on the paved road marked Youngs River Falls. Continue 4 miles to the wide, unmarked parking area at a hairpin turn in the road. A short, easy trail leads to the base of the falls where Youngs River curtains 30 to 50 feet into the Klaskanine Valley.

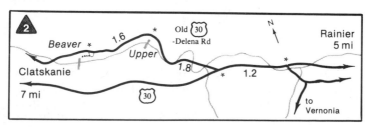

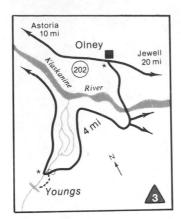

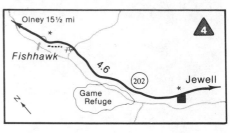

4. JEWELL

Fishhawk Falls
Type: fan; map: USGS Vinemaple 7½'

Drive 4.4 miles northwest from Jewell along S.R. 202 to Lee Wooden County Park. Trails lead upstream to the base of the falls in 0.2 mile. Fishhawk Creek ripples 40 to 60 feet downward. You can also drive 0.2 mile farther to an undesignated viewpoint above the falls.

Between Jewell and Fishhawk Falls is Jewell Meadows Wildlife Area. Elk and deer are often seen browsing in this state game refuge. There are marked viewpoints next to the highway.

5. NEHALEM RIVER ROAD

Two minor falls are found along the leisurely drive down winding Nehalem River Road. The road faithfully follows the meandering river for 27 miles through Tillamook State Forest between U.S. 26 and S.R. 53.

Little Falls
Type: cascade; map: USGS Elsie 7½'

Turn off U.S. 26 near Elsie at the southbound turn marked Spruce Run County Park. Drive 5.2 miles to the park, then 1 mile farther to a sharp right (west) turn in both the road and the river. Park where the road widens. Fishing access paths lead to the falls where water cascades 5 to 10 feet over the 75- to 100-foot wide Nehalem River.

Nehalem Falls
Type: cascade; map: USGS Foley Peak 7½'

Turn northeast off U.S. 101 onto S.R. 53 near Wheeler. In 1.3 miles turn right (southeast) on Nehalem River Road and drive 7 miles to the entrance to Nehalem Falls Park. Stop along the road about 100 yards inside the entrance. The Nehalem River slides 5 to 10 feet nearby.

6. TILLAMOOK AREA

If this region's waterfalls have thus far left you uninspired, be patient. Buy some crackers and the famous Tillamook cheese and drive to the following entry.

Munson Creek Falls
Type: tiered; map: USGS Beaver 7½'

This fine-lined cataract dropping 266 feet is the highest waterfall in the Coast Range. Turn from U.S. 101 about halfway between Tillamook and Beaver at the sign for Munson Creek Falls County Park. Follow the signs 1.6 miles to the parking area and trailhead.

The easily hiked Lower Trail traverses through a lush forest to the base of the falls. For full views of the triple horsetail falls, follow the Upper Trail for 0.5 mile to an excellent gorge vista. The trails were built as part of youth programs in 1960–62 and 1978–79. The water features are named after Goran Munson, who came from Michigan and settled along the creek in 1889.

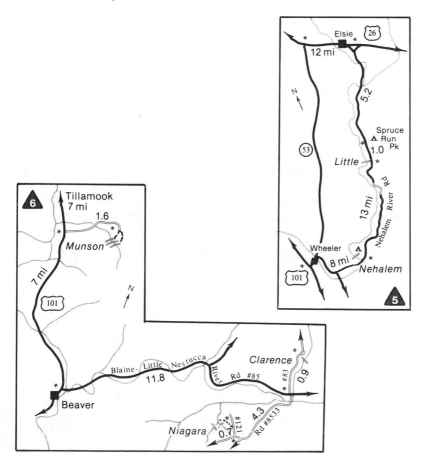

Clarence Creek Falls
Type: horsetail

Turn left (north) off U.S. 101 at Beaver to the Blaine–Little Nestucca River Road. Drive 11.8 miles, then turn left (north) on Clarence Creek Road #83. The gravel route ascends steeply, then levels off to a gentle slope in 0.9 mile. Clarence Creek slides 45 feet adjacent to the road.

Niagara Falls
Type: segmented

Technically two waterfalls, as Pheasant Creek plunges 80 to 100 feet beside a tributary cascading down 120 to 130 feet within Siuslaw National Forest. Follow the directions for Clarence Creek Falls (above), but instead of turning left on Clarence Creek Road #83, turn right (south) on Road #8533. Proceed 4.3 miles to Road #8533-121 and turn right; the trailhead is located 0.7 mile along this secondary route. The trail ends in 0.7 mile at the base of the waterfalls. The falls are not titled after their eastern namesake, but derived from nearby Niagra Point and its Niagara Creek drainage basin. Its impressiveness decreases as summer progresses.

7. DOLPH

Gunaldo Falls
Type: fan

Drive toward Dolph Junction, located where S.R. 22 and Little Nestucca River Road meet 11 miles south of Hebo and 14 miles northwest of Valley Junction. Take S.R. 22 from Dolph southeast for 1.2 miles to a wide expanse of the road immediately preceding a dirt road to the right (south). Listen for the falls. Scramble down the adjacent slope to the stream and continue to where an unnamed tributary sprays 65 feet into Sourgrass Creek 0.1 mile from the highway.

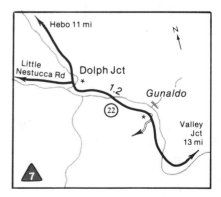

▲ *Lee Falls*

8. CHERRY GROVE

Cherry Grove is a small community nestled in the eastern foothills of the Coast Range. Two small waterfalls descend nearby along the refreshing waters of Tualatin River. Turn west off S.R. 47 at Patton Valley Road 6 miles south of Forest Grove and 11 miles north of Yamhill. Drive 6 miles to the town, staying on the main road through the village. At a sweeping curve to the right, the route becomes Summit Avenue. Continue to the end of the paved surface and turn left (west) on a dirt road.

Little Lee Falls

Type: punchbowl; map: USGS Turner Creek 7½'

Tualatin River splits into three parts before cascading 5 to 10 feet into a large pool. Drive along the dirt road past the scattered residential area into the forest to an unmarked turnout in 0.8 mile. The falls are a short walk away.

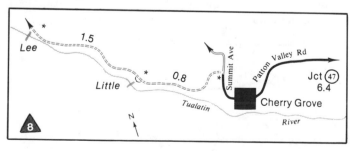

▲ *Falls City Falls*

Lee Falls
Type: segmented; map: USGS Turner Creek 7½'

Hike along the dirt road for an easy 1.5 miles past Little Lee Falls (above) to a gate blocking the way. Water pours 10 to 20 feet from a rocky escarpment adjacent to the road. **Haines Falls** is 1.75 miles farther upstream, but is not accessible.

9. FALLS CITY

Falls City Falls
Type: block; map: USGS Falls City 7½'

Little Luckiamute River sharply drops 25 to 35 feet into a tight gorge. To reach the community after which the waterfall is named, turn off S.R. 223 at the Falls City road 6 miles south of Dallas and 20 miles north of U.S. 20. Drive 4 miles to the town; continue toward the west side of town. After crossing the river, turn right at the South Main Street sign and drive 0.1 mile to Michael Harding Park. There are side views of the falls from the park.

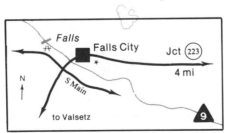

Oregon's South Coast Range

The southern portion of Oregon's Coast Range extends from the north along S.R. 34, which connects Waldport and Corvallis, south to the California border, where the range is commonly called the Klamath Mountains. There are 42 waterfalls mapped in this region; 24 of them are described here.

The landscape of the South Coast Range is geomorphically youthful. Its geology includes each of the three major classes of rocks. *Igneous* rocks, such as basalt, are common, as are *sedimentary* layers of sandstone and siltstone. Heat and pressure have transformed some of these rocks into the third category — *metamorphic* rocks, of which gneiss and quartzite are examples. Each type of rock has a varying degree of resistance to erosion from running water.

This region once had a low relief, but internal earth forces uplifted and deformed the flat, coastal plains between 1 million and 3 million years ago. The courses of most of the rivers flowing to the Pacific Ocean from the western flank of the Cascade Mountains were altered by this evolution of the Coast Range. Only two waterways, the Rogue River and the Umpqua River, were powerful enough to maintain their passages to the sea. Falls were shaped on these two rivers where rising bedrock with contrasting rates of erosion resistance met the streambeds.

Other major streams such as the Coquille River found new courses as the land surface rose. The rising bedrock of different forms also created waterfalls on these rivers. Additional descents formed where tributary creeks connected with larger rivers. As uplifting progressed, smaller streams generally eroded less effectively than the main channel. Therefore, a vertical drop is often seen near a tributary's confluence with the larger waterway. *Elk Creek Falls* is an example.

1. ALSEA AREA

Alsea, on the eastern flank of the Coast Range, is near these three waterfalls. The town is 25 miles southwest of Corvallis and 40 miles east of Tidewater on S.R. 34.

Fall Creek Falls
Type: punchbowl; map: USGS Alsea 7½'

Fall Creek drops only 5 to 10 feet, but a fish ladder bypasses it. Follow S.R. 34 west of Alsea for 13 miles. Turn right (north) on Fall Creek Road. The waterfall is to the left in 1.2 miles.

▲ *Green Peak Falls*

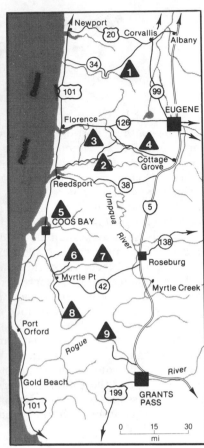

Alsea Falls

Type: cascade; map: USGS Glenbrook 7½'

South Fork Alsea Creek cascades 30 to 50 feet downward. Turn off S.R. 34 at Alsea and drive south for 1 mile. Then turn left (east) and continue 8.6 miles to Alsea Falls Picnic Area. This route is marked all the way from town. A short trail leads to the river and the falls.

Green Peak Falls

Type: fan; map: USGS Glenbrook 7½'

Water veils 30 to 40 feet downward along South Fork Alsea River. Enter Hubert K. McBee Memorial Park, located 0.7 mile northwest of Alsea Falls Picnic Area (above). Drive through the park for 0.5 mile to a junction with a dirt road. Park next to the road in slightly less than 0.2 mile. Short but very steep paths lead down to the river. Use the vegetative ground cover for hand- and footholds to help you carefully make your way down. Scrambling back up to the road won't be as difficult.

2. SMITH RIVER

Smith River Falls
Type: block; map: USGS Smith River Falls 7½'

A 5- to 10-foot drop along the otherwise placid Smith River. Turn east off U.S. 101 onto Smith River Road, located north of Umpqua River and Reedsport. Drive 22 miles eastward, 11 miles past the junction with North Fork Road #48 (do not turn at the junction). The waterfall, which is less impressive in summer, is located just before Smith River Falls Campground, run by the BLM. The features are named for Jedediah Strong Smith, an early 19th century fur trader and explorer.

3. MAPLETON RANGER DISTRICT

Three impressive waterfalls are nestled deep within this district of Siuslaw National Forest, each accessible from the superbly designed Kentucky Falls Trail. Drive Smith River Road 11 miles east of U.S. 101 to North Fork Road #48; turn north and continue 7.6 miles to Road #23, turning right (east). After an additional 10.5 miles, turn left (northwest) on Road #919 and proceed 2.8 miles to the trailhead.

Upper Kentucky Falls
Type: segmented

An easy 0.75-mile hike leads to a cliffside view of this 80- to 100-foot drop along Kentucky Creek.

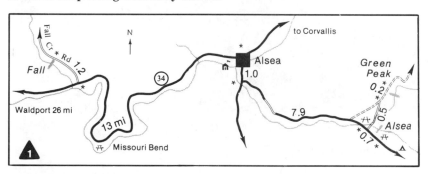

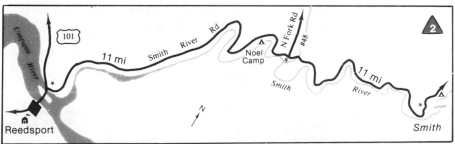

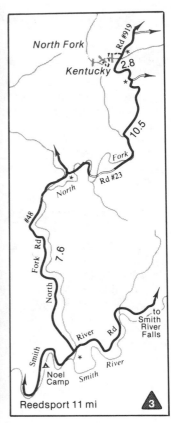

▲ *Lower Kentucky Falls*

Lower Kentucky Falls
Type: tiered

Kentucky Creek plunges 50 to 60 feet before diverging into two 15- to 20-foot waterfalls. The trail steepens considerably until its end 2 miles from the trailhead. A viewing platform has been built near the base of the falls.

North Fork Smith Falls
Type: fan; map: USGS Baldy Mtn 7½'

Also visible at the end of the trail is this 60- to 80-foot drop along North Fork Smith River. Also known as *North Fork Falls,* it appears as a segmented form during periods of low discharge. The cataract can be seen with Lower Kentucky Falls from selected vantages.

4. LORANE AREA

Siuslaw Falls

Type: block; map: USGS Letz Creek 7½'

Water stairsteps 5 to 10 feet over a 70-foot wide expanse of Siuslaw River. Drive 13 miles northwest on the Cottage Grove–Lorane Road from Cottage Grove to the hamlet of Lorane. Continue west 8.8 miles to an unnamed county park. Stop 0.5 mile down the park access road. The falls are a short walk away.

5. MILLICOMA RIVER DRAINAGE

Waterfalls are abundant on the various tributaries of Millicoma River. Unfortunately, most of them are inaccessible. But all is not lost. The most impressive falls of the area and indeed of the region are the star attractions at Golden and Silver Falls State Park. Turn off U.S. 101 south of downtown Coos Bay, on a road signed for Eastside and the state park. Drive through Eastside and on to the logging community of Allegany in 14 miles. The state park is at the road's end 10 miles farther.

Golden Falls

Type: horsetail; map: USGS Ivers Peak 15'

Glenn Creek plummets 125 to 150 feet over a rock wall. Take the marked trail at the end of the road an easy 0.25 mile to the base of the falls. The waterfall is named after Dr. C.B. Golden, First Grand Chancellor of the Knights of Pythias of Oregon.

Silver Falls

Type: segmented; map: USGS Ivers Peak 15'

Silver Creek trickles 80 to 120 feet over an unusual dome-shaped projection of weathered bedrock. Follow the second marked trail from the picnic area 0.25 mile to the falls.

6. FAIRVIEW AREA

Laverne Falls

Type: block; map: USGS Daniels Creek 7½'

Leave S.R. 42 at Coquille and drive 9 miles northeast to Fairview. Continue north 5.6 miles past Fairview to popular Laverne County

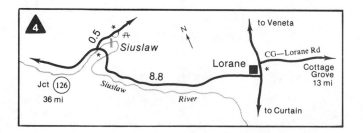

Park. The series of miniature falls, ranging from 3 to 5 feet, are near the camping area, downstream from the park entrance.

7. EAST FORK COQUILLE

There are many small waterfalls along the scenic East Fork Coquille River, and the historic Coos Bay Wagon Road follows beside it. Be careful when driving this narrow route. Logging trucks have replaced horse-drawn buggies! Be sure to find a safe place to park off the road when you locate each descent. Major accesses to this roadway are at Fairview from the west and Tenmile from the east.

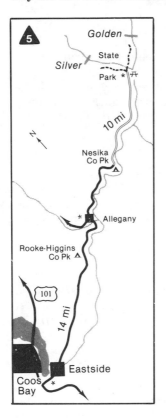

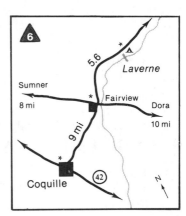

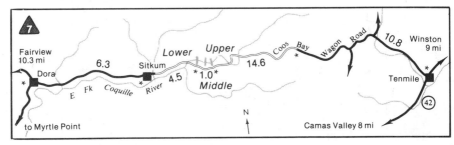

Lower Falls
Type: cascade

East Fork Coquille River tumbles 15 to 20 feet along a bend in the stream. The waterfall is located 4.5 miles east of Sitkum, 11 miles east of Dora, and 26.5 miles west of Tenmile.

Middle Falls
Type: segmented

Water pours 15 to 20 feet over a small rock escarpment. Drive 0.6 mile upstream from Lower Falls (above).

Upper Falls
Type: fan

This low-lying 5- to 10-foot descent occurs where East Fork Coquille River spreads downward next to a small, primitive campsite off the main road. The waterfall is 0.4 mile upstream from Middle Falls (above).

8. SISKIYOU NATIONAL FOREST

Siskiyou National Forest is a largely primitive portion of southwest Oregon's Coast Range. Many waterfalls here are currently inaccessible and unmapped. Also, seasonal descents are often seen along canyon roads during moist periods. Two of the most scenic cataracts are listed here.

Elk Creek Falls
Type: tiered; map: USGS China Flat 7½'

Elk Creek drops 80 to 120 feet over a bluff. Turn south off S.R. 42 onto South Fork Coquille River Road 3 miles southeast of Myrtle Point. Drive 19 miles to the ranger station at Powers, then continue 8.7 miles south to parking for Elk Creek Falls Trail #1150. Follow the path to the left, toward the stream. It's a short, easy stroll to the falls and there is a picnic table nearby. The cataract is not as impressive during late summer.

Coquille River Falls
Type: segmented

Superb year-round, as water crashes 40 to 60 feet along Coquille River. Drive 10.5 miles past Elk Creek Falls (above), turning left (east) on Road #3348 soon after crossing the river. Drive 1.5 miles to the trailhead. Coquille River Trail #1257 steadily switchbacks down the steep valley side for 0.5 mile. At trail's end, miniature falls can also be seen sliding into the river from Drowned Out Creek.

▲   *Coquille River Falls*

9. ROGUE RIVER

The Rogue River cuts through the Klamath Mountains portion of the Coast Range, creating a 2,000-foot-deep canyon. A 35-mile stretch of it is designated a Wild River, a federal classification intended to provide river recreation in a primitive setting and to preserve the natural, untamed integrity of the river and its surrounding environment. Such areas are generally accessible only by boat and trail.

An extended backpacking on the Rogue River Trail or float trip down the Rogue is essential to thoroughly enjoy the area. Additional travel information is *required* before embarking upon such a journey.

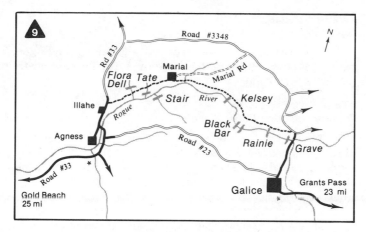

One excellent pamphlet is *The Wild and Scenic Rogue River*, published by the U.S. Forest Service and the Bureau of Land Management. Contact one of the following places to get this and other publications about the Rogue: Gold Beach Ranger District, 1225 S. Ellensburg, Box 7, Gold Beach, OR 97444; Gold Beach Chamber of Commerce, 510 S. Ellensburg, Gold Beach, OR 97444; Galice Ranger District, P.O. Box 1131, Grants Pass, OR 97526; or Grants Pass Visitor Bureau, P.O. Box 970, 206 N.E. Seventh, Grants Pass, OR 97526.

Grave Creek Falls
Type: cascade

Experienced white-water adventurers negotiate this 5-foot chute without much difficulty. Drive 7 miles north of Galice to the parking area past Grave Creek bridge. There are rapids next to the boat launch, and the falls are 1,200 feet downstream.

Rainie Falls
Type: block; map: USGS Galice 15'

This is the largest waterfall along the Rogue. Because of its 10- to 15-foot drop, this cataract is too dangerous to run, but an adjacent fish ladder provides boaters an alternative to portaging. The waterfall is 1.3 miles downstream from Grave Creek Falls (above). Hikers can start at the parking area and walk 1.3 miles to a spur trail leading to the river and the falls. The escarpment formed because its highly resistant quartzite eroded at a slower rate than the bedrock immediately below.

Upper Black Bar Falls
Type: cascade

Rogue River sharply drops a couple of feet downward 6.7 miles downstream from Rainie Falls (above). **Lower Black Bar Falls,** less severe than the upper falls, is 0.1 mile away. Neither waterfall is accessible by trail.

Kelsey Falls
Type: tiered

To reach this minor series of cascades along the Rogue, float 5.4 miles past Lower Black Bar Falls (above). The falls are upstream from Kelsey Creek Camp.

Stair Creek Falls
Type: tiered; map: USGS Marial 15'

This cataract tumbles from the side of the canyon into Rogue River. It is visible 2.3 miles downriver from Marial Lodge. The waterfall can also be seen from Inspiration Point, a trailside vista for hikers and backpackers 2.4 miles past Marial.

Tate Creek Falls

Tate Creek sprays 50 feet over sandstone into the Rogue River 6.5 miles past Stair Creek, or 2 miles upstream from Flora Dell Creek. The trail passes above the falls.

Flora Dell Falls
Type: punchbowl

Flora Dell Creek plunges 30 feet near the trail. Boaters can stop at the campsite 2 miles past Tate Creek. Backpackers hike 10 miles west from Inspiration Point. Or hike 4.3 miles east from a trailhead via the gravel road to Illahe. The pool below the falls makes a good swimming hole.

Oregon's Northern Cascade Range

This chapter describes waterfalls from Mount Hood, located immediately south of the Columbia Gorge, through the Cascades to Mount Washington, 75 miles southward. There are 106 cataracts known to occur throughout the region, with 52 of them mentioned here.

The major peaks along the Cascades are actually volcanoes. The appearance of each mountain shows the relative time since it last experienced volcanic activity. The smooth slopes of Mount Hood (11,235 feet) indicate its youth, while Mount Jefferson (10,495 feet) is slightly older and hence more rugged. Three Fingered Jack (7,841 feet) and Mount Washington (7,802 feet) have very jagged features, suggesting that their volcanic activity ceased longer ago, allowing glacial erosion to greatly modify the once-smooth form of these peaks.

Glaciation created the waterfalls associated with the volcanic mountains of the high Cascades. The alpine glaciers that top these peaks today once extended to lower elevations. Streams sometimes descend from adjacent walls into the valleys carved by glaciers. *Switchback Falls* is an example. Some cataracts are found on the valley floor where the glacier eroded unevenly, as at *Gatch Falls*, or where the present stream cuts over a highly resistant rock escarpment, as at *Downing Creek Falls*.

The many falls along the western flank of the Cascades formed in a manner related to the development of the range itself. About 20 million to 30 million years ago, lava flows and accumulations of ashfalls alternatively covered the region. The lava hardened to become *basaltic* bedrock. The volcanic ash mixed with dust to create rock layers called *tuffaceous sandstone*. The area was uplifted and folded 12 million years ago, forming the Cascade Range.

As streams carved courses from the high Cascades westward, their flowing waters eroded the softer sandstone much more rapidly than the resistant basalt. At descents in Silver Falls State Park and from McKenzie River, water plunges over ledges of basalt. Recesses beneath the falls are open amphitheaters where sandstone layers have been eroded away by the running water.

1. MOUNT HOOD WILDERNESS

One of 12 wilderness areas in Oregon, Mount Hood Wilderness has over 35 square miles of pristine sanctuary just a few miles from metropolitan Portland.

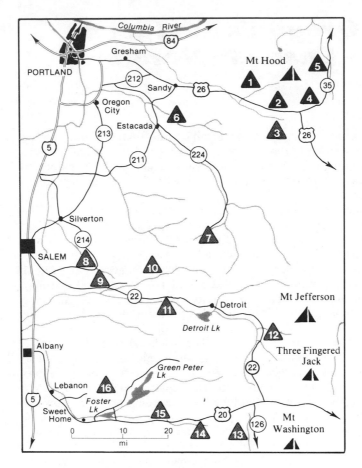

Ramona Falls
Type: fan; map: USGS Bull Run Lake 7½'

Turn north off U.S. 26 onto Lolo Pass Road #18 at Zigzag. Bear right in 3.75 miles on Muddy Fork Road #1825, driving to its end in 4 miles. Sandy River Trail #797 begins at the road's end. Hike 2 miles to where Sandy River veils 45 feet downward.

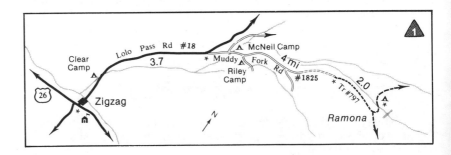

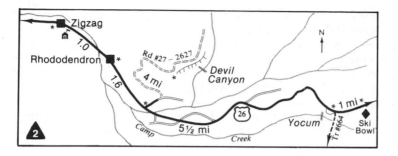

2. ZIGZAG RIVER DRAINAGE

Devil Canyon Falls

Type: plunge; map: USGS Government Camp 7½'

An unnamed stream plunges 50 to 75 feet within Devil Canyon. Drive 1.6 miles east of Rhododendron along U.S. 26 to Zigzag Mountain Road #27-2627 and turn north. The road soon deteriorates into a dirt surface, but is usually navigable by automobiles during summertime. Drive 4 miles to an overlook of Zigzag River Valley and the falls 0.5 mile up Devil Canyon.

Yocum Falls

Type: cascade

Drive along U.S. 26 to a Sno-Park wayside about 7 miles east of Rhododendron and 1 mile west of the entrance to Ski-Bowl Resort. Look down from the parking area for a view of Camp Creek sliding down hundreds of feet. Mirror Lake Trailhead is immediately upstream. The waterfall is named after Oliver C. Yocum, who developed the vicinity's Government Camp hotel and resort in 1900.

3. SALMON-HUCKLEBERRY WILDERNESS

Falls along the Salmon River

First the good news: there are seven waterfalls located within the Salmon River Canyon. Now the bad news: although all are audible, none are clearly visible from the canyon's main trail.

Proceed 0.25 mile west of Zigzag along U.S. 26, then turn left (south) on Salmon River Road #2618. Drive 5 miles to a parking area for Salmon River Trail #742. The trail is approximately 8 miles long, with all of the falls distributed along its southern portion. Alternatively, you can depart from the other end of the trail. Refer to a map of Mount Hood National Forest for additional route information.

Final Falls, so named because it is the farthest downstream, tumbles 45 feet. **Frustration Falls** plunges 55 feet, while **Vanishing Falls** descends 30 feet into a narrow box canyon. The 15-foot drop of **Little Niagara Falls** is a miniature replica of its eastern namesake.

Hideaway Falls hurtles 100 feet into the canyon from Iron Creek. **Split Falls** is a tiered cataract, one 35 feet high and the other about 55 feet. **Stein Falls** drops 75 feet, and is named in honor of Bobby and Johnny Stein, casualties of World War II. All of the waterfalls are located within the Salmon-Huckleberry Wilderness Area of Mount Hood National Forest, and were officially named in 1963 as suggested by W. Kirk Braun.

As a hiking aid, the USGS Rhododendron map depicts the northern part of the trail. Final, Frustration, Vanishing, and Hideaway falls are indicated on USGS High Rock. Although not shown, Little Niagara is situated several hundred feet downstream (west) from Goat Creek. Lastly, refer to USGS Wolf Peak to help you find Split and Stein falls. If you decide to leave the trail for better views, stay on stable terrain that is not dangerous to negotiate.

4. BENNETT PASS

Switchback Falls
Type: cascade; map: USGS Mt Hood South 7½'

North Fork Iron Creek cascades steeply 100 to 200 feet next to S.R. 35. The waterfall is aptly named for the winding path of the highway. Drive to the undesignated turnout 1 mile past Road #48 and 1.4 miles from the entrance to Mount Hood Meadows Ski Area. The falls are immediately above the road.

Sahalie Falls
Type: horsetail; map: USGS Mt Hood South 7½'

Bright water tumbles 60 to 100 feet along East Fork Hood River. Turn at the entrance to Mount Hood Meadows Ski Area, then bear right on an old paved road. Stop near the bridge crossing in 0.4 miles. The falls are a short distance upstream. Sahalie is a Chinook word meaning "high." The falls were named by George Holman as part of a competition sponsored by the *Portland Telegram.*

Umbrella Falls
Type: fan; map: USGS Mt Hood South 7½'

This 40- to 60-foot waterfall along East Fork Hood River is appropriately named. Drive 0.8 mile up the Mount Hood Meadows Ski Area access road to a sign marking Umbrella Falls Trail #667. Follow the trail 0.2 mile from the right (east) side of the road to the base of the falls.

Pencil Falls

Take Umbrella Falls Trail #667 from the left (west) side of the ski area road (see directions to Umbrella Falls, above). Hike 1.3 miles to the trail's end at Timberline Trail #600 and turn right (northeast). Pass a ski lift on the way to the falls in 0.5 mile.

▲   *Tamanawas Falls*

5. NORTHEAST MOUNT HOOD

Tamanawas Falls

Type: plunge; map: USGS Dog River 7½'

Cold Spring Creek plunges 100 to 150 feet over a rock ledge in a deep woods setting.

Drive on S.R. 35 to Sherwood Campground 9 miles north of Bennett Pass or 10.5 miles south of the town of Mount Hood. The parking area to the trail system is 0.25 mile north of the camp. Easily hiked Trail #650 leads 2 miles to the falls. Tamanawas is a Chinook word for "friendly or guardian spirit."

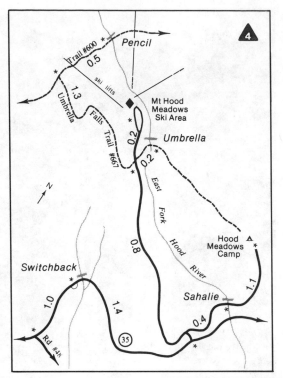

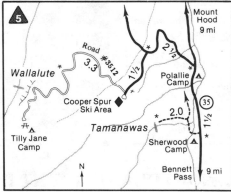

Wallalute Falls
Type: plunge; map: USGS Mt Hood North 7½'

This waterfall roars down more than 100 feet along Eliot Branch.
Turn west off S.R. 35 onto Cooper Spur Road. After 4 miles, turn right
(northwest) on Cloud Cap Road #3512. Follow this steeply graded,
winding road to the viewpoint in 3.3 miles. Look at the northeast base
of Mount Hood (to your lower left) to find the distant cataract.
Wallalute is a Wasco Indian term meaning "strong water." The falls
were named in 1893 by Miss A.M. Long. She is believed to be the first
white person to see the falls.

▲ *Mount Hood; Wallalute Falls to the lower left.*

6. EAGLE CREEK

These two small waterfalls are not far from the Portland metropolitan area. Turn southeast off S.R. 211 onto Southeast Eagle Creek Road, located 0.1 mile east of the junction with S.R. 224. Go 1.2 miles and turn left (east) from Southeast Eagle Creek Road onto Southeast Wildcat Road, go 1.8 miles, then bear right (south) on County Road #40.

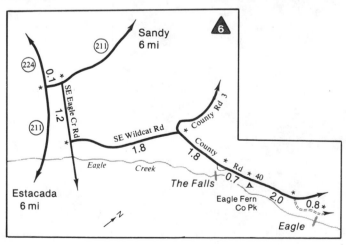

The Falls
Type: segmented; map: USGS Estacada 7½'

Drive 1.8 miles along County Road #40 to a yellow-gated turnout to the right. Eagle Creek descends 20 to 30 feet a short walk down a well-worn path from the turnout.

Eagle Creek Falls
Type: block; map: USGS Estacada 7½'

Continue 2.7 miles past The Falls (above) on County Road #40. Park at the yellow-gated road to the right (south). Walk along the dirt road for 0.8 mile until the falls are heard. A short path leads to the base of a 20- to 30-foot block-type waterfall. Fishing is prohibited. I've called the falls by the name of its stream.

7. BAGBY HOT SPRINGS AREA

Pegleg Falls
Type: block; map: USGS Bagby Hot Springs 7½'

Water descends 10 to 15 feet along Hot Springs Fork, with a fish ladder bypassing the falls. Drive 27 miles southeast from Estacada on S.R. 224 to Clackamas River Road #46, 0.5 mile past Ripplebrook Ranger Station. Turn right (south) on Road #46, and after 3.6 miles bear right (south) on Collawash River Road #63. Turn right once more in another 3.5 miles onto Road #70, with Pegleg Falls Campground in 5.6 miles. Drive into the camp and stop at the first parking area. The falls are located just upstream.

▲ *Pegleg Falls*

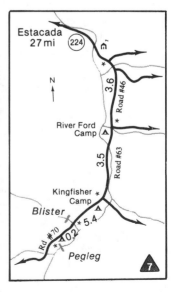

Blister Creek Falls

Type: horsetail; map: USGS Bagby Hot Springs 7½'

Blister Creek streams 25 to 35 feet into a small pool. The falls can be seen from a bridge 0.2 mile before Pegleg Falls Camp (see directions to Pegleg Falls, above). Fishermen's paths offer closer views of the cataract, which I've named after the stream.

8. SILVER FALLS STATE PARK

This is a paradise for waterfall seekers. Silver Creek Canyon has 10 major waterfalls, all of them within moderate walking distances of the main highway. S.R. 214 goes through the park 14 miles southeast of Silverton and 25 miles east of Salem.

Upper North Falls

Type: plunge; map: USGS Elk Prairie 7½'

North Silver Creek drops 65 feet. Find the trail at the south side of the parking lot at the east end of the park. Cross under the highway and walk east 0.3 mile to the falls.

North Falls

Type: plunge; map: USGS Elk Prairie 7½'

Take the previously mentioned trail 0.3 mile west to exciting views beside and behind this impressive 136-foot waterfall.

Twin Falls

Type: segmented; map: USGS Silver Creek Falls 7½'

North Silver Creek diverges in two streams as it tumbles 31 feet over weathered bedrock. Follow trail 0.9 mile downstream from North Falls (above) a total of 1.2 miles from the trailhead.

Middle North Falls

Type: plunge; map: USGS Silver Creek Falls 7½'

This unique waterfall hurtles through the air for two-thirds of its 106-foot drop, then veils over bedrock for the final portion. Walk 0.5 mile downstream from Twin Falls (above), a total of 1.7 miles from the trailhead, or 0.7 mile past Winter Falls (described below) to view this entry. A side trail goes behind and around the waterfall.

Drake Falls

Type: horsetail; map: USGS Silver Creek Falls 7½'

Hike 0.2 mile downstream from Middle North Falls (above), a total of 1.9 miles from the trailhead, to this 27-foot curtain of water.

Double Falls

Type: tiered; map: USGS Silver Creek Falls 7½'

Water drops a total of 178 feet in tiered form. The lower portion descends four times as far as the upper part. Walk 0.3 mile past Drake

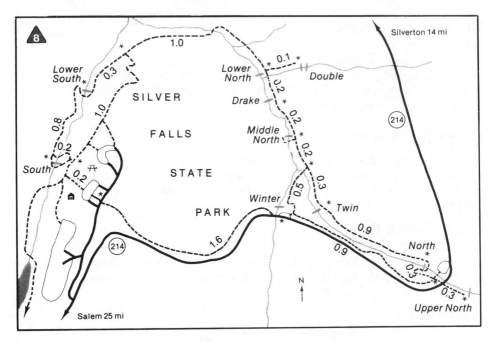

Falls (above), a total of 2.2 miles from the trailhead, to the spur trail at Hullt Creek.

Lower North Falls
Type: block; map: USGS Silver Creek Falls 7½'

This 30-foot drop is immediately downstream from the mouth of Hullt Creek along North Silver Creek (see directions to Double Falls above), about 2.3 miles from the trailhead.

Winter Falls
Type: plunge; map: USGS Silver Creek Falls 7½'

Winter Creek falls 134 feet in two forms. Initially it plunges down, then becomes a horsetail. Walk a short distance north from the designated turnout on S.R. 214, as shown on the accompanying map.

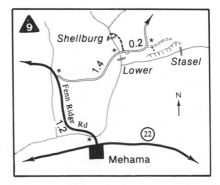

South Falls
Type: plunge; map: USGS Silver Creek Falls 7½'

This is the highlight of the park. South Silver Creek drops 177 feet over a ledge of basalt. Walk about 0.4 mile west from the parking areas in the western portion of the park. Vistas and trailsides reveal the many faces of the falls. There is a lodge and gift shop between the main parking area and South Falls.

Lower South Falls
Type: plunge; map: USGS Silver Creek Falls 7½'

The trail passes behind this 93-foot waterfall located 0.8 mile downstream from South Falls (above), a total of 1.2 miles from the trailhead.

9. MEHAMA

Several falls occur within the area, three of which are accessible. The first one is located on a Bureau of Land Management parcel, while the following two are both situated in Santiam State Forest. Turn north off S.R. 22 onto Fenn Ridge Road at Mehama. Drive uphill 1.2 miles, then take a sharp right (east) turn onto an unsigned gravel road.

Stasel Falls
Type: horsetail; map: USGS Lyons 7½'

This 100- to 125-foot descent along Stout Creek would deserve a higher rating, but the side view is partially obstructed. Drive 1.6 miles from Fenn Ridge Road, parking next to a dirt road junction. Follow this unimproved route about 100 yards to paths leading to the top of abrupt cliffs and obstructed views upstream to the falls.

Lower Shellburg Falls
Type: plunge; map: USGS Lyons 7½'

Drive 1.4 miles eastward on the unsigned gravel road from Fenn Ridge Road, or backtrack 0.2 mile from the previous entry and park near Shellburg Creek and its lower 20- to 40-foot falls.

Shellburg Falls
Type: plunge; map: USGS Lyons 7½'

This 80- to 100-foot plume descends over an extension of basalt along Shellburg Creek. From Lower Shellburg Falls, find the unmarked trail on the north side of the road. The easily hiked trail goes behind the base of this waterfall in 0.2 mile.

10. NORTH FORK DRAINAGE

Access to the pleasant Elkhorn Valley and waterfalls upstream is easiest eastbound on North Fork Road #2209 from S.R. 22, 1 mile east of Mehama. Alternatively, adventurous drivers with a reliable vehicle

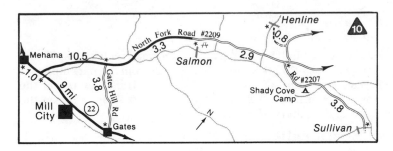

may wish to tackle Gates Hill Road. This gravel route travels up, up, up, then down, down, down from Gates to Elkhorn Valley.

Salmon Falls
Type: segmented; map: USGS Elkhorn 7½'

A high-volume 25- to 35-foot waterfall drops down along Little North Santiam River. Drive 3.3 miles up the valley (east) from the junction of Gates Hill Road and North Fork Road #2209. Turn at the sign for Salmon Falls County Park. A fish ladder bypasses the cataract.

Henline Falls
Type: plunge; map: USGS Elkhorn 7½'

Henline Creek falls 75 to 100 feet over a mountainside. Continue past Salmon Falls for 2.9 miles, then bear left 0.1 mile along Road #2209. Park and walk up the tributary road to the left. After about 0.5 mile, turn left onto a dirt road, which quickly becomes a well-worn trail. The falls are reached in 0.25 mile. The entrance to the old Silver King Mine is near the base of the falls. Look, but don't enter!

Sullivan Creek Falls
Type: cascade; map: USGS Mill City 7½'

This steep 40- to 60-foot cascade would deserve a higher rating, but the surrounding clear-cut land detracts from the scene. Turn right off Road #2209 onto Road #2207 about 2.9 miles past Salmon Falls. Drive along this gravel road 3.8 miles to the falls directly above a bridge over Sullivan Creek. I've called this waterfall after its stream.

11. NIAGARA PARK

Niagara Park was the site of a small town from 1890 to 1934. A rubble masonry dam was built in the late 1890s to provide power for a

paper mill. Difficulties in constructing the dam caused the mill project to be abandoned and the village faded. Historic remnants of the town can be seen at a marked turnout along S.R. 22, 4.2 miles east of Gates and 13 miles west of Detroit.

Sevenmile Creek Falls
Type: punchbowl

Walk down a short pathway from Niagara Park to North Santiam River. Scramble on interesting rock formations to view Sevenmile Creek descending into the far side of the river. I've named it after the stream.

12. MARION FORKS AREA

Whispering Falls
Type: horsetail

Misery Creek falls 40 to 60 feet into North Santiam River. Drive to Whispering Falls Campground, located on S.R. 22, 4 miles east of Idanha. The waterfall is across the river from the camp. Probably it got its name from the fact that the busy North Santiam drowns out the sound of the falls.

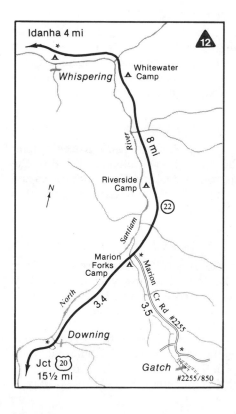

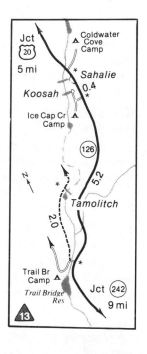

Gatch Falls
Type: block; map: USGS Mt Jefferson 15'

This beautiful 75- to 100-foot waterfall from Marion Creek is also known as *Gooch Falls*. Turn southeast off S.R. 22 at Marion Forks onto Marion Creek Road #2255. Follow the gravel road for 3.5 miles, then turn right on Road #2255/850. Park where the dirt road widens in less than 0.2 mile. Walk carefully toward the creek for a natural, *unfenced* view above and into the falls.

Downing Creek Falls
Type: cascade; map: USGS Mt Jefferson 15'

Drive 3.4 miles south from Marion Forks on S.R. 22 to an undesignated turnout and camping site on the left (east) side of the highway. Walk a short distance upstream to where Downing Creek flows 20 to 30 feet down a chute. I've called the falls by the name of the stream.

13. McKENZIE RIVER

The waterfalls along the McKenzie River descend with fury, except for Tamolitch, which has been artificially turned off.

Sahalie Falls
Type: segmented; map: USGS Three Fingered Jack 15'

This roaring 140-foot torrent can be seen from developed viewpoints. Turn at the point-of-interest sign along S.R. 126 located 5.2 miles south of U.S. 20 and 6 miles north of Belknap Springs. Sahalie is a Chinook word meaning "high." The smaller of the two segments disappears during periods of lower discharge.

Koosah Falls
Type: block; map: USGS Three Fingered Jack 15'

McKenzie River thunders 80 to 120 feet over a sharp escarpment. Drive 0.4 mile south of Sahalie Falls (above) along S.R. 126 to the entrance marked Ice Cap Campground and turn. The parking area and developed viewpoints are in 0.3 mile. The falls appear as a segmented form during late summer.

Tamolitch Falls
Type: punchbowl; map: USGS Echo Mountain 15'

A 60-foot dry rock wall is the only thing left where water once poured from McKenzie River. But by all means, visit this location! Turn off S.R. 126 at the north end of Trail Bridge Reservoir, 0.5 mile north of Belknap Springs or 5.2 miles south of Koosah Falls. Drive about 0.75 mile to the McKenzie River Trailhead.

Hike up the trail along the river for 2 miles to a crystal clear, cyan-colored pool with the dry falls at its head. This circular basin inspired the name Tamolitch, which is Chinook for "tub" or "bucket." At this site, you will see a very rare phenomenon — a full-sized river

▲ *Sahalie Falls*

beginning at a single point. Springs feed the plunge pool at the base of the dry cataract. Superb!

What happened to the falls? The river has been diverted 3 miles upstream at Carmen Reservoir. A tunnel directs the water to Smith Reservoir and the power generating facilities in the adjacent drainage.

14. HOUSE ROCK

House Rock Falls
Type: cascade; map: USGS Harter Mtn 7½'

This 20- to 30-foot drop along South Santiam River would be more scenic except it is nearly covered by several large boulders that have fallen into the stream from the north slope of the gorge. Drive to House Rock Campground, located 1.9 miles east of Upper Soda along U.S. 20. Proceed 0.4 mile into the camp and park just before a creek crossing at House Rock Loop Trail #3406. A 0.3-mile walk to the falls along a nice trail.

15. CASCADIA

Lower Soda Falls
Type: tiered; map: USGS Cascadia 7½'

Soda Creek tumbles 150 to 180 feet in three tiers among moss-covered rocks. Start at Cascadia State Park, located 13 miles east of Sweet Home along U.S. 20. Find the unmarked trail at the far north

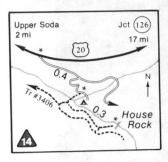

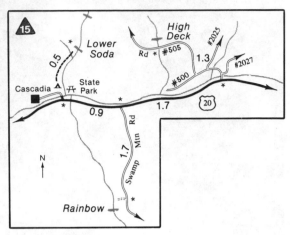

end of the campsite area and hike a moderate 0.5 mile to the falls. **Upper Soda Falls** is not accessible.

Rainbow Falls
Type: punchbowl; map: USGS Cascadia 7½'

Drive 0.9 mile east from Cascadia, turning right (south) from U.S. 20 onto Swamp Mountain Road. Follow this gravel route for 1.7 miles, parking at an old dirt road to the right. Follow it for about 100 feet, then descend to a small ridge from which you can see Dobbin Creek pouring 20 to 30 feet into a pool.

High Deck Falls
Type: cascade

Water cascades steeply for more than 100 feet along an unnamed creek. Continue east along U.S. 20 for 1.7 miles past Swamp Mountain Road to Moose Creek Road #2027. Follow the turns as shown on the accompanying map to Road #505 and the falls in 1.3 miles. I've called the waterfall by the name of the nearby mountain.

16. McDOWELL FALLS AREA

Four of the five waterfalls described in this subsection are within McDowell Creek Falls County Park, a pleasant and thoughtfully planned day-use recreation area. Turn off U.S. 20 at Fairview Road. Turn left at the first junction, then right onto McDowell Creek Road after a total of 1 mile. The county park and first parking turnout are 6.5 miles farther east.

Lower Falls
Type: tiered; map: USGS Sweet Home 7½'

This minor pair of 5- to 10-foot drops along McDowell Creek are located immediately downstream from the footbridge at the southern beginning of the trail, at the parking turnout.

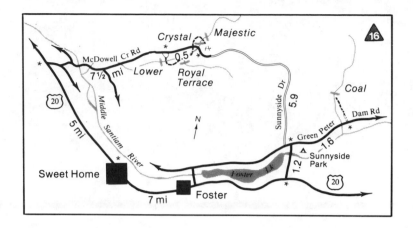

Royal Terrace Falls
Type: tiered; map: USGS Sweet Home 7½'

Fall Creek sprays 119 feet down in a fountainlike tiered display. Walk an easy 0.3 mile upstream from Lower Falls (see directions above) to this waterfall. A marked spur path goes to a viewpoint from the top of the cataract.

Majestic Falls
Type: block; map: USGS Sweet Home 7½'

A porchlike overlook allows a close-up view of this 30- to 40-foot drop tumbling from McDowell Creek. Drive to the north end of the park. A stairway leads shortly to the vista.

Crystal Falls
Type: punchbowl

McDowell Creek skips 10 to 15 feet into punchbowl-shaped Crystal Pool. Continue on foot 0.1 mile past Majestic Falls to an overview of this waterfall.

Coal Creek Falls
Type: plunge; map: USGS Green Peter 7½'

Reach Green Peter Dam Road, 6 miles southeast of McDowell Creek Falls County Park, via Sunnyside Drive, or north from U.S. 20 at the east end of Foster Lake. Once you come alongside Middle Santiam River, drive east 1.6 miles and park at the dirt road to the left (north). Walk to the end of the road, then scramble up the crumbly slope to a faint path. A short distance farther you can see the 40- to 60-foot drop. The walk totals 0.25 mile. I've called this waterfall by the name of its stream.

Oregon's Southern Cascade Range

South-central Oregon presents a collage of scenic outdoor settings typical of the Cascade Range. The area's major peaks include Three Sisters, Bachelor Butte, Diamond Peak, and Mount McLoughlin — all of them volcanic in origin. The region also boasts five national forests, four wilderness areas, an abundance of mountain lakes, and Crater Lake National Park.

Waterfalls are well distributed throughout the South Cascades. Most of the 84 recognized falls in the region are relatively accessible; 54 of them are listed in this book. Many are among the most majestic in the Pacific Northwest.

Falls are commonly found streaming down canyon walls carved by alpine glaciers. During the last major Ice Age, 10,000 to 14,000 years ago, these glaciers extended their range to areas below 2,500 feet in elevation in the South Cascades. Large, U-shaped glacial troughs remain as evidence of the intense erosive powers of these glaciers. Today, rivers follow the valleys abandoned by the retreating glaciers. As tributary streams flow into the troughs, they often drop sharply as waterfalls. *Rainbow Falls*, *Proxy Falls*, and *Vidae Falls* are examples. Many physical geographers and geologists refer to this type of descent as *ribbon falls*.

The western portion of the South Cascades formed in the same manner as the northern extension described in the preceding chapter. Where layers of resistant basalt and weak sandstone meet along a stream's course, the sandstone erodes faster than the basalt. The graceful *Toketee Falls* and *Grotto Falls* are good examples of cataracts shaped in this way.

1. THREE SISTERS WILDERNESS

The peaks of North Sister (10,085 feet), Middle Sister (10,047 feet), and South Sister (10,358 feet) dominate the Cascade scenery along S.R. 242. The major waterfalls of this wilderness area are easily accessible.

Rainbow Falls

Type: horsetail; map: USGS Three Sisters 15'

Turn south off S.R. 126 onto Foley Ridge Road #2643 about 0.5 mile east of McKenzie Bridge Ranger Station. Follow Road #2643 for

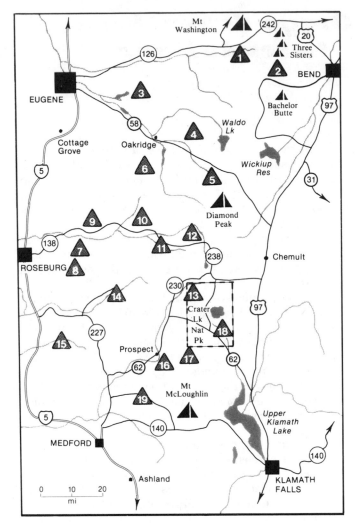

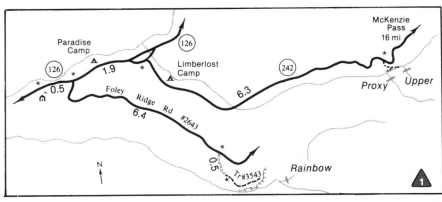

6.4 miles, then turn right on the marked dirt road to the start of Rainbow Falls Trail #3543. The moderately easy trail ends in 0.75 mile at the unfenced viewpoint. Rainbow Creek distantly descends 150 to 200 feet on the other side of the valley with Three Sisters in the background.

Upper Falls

Type: segmented

Water steeply cascades 100 to 125 feet from springs issuing from a high canyon wall. Turn southeast off S.R. 126 onto S.R. 242 and drive 6.3 miles east to the turnout for Proxy Falls Trail #3532. Hike about 0.5 mile, then take a short left fork to the Upper Falls.

Proxy Falls
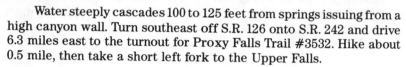

Type: fan; map: USGS Three Sisters 15'

Proxy Creek pours 200 feet in impressive fashion. Follow the right spur of Trail #3532, labeled Lower Falls (see directions to Upper Falls, above). It leads shortly to a developed viewpoint overlooking the falls.

2. CASCADE LAKES HIGHWAY

Fall Creek Falls
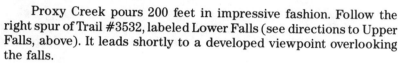

Type: block

Drive west from Bend for 28 miles on the Cascade Lakes Highway, also known as Century Drive and County Road #46. Turn at the marked access road for Green Lakes Trail #17, located on the west

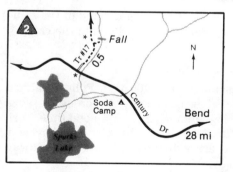

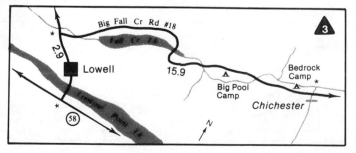

side of Fall Creek. Drive 0.2 mile to the trail, then hike 0.3 mile to a short spur trail to Fall Creek Falls.

3. BIG FALL CREEK

There are several interesting scenes on the way to Chichester Falls. Turn off S.R. 58 at the Lowell exit, where an old covered bridge looks out of place above the reservoir of Lookout Point Lake. Follow the Lowell-Jasper Road through town and turn right (east) in 2.9 miles on Big Fall Creek Road just before reaching a second covered bridge. Take this secondary road, which becomes Road #18, for 15.9 miles to a turnout at Andy Creek.

Chichester Falls
Type: punchbowl; map: USGS Saddleblanket Mtn 7½'

This 20- to 30-foot punchbowl waterfall along Andy Creek is easiest and safest to view from the bridge. A casual observer may disagree with the rating, but a closer look reveals an interesting grotto around the plunge pool. Moss and plants enhance the setting.

4. SALMON CREEK DRAINAGE

To reach these two waterfalls east of Oakridge, turn north off S.R. 58 at Fish Hatchery Road. Follow the route 1.4 miles to its end, and turn right (east) on Salmon Creek Road.

Salmon Creek Falls
Type: segmented; map: USGS Huckleberry Mtn 7½'

This small 5- to 10-foot drop is at the campground of the same name. Drive 3.7 miles east along Salmon Creek Road to the camp.

Lithan Falls
Type: cascade; map: USGS Waldo Lake 15'

Nettie Creek steeply cascades 50 to 100 feet. Follow Salmon Creek Road #24 east to the end of the pavement at the creek crossing. Continue 2.5 to 3 miles, crossing Salmon Creek a second time. Turn right (south) at Black Creek Road #2421; go about 8 miles to its end. Black Creek Trail #3551 starts here, with the falls about 2 miles away. It is also known as *Lillian Falls.*

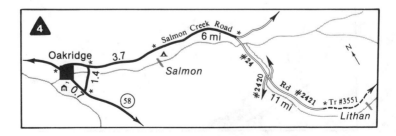

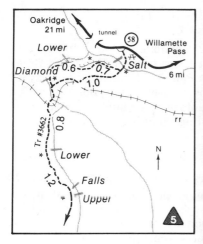

▲ *Salt Creek Falls*

5. SALT CREEK DRAINAGE

There are six cataracts within 2 square miles of this area. Drive 21 miles east from Oakridge or 6 miles west from Willamette Pass along S.R. 58. Park at the Salt Creek Falls turnout, or in Salt Creek Falls Picnic Area.

Salt Creek Falls

Type: plunge; map: USGS Diamond Peak 7½'

This 286-foot plunge is near the road and can be viewed year-round. Trails and fenced vistas provide a variety of views of this impressive waterfall, which was discovered by Frank S. Warner and Charles Tufti in March 1887.

Lower Diamond Creek Falls
Type: tiered; map: USGS Diamond Peak 7½'

Although the falls are 200 to 250 feet high, the low rating is due to obscured views of the magnificent lower portion. From Salt Creek Picnic Area, follow Diamond Creek Falls Trail #3598 for an easy 0.7 mile along Salt Creek Canyon to one of several viewpoints. In 1988, a couple of trees prevented a clear vantage of the falls. If this situation has been remedied, my two-star rating should be ridiculed.

Diamond Creek Falls
Type: fan; map: USGS Diamond Peak 7½'

Another superb cataract occurs where Diamond Creek pours 70 to 90 feet downward. Follow Trail #3598 for 1.3 miles from the trailhead (0.6 mile past the previously described vista), or embark from Vivian Lake Trail #3662 (which diverges from Trail #3598 less than 0.1 mile from the trailhead) for a 1-mile jaunt. There is a viewpoint above the falls, plus a short spur trail that quickly leads to its base.

Lower Falls Creek Falls
Type: tiered

This double waterfall totals 30 to 50 feet. Near Diamond Creek Falls (above), take Vivian Lake Trail #3662 for a moderately steep 0.8-mile hike (1.8 miles from the trailhead) to views just off the trail.

Falls Creek Falls
Type: plunge; map: USGS Diamond Peak 7½'

This 40- to 60-foot plunge is visible from Trail #3662. Continue climbing steeply 1 mile past Lower Falls Creek Falls (above). A sign tacked to a tree marks the viewpoint for the moderately distant falls, 2.8 miles from the trailhead.

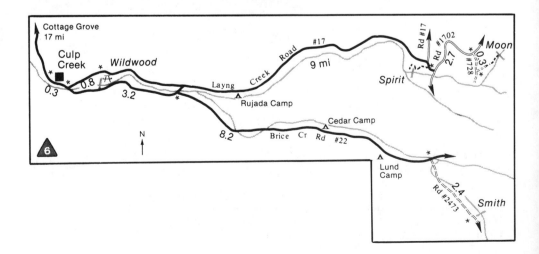

Upper Falls Creek Falls
Type: fan

The best of the waterfalls from Falls Creek is visible from the trail. Continue climbing about 0.2 mile along Trail #3662 past the main falls, 3.0 miles from the trailhead. The upper waterfall descends 50 to 80 feet.

6. ROW RIVER DRAINAGE

Several waterfalls are to be found on the Row River and its tributaries further upstream. All but the first descent are located within Umpqua National Forest. Access the area by departing Interstate 5 at Cottage Grove (Exit 174) and driving east on the Cottage Grove–Dorena Road for 17 miles to Culp Creek townsite.

Wildwood Falls
Type: punchbowl; map: USGS Culp Creek 7½'

A 10- to 15-foot drop along Row River. Drive to the east side of Culp Creek townsite, then bear left on an unsigned road, staying on the north side of the river. Views of the falls at Wildwood Falls Picnic Area in 0.8 mile, as well as a developed roadside vista just before the picnic area.

Smith Falls
Type: segmented; map: USGS Fairview Peak 7½'

Champion Creek tumbles 15 to 25 feet along a route dubbed the "Tour of the Golden Past," once a thoroughfare to the now historic Bohemia Mining District. Drive east from Culp Creek to Disston, bearing right (southeast) on Brice Creek Road #22 (which may also be designated as Road #2470). After 8.2 miles, turn right (south) upon Champion Creek Road #2473. Cautious individuals can usually drive automobiles up the road in the summer, though the journey of 2.4 miles will be at a slow pace. At the falls is the Jerome #9 Placer Claim, as signified by a nearby marker.

Spirit Falls
Type: fan; map: USGS Rose Hill 7½'

This aptly named 60-foot waterfall somehow seems surrealistic, with water from Alex Creek gouging into a bulging mass of moss-covered substrate. Take Road #17 northeast from Disston for 9 miles to the trailhead for the falls. A 0.5-mile trail moderately leads down to a picnic table near the base of the cataract.

Moon Falls
Type: fan; map: USGS Holland Point 7½'

Further upstream from Spirit Falls (above), Alex Creek drops 120 feet. Proceed 0.2 mile to Road #1702. Turn left on #1702 and drive 2.7 miles; turn right on Road #1702-728. Take its unimproved surface 0.3 mile before turning left on Road #1702-203. Trailhead in another

▲ *Spirit Falls*

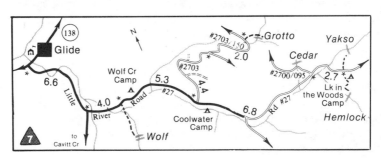

0.1 mile. Hike an easy 0.5 mile to the falls, complete with a picnic table.

7. LITTLE RIVER DRAINAGE

Pass one waterfall after another as you progress up the Little River Valley. To enter the valley, turn southeast off S.R. 138 at Glide onto Little River Road #27.

Wolf Creek Falls
Type: tiered; map: USGS Red Butte 15'

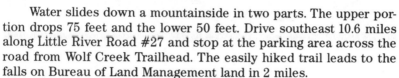

Water slides down a mountainside in two parts. The upper portion drops 75 feet and the lower 50 feet. Drive southeast 10.6 miles along Little River Road #27 and stop at the parking area across the road from Wolf Creek Trailhead. The easily hiked trail leads to the falls on Bureau of Land Management land in 2 miles.

Cedar Creek Falls
Type: plunge

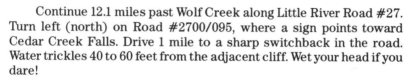

Continue 12.1 miles past Wolf Creek along Little River Road #27. Turn left (north) on Road #2700/095, where a sign points toward Cedar Creek Falls. Drive 1 mile to a sharp switchback in the road. Water trickles 40 to 60 feet from the adjacent cliff. Wet your head if you dare!

Hemlock Falls
Type: horsetail; map: USGS Quartz Mtn 15'

Drive along Little River Road #27 for 2.7 miles past Road #2700/095 and turn at Lake in the Woods Camp. Hemlock Falls Trail #1520 begins just before you reach the campsites. Follow it down steeply 0.5 mile to an 80-foot rush along Hemlock Creek.

Yakso Falls
Type: fan

Yakso Falls Trail #1519 starts across the road from the entrance to Lake in the Woods Camp (see directions to Hemlock Falls, above). Walk 0.7 mile to the base of the 70-foot falls.

Grotto Falls
Type: segmented; map: USGS Mace Mountain 15'

The shimmering waters of this pleasant waterfall plunge 100 feet along Emile Creek. Backtrack 9.5 miles from Lake in the Woods Camp or from Wolf Creek Falls (above), continue 5.3 miles east on Little River Road #27 to Road #2703. Turn north, drive 4.4 miles, and turn left on Road #2703/150, following the gravel route 2 miles farther to Grotto Falls Trail #1503 on the far side of Emile Creek bridge. The trail goes behind the descent in 0.3 mile. This waterfall is also known as *Emile Falls*, after Emile Shivigny, who homesteaded nearby in 1875.

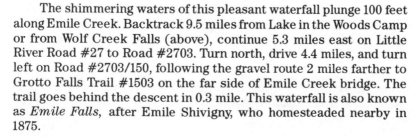

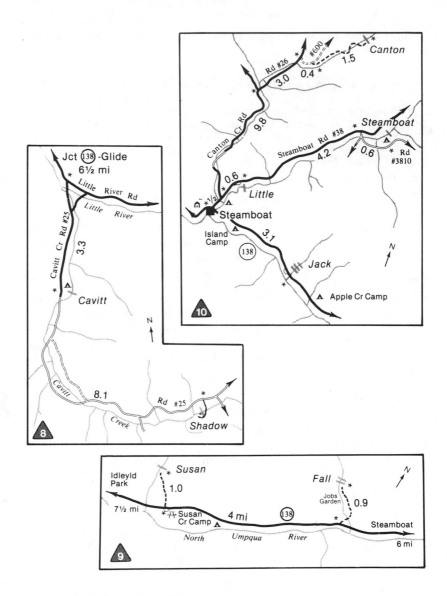

8. CAVITT CREEK

Cavitt Falls
Type: punchbowl

Take a footbath in the refreshing pool at the base of this 10- to 15-foot descent. Turn right (south) off Little River Road onto Cavitt Creek Road 6.6 miles from Glide. In 3.3 miles, turn at the Bureau of Land Management-administered Cavitt Falls Park. The waterfall is in the park.

Shadow Falls
Type: tiered; map: USGS Red Butte 15'

This triple waterfall totaling 80 to 100 feet along Cavitt Creek is aptly named. Drive southeast 8.1 miles past Cavitt Falls Park on Cavitt Creek Road #25. Stop at the turnout and follow Shadow Falls Trail #1504 to the descent in 0.8 mile.

The waterfall has worked its way headward over time, eroding upstream through a rock fracture to form a narrow, natural grotto. Immediately downstream from the falls, next to the trail, are interesting weathered bedrock formations.

9. IDLEYLD PARK AREA

Scenic S.R. 138 serves as a convenient corridor, passing many waterfalls on the way from Glide to Crater Lake.

Susan Creek Falls
Type: fan

A trail built by the Bureau of Land Management is an easy 1 mile to this 30- to 40-foot waterfall. Drive S.R. 138 7.5 miles east from Idleyld Park to Susan Creek Picnic Area.

The trailhead is across the road from the parking area. Indian mounds to be seen farther up the trail.

Fall Creek Falls
Type: tiered; map: USGS Mace Mountain 15'

Drive 4 miles east from Susan Creek State Park to the marked turnout on S.R. 138. Fall Creek Falls National Recreation Trail winds around and through slabs of bedrock and past the natural, lush vegetation of Job's Garden. This beautiful path leads 0.9 mile to a double falls with each tier 35 to 50 feet in height.

10. STEAMBOAT

Fishing is prohibited in the entire drainage basin encompassing Steamboat Creek in order to provide undisturbed spawning grounds for the salmon and steelhead of the North Umpqua River drainage.

Little Falls
Type: segmented; map: USGS Illahee Rock 15'

Watch the fish negotiate this 5- to 10-foot break along Steamboat Creek. Turn northeast off S.R. 138 onto Steamboat Road #38 at Steamboat. Drive 1.1 miles to the undesignated turnout next to the falls and the adjacent bedrock slabs.

Steamboat Falls
Type: block; map: USGS Illahee Rock 15'

Continue northeast along Steamboat Road #38 for 4.2 miles past Little Falls (above). Turn right (southeast) on Road #3810 and continue to Steamboat Falls Campground entrance in 0.6 mile. A developed viewpoint showcases a 20- to 30-foot waterfall. Some fish attempt to jump the cataract, while others use the adjacent fish ladder.

Jack Falls
Type: tiered

Park at the undesignated turnout at mile marker 42, located 3.1 miles southeast of Steamboat junction along S.R. 138. Walk 100 yards farther to Jack Creek. Follow the brushy streambank to three closely grouped falls. The lower descent slides 20 to 30 feet in two segments. The middle and upper falls are of the horsetail type, descending 25 to 40 feet and 50 to 70 feet respectively.

Canton Creek Falls
Type: horsetail

View this 60- to 80-foot drop from the top of the falls. From S.R. 138 turn northeast on Steamboat Road #38, then left on Canton Creek Road in 0.5 mile. Follow this route for 9.8 miles to Upper Canton Road #26 and turn right. Take Road #26 for 3 miles and turn right (east) on Saddle Camp Road #2300-600. Trailhead in 0.4 mile. The falls are located 1.5 miles from the start of Canton Creek Falls Trail #1537.

11. TOKETEE

Toketee Falls
Type: tiered; map: USGS Toketee Falls 7½'

The Indian word Toketee means "graceful." It is an apt title for this inspiring waterfall. The major lower portion plunges 90 feet over a sheer wall of basalt, while the upper drops 30 feet. Turn north off S.R. 138 toward Toketee Lake on Road #34 (formerly #268). Drive 0.3 mile to the marked left (west) turn to the beginning of Toketee Falls Trail #1495. Follow the easily hiked path 0.6 mile to a viewpoint looking into the falls.

The Toketee Pipeline can be seen from the trailhead. Pacific Power diverts water from Toketee Lake via this 12-foot redwood stave pipe. It bypasses North Umpqua River for 1,663 feet to a mile-long tunnel. The water then plunges down a steel penstock pipe to the Toketee Powerhouse, where it can generate as much as 210,000 kilowatts of electricity.

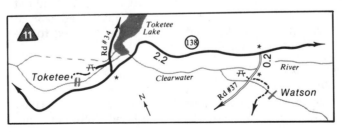

Watson Falls

Type: plunge; map: USGS Garwood Butte 15'

Drive east 2.2 miles past Toketee Lake along S.R. 138 to Fish Creek Road #37; turn right (south). Follow it 0.2 mile to Watson Falls Picnic Ground. Follow Watson Falls Trail #1495 from the picnic area. A footbridge 0.3 mile from the trailhead provides a full view of Watson Creek hurtling down 272 feet.

12. NORTHEASTERN UMPQUA

Whitehorse Falls

Type: punchbowl; map: USGS Garwood Butte 7½'

Relax on the porchlike vista overlooking this 10- to 15-foot punchbowl falls along Clearwater River. Turn off S.R. 138 at the marked turn for Whitehorse Falls Camp, 4.5 miles east of Toketee. Park at the picnic area adjacent to the falls.

Clearwater Falls

Type: segmented; map: USGS Diamond Lake 7½'

Drive 3.5 miles east on S.R. 138 from Whitehorse Falls to the turnoff for Clearwater Falls Camp. Follow the access road 0.2 mile to the picnic area. The 30-foot cascade is a short walk up Clearwater River.

Lemolo Falls

Type: horsetail; map: USGS Lemolo Lake 7½'

The previous entries are conducive to meditation, but this 75- to 100-foot monster along the North Umpqua River won't allow such tranquility. Turn north from S.R. 138 onto Lemolo Lake Road #2610, 3 miles east of Clearwater Falls, and drive toward Lemolo Lake. Bear left (north) after 4.3 miles to Thorn Prairie Road #3401, go 0.4 mile, then turn right on Lemolo Falls Road #3401/800. The trailhead is 1.8 miles farther. Lemolo Falls Trail #1468 descends steeply 1 mile to the base of the falls. The cataract is also accessible from Trail #1414 on the north side of the river; consult the accompanying map. Lemolo is Chinook for "wild" or "untamed."

Warm Springs Falls

Type: block

Warm Springs plunges 50 to 70 feet over basalt cliffs. Follow the directions to Lemolo Falls (above), but instead of turning on Road #3401 for Lemolo Falls, continue 0.9 mile on Lemolo Lake Road #2610 to the far side of Lemolo Dam. Turn left (northwest) on Road #600, driving 3 miles to Road #680. Turn left here and proceed 1.7 miles to the start of Warm Springs Falls Trail #1499. An unguarded vista of the falls at the trail's end in an easy 0.3 mile.

 Warm Springs Falls

13. FALLS OF THE UPPER ROGUE

Upper Falls
Type: cascade; map: USGS Hamaker Butte 7½'

Upper Rogue River Trail #1034 passes next to two falls along its northerly route. The closest trailheads are at Mazama Viewpoint, 0.6 mile west of S.R. 138 on S.R. 230, and Hamaker Campground, 11 miles north of S.R. 62 off S.R. 230. The steep 30- to 50-foot cascades of the upper cataract are 3.5 miles south of Mazama Viewpoint. The 15- to 25-foot drop of **Middle Falls** is 1.5 miles downstream from the upper falls, or 2.5 miles upstream from Hamaker Camp.

Muir Creek Falls
Type: tiered; map: USGS Hamaker Butte 7½'

Leave S.R. 230 at Road #6560, across from the access road to Hamaker Camp. Drive about 1 mile to a turnout for Buck Canyon Trail #1042. Hike 1 mile downstream to where Sherwood Creek can be seen falling 15 to 25 feet in tiers into Muir Creek on the other side of the canyon.

Lower Falls
Type: block; map: USGS Hamaker Butte 7½'

This block-type waterfall drops 10 to 15 feet where S.R. 230 follows a sweeping bend in the Rogue River. Drive to an undesignated turnout 1.8 miles south of Road #6560, or 2.7 miles north of Road #6530.

National Creek Falls
Type: segmented; map: USGS Hamaker Butte 7½'

National Creek pours 30 to 50 feet downward in three segments. From S.R. 62, turn north on S.R. 230. In 5.8 miles, turn right (east) on Road #6530. Follow this secondary route 3.5 miles to the marked parking area for National Creek Falls Trail #1053. The path descends moderately to the base of the falls in 0.5 mile.

14. SOUTH UMPQUA

Campbell Falls
Type: punchbowl; map: USGS Red Butte 15'

Drive to the hamlet of Tiller along S.R. 227. Turn northeast onto South Umpqua Road #28 (northwest of the ranger station) and continue 12 miles to Boulder Creek Camp. The 10- to 15-foot drop is on the Umpqua above the mouth of Boulder Creek. The name honors Robert G. Campbell, a former U.S. Forest Service employee who was killed in action during World War II.

South Umpqua Falls
Type: cascade; map: USGS Quartz Mtn 15'

Water slides 10 to 15 feet over wide slabs of bedrock. Drive southeast on South Umpqua Road #28, 6.6 miles past Boulder Creek Camp (above) to South Umpqua Falls Picnic Area and Observation Point. A fish ladder bypasses the falls.

Deer Lick Falls
Type: tiered; map: USGS Quartz Mtn 15'

Peer into a series of five blocklike descents ranging from 5 to 20 feet in height. Reach them by driving 4.1 miles northeast past the previous entry along South Umpqua Road #28. Do not cross the river, but bear left on Road #28 toward Camp Comfort. The waterfall is along Black Rock Fork 4 miles beyond the campground.

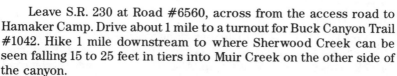

15. AZALEA AREA

Cow Creek Falls

Type: cascade

Cow Creek drops 25 to 40 feet along a series of rock steps. Turn off Interstate 5 at Azalea (Exit 88) and follow Cow Creek Road east for 17.2 miles to Devils Flat Camp. A short loop trail across the road from the campground passes the falls. Two historic buildings from homestead days provide landmarks near the trail.

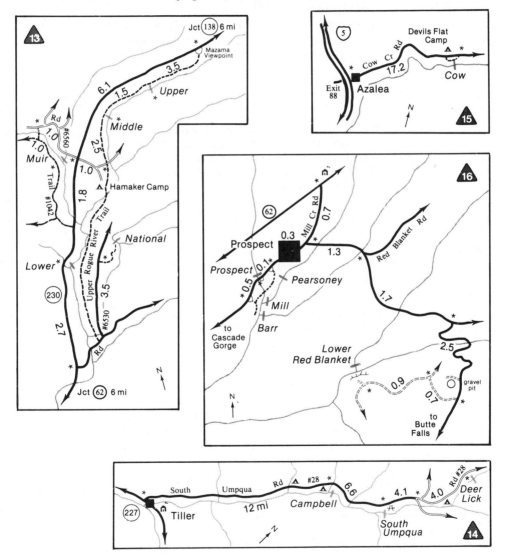

16. MILL CREEK SCENIC AREA

Three of the following five waterfalls are part of Boise Cascade Corporation's Mill Creek Falls Scenic Area. The timber company has constructed public trails on a tract of pristine land.

Mill Creek Falls
Type: plunge; map: USGS Rustler Peak 15'

Look across a canyon cut by the Rogue River to this thundering 173-foot plunge. Turn off S.R. 62 onto Mill Creek Road at either Cascade Gorge or Prospect. Park at the turnout marked by a large trail system sign. Start on the interpretive trail immediately south of the parking area and walk 0.3 mile to the viewpoint.

Barr Creek Falls
Type: fan

Follow the trail 0.1 mile past Mill Creek Falls, or 0.4 mile from trailhead (see directions, above), to a rocky outcrop with a superb view across the canyon to this 175- to 200-foot display. The cataract is also known as *Bear Creek Falls.*

Prospect Falls
Type: cascade

Drive 0.5 mile northeast past the Mill Creek parking area (above) to an undesignated turnout on the east side of the bridge over Rogue River. A well-trodden path leads to many good views of Rogue River tumbling 50 to 100 feet. I've named the waterfall after the nearby town.

Pearsoney Falls
Type: segmented

Continue 0.1 mile north of the bridge over the Rogue (see directions to Prospect Falls, above) to a parking area off Mill Creek Road. Follow the main trail 0.2 mile to where Mill Creek drops 15 to 25 feet. The waterfall is named after two early pioneer families of the Prospect area: the Pearsons and the Mooneys.

Lower Red Blanket Falls
Type: tiered; map: USGS Prospect 15'

Take Red Blanket Road east from Prospect and turn right after 1.3 miles. Continue 1.7 miles, then bear right (south) toward Butte Falls. After the route switchbacks uphill, look for a jeep trail to the right (west). It's the first road past a short gravel road ending at a gravel pit.

Follow the jeep trail for 1.6 miles as shown on the accompanying map. Park at the short, abandoned jeep trail, which leads toward the canyon rim. Follow the trail for a few hundred yards, then cut through the woods toward the roaring sound of the falls. Pick a route partway down the moderately steep slope for good views of Red Blanket

Creek plummeting 90 to 140 feet into the opposite side of the Rogue River. The walk is about 0.3 mile, but I recommend it for experienced hikers only.

17. SKY LAKES WILDERNESS

Red Blanket Falls
Type: punchbowl; map: USGS Union Peak 7½'

Follow Red Blanket Road east for 15 miles from Prospect to the parking area for Upper Red Blanket Trail #1090. Red Blanket Creek drops 20 feet about 2.5 miles upstream from the trailhead.

Stuart Falls
Type: fan; map: USGS Union Peak 7½'

Continue 2 miles past Red Blanket Falls (above) to the end of Trail #1090 a total of 4.5 miles from the trailhead. Follow Stuart Falls Trail #1078 to the left (north) for 0.5 mile to where Red Blanket Creek veils down 25 feet. A campsite is nearby.

18. CRATER LAKE NATIONAL PARK

The center of attraction in the park is the *caldera,* an enormous depression presently occupied by Crater Lake. It formed as a result of a cataclysmic eruption of volcanic Mount Mazama 6,600 years ago. Heavy annual precipitation maintains the lake level. In addition to the lake, the park has a pair of falls.

Annie Falls
Type: cascade; map: USGS Maklaks Crater 7½'

For a canyon rim view of water rushing 30 to 50 feet along Annie Creek, drive 4.7 miles north of the south park entrance to a turnout off S.R. 62. *Heed the warning signs at the canyon rim.* The slopes are very unstable and impossible to walk on. **Duwee Falls** makes its descent a few miles upstream, but the shape of the gorge hides it from view.

Vidae Falls
Type: fan; map: USGS Crater Lake East 7½'

Vidae Creek sprays from Crater Lake's south rim near Applegate Peak. Drive 3 miles southeast from the park headquarters to a turnout near the falls.

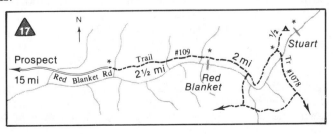

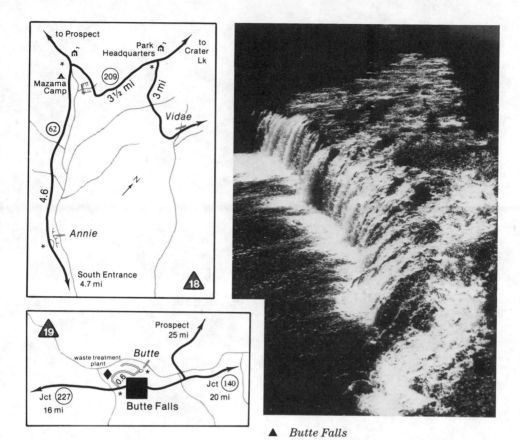

▲ *Butte Falls*

19. BUTTE FALLS

Butte Falls
Type: block; map: USGS Butte Falls 15'

    The nearby community is named after this 10- to 15-foot block waterfall. Turn off S.R. 62 at the Butte Falls junction, 5 miles north of Eagle Point. Reach the town of Butte Falls in 16 miles. Upon entering the village, look for Pine Street to the left (north). Backtrack one block to an unmarked gravel road. Take this unpaved route north past a waste treatment plant to an undesignated parking area in 0.6 mile. Well-worn paths quickly lead to the falls.

The Columbia Plateau

The landscape of eastern Oregon is dominated by a broad region of generally low relief called the Columbia Plateau. This plain, which extends into southeastern Washington, northern Nevada, and southwestern Idaho, is composed of thick layers of basalt which formed from widespread lava flows 30 million years ago. Waterfalls are scarce in the Oregon portion of the plateau. Cataracts are lacking along most of the region's major rivers because of the consistent erosion resistance of the basaltic bedrock. In addition, low annual precipitation means that few tributary streams flow over the rims of the larger river canyons. Twenty of the region's 46 known waterfalls are listed in this chapter.

Most of the cataracts in this region are found where other geomorphic processes have contributed to waterfall formation. Recent lava flows inundated the course of the Deschutes River 5,000 to 6,000 years ago. When the lava cooled, jumbled basaltic rock was formed. The river cuts into and tumbles over these rocky obstructions.

The Strawberry Mountains near the town of John Day were shaped by the accumulation of basalt, rhyolite, and breccia due to volcanic activities 10 million to 13 million years ago. The extreme differences in the erosion resistance of these rock types produce waterfalls where streams flow across their contact points.

The Wallowa Mountains of northeastern Oregon are in one of the few nonvolcanic areas of the region. Large masses of granite and sedimentary rocks were displaced thousands of feet above the surrounding plain 100 million to 150 million years ago. Its high relief stopped subsequent lava at its western perimeter. Since the Wallowas rise over 8,000 feet above sea level, their climate was sufficiently cold and moist for alpine glaciation to have occurred. The erosive work of these glaciers left vertical breaks for stream courses to plunge over.

1. REDMOND

The Deschutes River (meaning "River of the Falls") is aptly titled, since it has nine cataracts along its course from La Pine to Culver. Of the five falls near Redmond, only Cline Falls (below) is accessible. The unapproachable descents are **Awbrey Falls,** named after Marshall Clay Awbrey, who served in the Rogue River Indian War of the

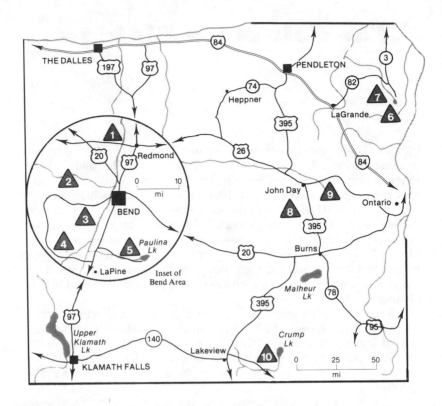

mid-1800s; **Big Falls**; **Odin Falls,** titled after the mythological Norse god of wisdom and heroes; and **Steelhead Falls,** presumably named for the fish.

Cline Falls
Type: segmented; map: USGS Cline Falls 7½'

The force of this cascade is reduced because a portion of the river has been diverted to a rustic powerhouse nearby. Drive 4.5 miles west of Redmond on S.R. 126. Turn right (north) at the west side of the Deschutes River on SW Eagle Drive. Park at the entrance to a dirt road 0.3 mile farther and look into the canyon at the falls and power facility. The waterfall was named for Dr. C.A. Cline, who once owned the falls.

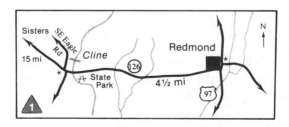

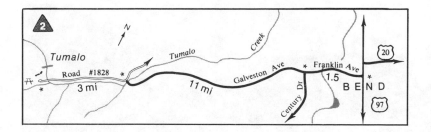

2. TUMALO CREEK

Tumalo Falls

Type: plunge; map: USGS Broken Top 15'

Turn off U.S. 97 in Bend onto westbound Franklin Avenue. The street becomes Galveston Avenue in 1 mile at Drake City Park. Proceed west 11 miles and turn left (west) on graveled Road #1828. Continue 3 miles to Tumalo Falls Picnic Area.

This 97-foot plummet is framed by stark tree snags — brown remnants of a forest fire during the summer of 1979. Think of your favorite vacation spots and imagine them devastated by fire. The Tumalo scene is a graphic reminder that "only you can prevent forest fires."

3. LAVA BUTTE GEOLOGICAL AREA

The Deschutes River drops in three places on the western fringe of Lava Butte Geological Area. Drive west on Franklin Avenue toward Tumalo Falls (see Tumalo Falls, above), but turn left (south) on Cascade Lakes Highway (also known as Century Drive) from the west side of Bend. Continue 6.3 miles and turn left (south) on gravel Road #41 at the sign to Dillon Falls.

Lava Island Falls

Type: segmented; map: USGS Benham Falls 7½'

The waterfall is minor, but the jumbled lava rock being split by the Deschutes is intriguing. Follow Road #41 south for 0.4 mile from Century Drive. Turn left (east) on dirt Road #620 and continue to its north end in 0.8 mile.

Dillon Falls

Type: cascade; map: USGS Benham Falls 7½'

Take Road #41 south 3 miles from Century Drive. Turn left (southeast) on dirt Road #500 and drive to its end in 0.9 mile. A trail goes from the parking area to views of a quarter-mile-long chasm where water froths 40 to 60 feet. There are no fenced observation points from the rim. The waterfall is named for homesteader Leander Dillon.

▲   *Dillon Falls*

Benham Falls
Type: cascade; map: USGS Benham Falls 7½'

Bear south on Road #620 at its four-way intersection with Road #500. Park where the road meets the river in 3.3 miles. The falls are immediately downstream. A short pathway leads to secure, but unfenced views of the river shooting down 40 to 60 feet through a narrow canyon. The waterfall is named for J.R. Benham, who unsuccessfully filed for land nearby in 1885.

4. LA PINE AREA

Fall River Falls
Type: fan; map: USGS Pistol Butte 7½'

Leave U.S. 97 at South Century Drive 13 miles south of Bend. Drive west 10.5 miles and turn left (south) on dirt Road #4360. Park at the wide turnout preceding the Fall River bridge. Follow the jeep trail 0.2 mile from the parking area to grassy banks surrounded by pines. The river tumbles 10 to 15 feet.

Pringle Falls
Type: cascade; map: USGS LaPine 7½'

Although pictured in travel guides and labeled on road maps, the main part of this series of small falls and cascades can no longer be seen by the public. A housing development currently lines the Des-

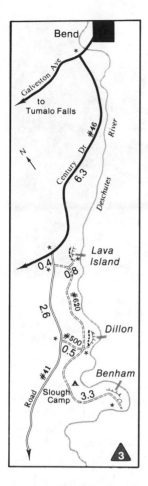

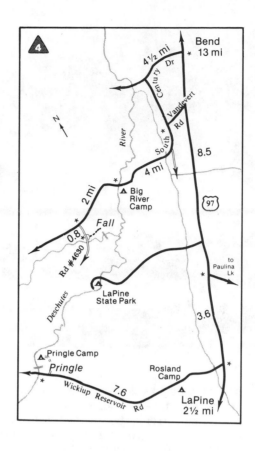

chutes along the falls. From the security system, it is clear that visitors are not welcome. Only uninspiring views of the beginning and end of the falls remain.

Turn toward Wickiup Reservoir 2.5 miles north of La Pine at the junction of U.S. 97 and Wickiup Reservoir Road. Drive 7.6 miles to the bridge crossing at the headwaters of the falls. Pringle Falls Camp is immediately downstream from the end of the falls. Follow dirt Road #218 to the campground. The falls are named for O.M. Pringle, who bought land nearby in 1902.

5. NEWBERRY CRATER

A dominant feature of the geology south of Bend is a *shield volcano*. It postdates and contrasts with the great *composite volcanoes* of the Cascade Range (Mount Rainier, Mount Hood, Mount Shasta, and others). Shield volcanoes are typically larger, but have gentler slopes than the composite type. The Paulina Mountains are

▲   *Fall River Falls*

part of a shield volcano. Its Newberry Crater represents a *caldera*, where the central portion of the volcano collapsed. Paulina Lake and East Lake currently fill the depression. As Paulina Creek flows from Paulina Lake, its erosive power has cut through the volcano's layers of basalt at a greater rate than through more resistant rhyolite. Waterfalls occur where these two rock layers meet along the stream's course.

Lower Falls
Type: tiered; map: USGS Paulina Peak 7½'

Paulina Creek descends a total of 50 to 80 feet as the creek diverges along its upper portion before fanning out below. Turn east off U.S. 97 at Paulina Lake Road, 6 miles north of La Pine. Drive 10 miles to a large, undesignated parking area to the left (north). Hike along an old jeep trail beginning at the far end of the turnout. At a junction in 0.4 mile, bear left (west) and walk 0.6 mile until the falls

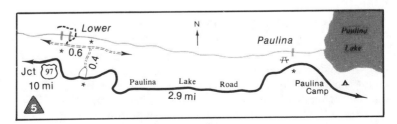

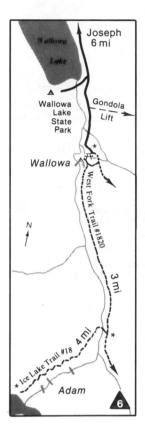

▲   *Paulina Creek Falls*

can be heard. An unmarked trail from the jeep route leads across a footbridge over the creek and downstream to views of the falls. The rating decreases during the low water periods of late summer.

Paulina Creek Falls

Type: segmented; map: USGS Paulina Peak 7½'

This 100-foot segmented waterfall is best seen in early summer when the streamflow is at its peak. Continue 2.9 miles east past Lower Falls along the paved road. Stop at Paulina Creek Falls Picnic Ground. A short trail leads to a developed vista with superb views. The waterfall is also known as *Upper Falls*.

6. WALLOWA LAKE AREA

Wallowa Lake is a beautiful example of a *paternoster lake,* a body of water formed by a natural dam blocking part of a glacial valley. Drive through Joseph on S.R. 82 to Wallowa Lake State Park in 6 miles. Turn left (south) toward the picnic area and away from the main boating and camping facilities.

Wallowa Falls
Type: punchbowl; map: USGS Joseph 15'

West Fork Trail #1820 toward Ice Lake starts at the picnic area. A footbridge crosses East Fork Wallowa River, then ascends shortly to a rocky outcrop adjacent to the West Fork in 0.1 mile. From this natural vista, follow the ridge a short distance downstream to a well-worn path above the river. From the path you can see West Fork Wallowa River pouring down 30 to 50 feet.

Adam Creek Falls
Type: tiered

The hiker views this series of falls individually; they can also be seen collectively. Hike 3 miles along West Fork Trail #1820, then turn right (west) on Ice Lake Trail #18. You will pass several waterfalls along the 4-mile route, which ends at Ice Lake.

Tourists atop Mount Howard can view the tiered falls as silvery mountainside threads. Take the High Wallowas gondola 3,700 feet above the valley for unforgettable views of Eagle Cap Wilderness, Wallowa Lake, and the Columbia Plateau. Look for the falls to the southwest.

7. HURRICANE CREEK DRAINAGE

Falls Creek Falls
Map: USGS Enterprise 15'

To reach this waterfall near the northeastern flank of the High Wallowas, drive along S.R. 82 to the Western-style community of Joseph. At the north end of town, turn right (west) at the marked turnoff to Imnaha. (Be sure to take the road *away* from Imnaha at the junction, not the road toward it.) In 2.5 miles, bear left at Hurricane Creek. The gravel road ends at a campsite in 2 miles. Hike 2 miles from the campground along Hurricane Creek Trail #1807 to the first trail junction to the right (west). This spur path leads up Falls Creek to its descent in 0.25 mile.

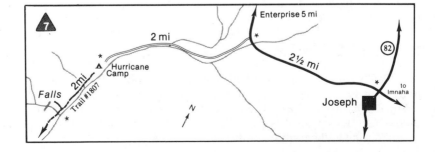

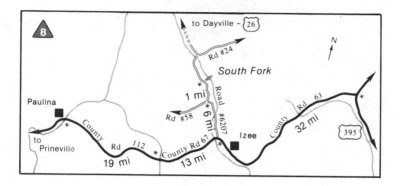

8. OCHOCO EAST

South Fork Falls
Type: cascade; map: USGS Suplee Butte 7½'

Water reportedly tumbles 75 feet over a 200- to 300-foot reach of the South Fork John Day River. Drive 32 miles west from U.S. 395 on County Road #63, or 32 miles east from Paulina along County Roads #112 and #67, to BLM Road #6207. Proceed north, following the river, for approximately 6 miles to Forest Road #58. Stay north on #6207; the cataract should be about 1 mile farther, where the road bends sharply. Located on BLM land, the cascades are locally known as *Izee Falls*.

9. STRAWBERRY MOUNTAINS WILDERNESS

The Strawberry Mountains rise 3,500 to 5,000 feet above the surrounding Columbia Plateau. Their climate, cooler and moister than the lower plateau, is suitable for forest growth.

Drive to Prairie City on U.S. 26 and obtain a backpacking permit at the local ranger station. The wilderness trails are generally clear of snow from mid-June to mid-November. Leave the main highway at Prairie City, turning south on Main Street. In 0.5 mile turn right on Bridge Street, which becomes Road #1428 after leaving town. Follow the Strawberry Lake signs south from town. Gravel Strawberry Road #1428 ends and the trail begins at Strawberry Camp in 12.5 miles.

Strawberry Falls
Map: USGS Prairie City 15'

Start hiking on Strawberry Basin Trail #375 from the south end of the campground. Reach Strawberry Lake in 1.5 miles and the base of the falls in a total of 3.5 miles. The trail continues to the top of the cataract in 0.2 mile. Strawberry Creek reportedly drops 75 feet.

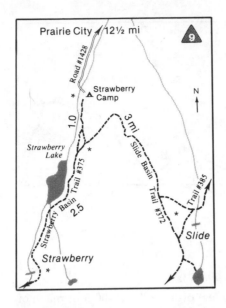

Slide Falls

Hike 1 mile along Strawberry Basin Trail #375, then bear left (east) at Slide Basin Trail #372. This pathway steepens until it reaches the ridgetop in 1 mile, then follows along Slide Creek Valley. After 3 miles more, a sign points east toward the waterfall along Slide Creek.

10. ADEL

Deep Creek Falls
Type: block; map: USGS Adel 7½'

This 30- to 50-foot cataract is framed by columns of basalt in a sagebrush setting. It is next to S.R. 140 at the floor of narrow and steep Deep Creek Canyon. Drive about 2.75 miles west from Adel or 35 miles east from Lakeview for roadside views.

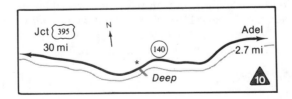

The Idaho Panhandle

The Panhandle of northern Idaho separates Washington from Montana. Stretching from the Canadian border 170 miles south to Lewiston, its width varies from 45 to 125 miles. Although many states have unusual shapes, Idaho's is unique in its historical and political significance. No other state was shaped wholly by the boundaries originally defined by its neighbors. Idaho is the land not annexed by Montana, Wyoming, Utah, Nevada, Oregon, or Washington.

The Panhandle is a region of large lakes and rolling to rugged mountains. Lake Coeur d'Alene, Lake Pend Oreille, Priest Lake, and Dworshak Reservoir cover large areas. All but Dworshak are natural. Mountain ranges such as the Selkirks, the Purcells, the Bitterroots, and the Clearwaters are distributed through the region. The Panhandle has 31 recognized waterfalls, of which 25 are described here.

Geomorphologists, scientists who study landforms, classify waterfalls as *destructive* or *constructive*. Most cataracts, including almost all of the ones in the Pacific Northwest, are of the destructive variety. The force of running water slowly erodes the streambeds, sometimes causing the falls to recede upstream. Constructive descents, on the other hand, mostly flow over mineral deposits and migrate downstream as the deposits accumulate. (*Fall Creek Falls*, listed in the "Snake River Plain" chapter, is a constructive falls.)

Destructive falls are further classified by how they developed. *Consequent falls* are located where a preexisting break occurs along the course of a stream. An example is water plunging into a glacier-carved valley, as at *Copper Falls*. When streams erode along rock materials of varying rates of erosional resistance, *subsequent falls* may form, as at *Snow Creek Falls*.

The waterfalls of the Northwest can be enjoyed for their beauty alone, but they are even more interesting when the forces that created them are pondered.

1. PRIEST RIVER DRAINAGE

Torrelle Falls

Type: punchbowl; map: USGS Quartz Mountain 7½'

A rustic restaurant built over the stream at the base of this 10- to 15-foot waterfall makes it unique. Drive 8.5 miles north from the town of Priest River on S.R. 57. The waterfall is on the left (west) side of the highway along West Branch Priest River.

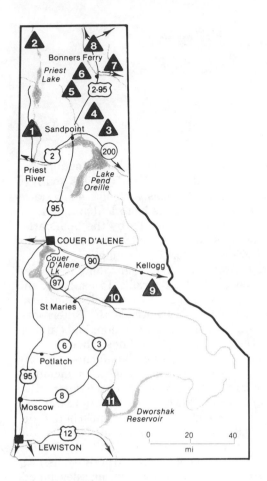

Mission Falls
Type: cascade; map: USGS Outlet Bay 7½'

Continue north on S.R. 57 for 11.5 miles past Torrelle Falls (above). Park at the northeast side of the bridge crossing Upper West Branch Priest River.

Follow a jeep trail next to a bridge for 0.2 mile to a road junction. Take the right fork; the left quickly leads back to the paved road. Follow the dirt route for 1.7 miles, bearing right at all junctions. When you near the river, a well-worn trail leads to the falls in a few hundred yards.

2. PRIEST LAKE

Recreational activities continue year-round near the 26,000 acres of Priest Lake, but the area's waterfalls are remote and should be visited from early summer to late autumn.

Granite Falls

Type: horsetail; map: USGS Helmer Mtn 7½'

Drive 37 miles north of Priest River along S.R. 57 to Nordman. Continue 13 miles and turn onto the entrance road to Stagger Inn Camp and Granite Falls. (S.R. 57 becomes Granite Creek Road #302 about 2 miles past Nordman.) The trailhead is at the south end of the camp. The sign to the falls may be misleading. Do not cross the log over the stream to which the arrow points. Instead walk straight past the sign. Granite Creek slides 50 to 75 feet less than 100 yards away. This waterfall is actually in Washington, but I've listed it in the Panhandle section because the primary access is from Idaho.

Upper Priest Falls

Type: fan; map: USGS Continental Mtn 7½'

Upper Priest River noisily crashes 100 to 125 feet within the secluded northwest tip of Idaho. Drive 1.75 miles north on Road #302 past Stagger Inn Camp (see Granite Falls, above), turning right (northeast) on Road #1013, which eventually turns to Road #637. Proceed approximately 11.5 miles to the Upper Priest River Trailhead #308. This path follows the river for 9 miles, ending at the falls.

There is another route to the falls, if your vehicle has good road clearance. Take Road #637 for about 11 miles to the Continental Trail #28. Hike 0.7 mile north on Trail #28 and turn right on Trail #308, about 1.5 miles more to the descent. The cataract is also known as *American Falls* to distinguish it from the similar drop of **Canadian Falls,** located upstream in British Columbia.

3. PEND OREILLE

A few years ago, the easiest route to Char Falls and Wellington Creek Falls was on Lightning Creek Road from Clark Fork. But severe flooding in 1980 all but destroyed the middle and lower parts of the road. Fortunately, an alternate route is available. The trip is rough, but worthwhile. However, you must wait until the snow melts in mid-summer.

Rapid Lightning Falls

Type: cascade

Water rushes 20 to 30 feet along Rapid Lightning Creek. Turn east off U.S. 2/95 onto S.R. 200 and drive 6.2 miles before turning left (north) on Colburn-Culver Road. In 2.9 miles, turn right (east) at the schoolhouse onto the road marked Rapid Lightning Creek (Road #629). Park at an undesignated turnout 3.4 miles farther. The cataract is accessible from short, well-trod paths.

Char Falls

Type: horsetail

Drive along S.R. 200 6.2 miles east past Colburn-Culver Road to Trestle Creek Road #275. Turn left (east) and go 13 miles to Lightning

▲   *Char Falls*

Creek Road #419. Turn right (south) and continue 0.6 mile to a primitive road to the left. Park and follow the rocky road 0.5 mile to a wide trail at its end. Take the trail only 20 yards, then find a faint path to the right. It leads to an overlook of the falls in less than 100 yards. Lightning Creek descends powerfully for 50 to 75 feet.

Wellington Creek Falls
Type: punchbowl

Continue 4.2 miles past Char Falls (above) along Lightning Creek Road #419 to Auxor Road #489, and turn right (west). Cross Lightning Creek and drive or hike down the primitive road to the left. Bear right at the fork in 0.4 mile and continue 0.4 mile on the bumpy road to

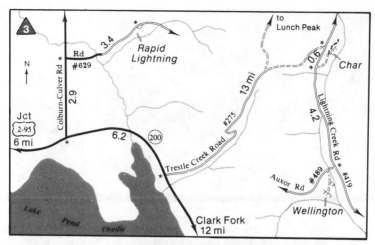

its end. Walk toward the creek and a bit upstream, listening for the falls. Continue toward Wellington Creek for good overviews of the wonderful 50- to 75-foot waterfall and the lush vegetation surrounding it. *Be careful near the edge of the precipice.*

4. COLBURN AREA

Grouse Falls

Type: cascade

Grouse Creek cuts through bedrock in a small series of descents totaling 15 to 20 feet. Turn east off U.S. 2/95 at Colburn onto Colburn–Culver Road. Drive east 4.5 miles and turn left on the gravel road. Continue 6 miles up Grouse Creek Valley to a turnout near a dirt road to the right. Park and follow the road, which becomes a trail in 0.3 mile. The waterfall is 0.2 mile farther.

5. PACK RIVER DRAINAGE

Jeru Creek Falls

Type: horsetail; map: USGS Dodge Peak 7½'

Turn northwest off U.S. 2/95 at Samuels onto Pack River Road #231. Drive 9 miles to the undesignated turnout on the north side of

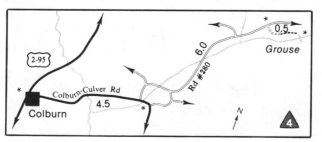

▲   *Moyie Falls*

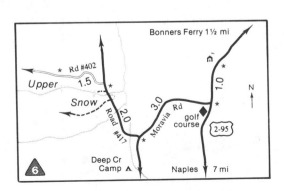

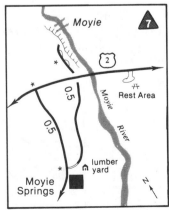

Jeru Creek. The 1-mile trek from the road starts on an obsolete four-wheel-drive route and eventually turns into a seldom used, unmaintained trail. When the path seems to end, you should be near the 100- to 150-foot waterfall. There is a similar, unnamed waterfall along nearby Hellroaring Creek, but unfortunately it is not accessible.

6. BONNERS FERRY

Snow Creek Falls
Type: segmented; map: USGS Moravia 7½'

Drive 2.5 miles south of Bonners Ferry on U.S. 2/95. Turn right onto Moravia Road at the golf course. Bear right in 3 miles on West Side Road #417 and drive 2 miles to a turnout and informal campsite. The unnamed trail on the north side of Snow Creek leads shortly to the base of the segmented 50- to 75-foot falls. The named trail south of the creek goes up the ridge and does not provide any views of the falls.

The 75- to 125-foot drop of the **Upper Falls** is more impressive than its lower counterpart, but there is no direct access. You can catch a bird's-eye glimpse of the falls from Snow Creek Road #402 about 1.5 miles west from where it intersects West Side Road #417.

7. MOYIE RIVER

Moyie Falls is purported to be one of Idaho's great scenic attractions. No argument here. But contrary to what some sources imply, you can't get good views from the main highway. The following description, however, directs you to a picture-perfect vista.

Moyie Falls
Type: tiered; map: USGS Moyie Springs 7½'

Turn off U.S. 2 at the Moyie Springs exit immediately west of the Moyie River bridge. After 0.5 mile, turn left on the street adjacent to a lumber yard. Follow this residential road 0.5 mile to various turnouts offering good views into a canyon carved out over thousands of years. Moyie River absolutely thunders through in a tiered cataract. The larger upper portion crashes 60 to 100 feet beneath an antiquated span crossing the canyon. The lower portion cascades 20 to 40 feet.

8. BOUNDARY LINE

Smith Falls
Type: plunge; map: USGS Smith Falls 7½'

Turn north onto S.R. 1 from U.S. 95 at the junction about 15 miles north of Bonners Ferry. Drive 1 mile, then turn left (west) on an unsigned road and continue 5 miles on the paved surface, crossing Kootenai River at the halfway point. Turn right (north) on West Side Road #417 and drive 8 miles to a marked turnout to the falls. A heavy

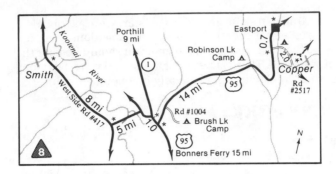

volume of water plunges 60 feet along Smith Creek. The falls and the viewpoint are on private property. Please obey the posted restrictions so others can continue to enjoy this setting.

Copper Falls
Type: plunge

Turn east off U.S. 95 onto Road #2517 less than 0.75 mile south of Eastport border crossing or 14 miles northeast of the junction with S.R. 1. Follow this bumpy gravel road for 2 miles to Copper Falls Trail #207. Hike 0.25 mile along the moderately steep trail to the falls. Copper Creek hurtles down 160 feet.

9. MULLAN

Pass the historic mining towns of Kellogg, Wallace, and Mullan as you travel east from Coeur d'Alene along Interstate 90. (They may become *exclusively* historic if the depressed mining industry continues its slide through the 1980s). Several nice waterfalls accessible from late summer to early autumn are located near the Bitterroot Divide, which separates Idaho from Montana.

Willow Creek Falls
Type: cascade

Leave I-90 at Mullan (Exit 68). Drive through the town and continue east. The route turns right after 1.5 miles and becomes Willow Creek Road. Continue 1.5 miles, passing I-90, to the road's end near an old set of railroad tracks. Willow Creek Trail #8008 leads moderately upstream for 2 miles to the 10- to 20-foot cascade along East Fork Willow Creek.

Stevens Lake Falls
Type: tiered

The tiers of this waterfall can be viewed collectively or individually. The cataracts are not easily visible from Willow Creek Trail #8008 (see Willow Creek Falls, above), but there are good vantage points just off the path. The trail steepens considerably past Willow Creek Falls as it follows the East Fork for 0.2 mile (2.2 miles from the

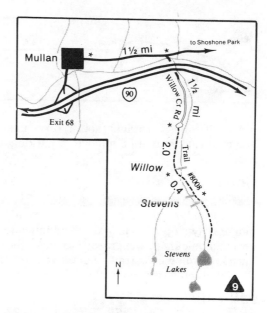

trailhead) to the 30- to 50-foot plunge of the lower portion. Hike 0.2 mile farther for a close-up view of the horsetail form of the 30- to 50-foot upper drop. Both portions can be glimpsed along the trail before they are reached.

10. ST. JOE DRAINAGE

The St. Joe River is particularly known for two things: first, it is navigable to one of the highest elevations of any river in North America. Second, its sport fishing is regarded as excellent, especially along the remote upper reaches where you can practically jump across the "mighty" St. Joe.

Falls Creek Falls
Type: block

If you're heading upstream to catch some trout, pause at this 20- to 30-foot waterfall. Turn east off S.R. 3 onto the St. Joe River Road 0.5 mile northeast of St. Maries. The falls are 15 miles up the River Road, or 4.5 miles past Shadowy St. Joe Camp. Park at the turnout nearest Falls Creek bridge.

11. ELK CREEK FALLS
RECREATION AREA

Many waterfalls are to be found within this portion of Clearwater National Forest, designated as a Recreation Area primarily to preserve the scenic surroundings. Access in the area is tolerable, but may not be clearly posted. Drive south from Bovill toward Elk River on S.R.

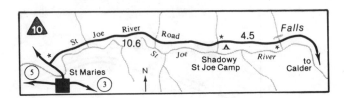

8. After 16 miles, turn right (south) on an unsigned road next to a large gravel pile. Continue 1.6 miles to a parking area next to a fork in the road.

Upper Elk Falls
Type: punchbowl; map: USGS Elk Creek Falls 7½'

Hike along the left fork of the road, which soon becomes a moderately sloped trail. Walk for 2 miles to a small open area, then descend quickly to the grassy slopes of the north rim of the canyon. Turn left, following a trail back into the woods and toward the creek. The 30- to 50-foot drop is about 0.3 mile upstream.

Elk Falls
Type: horsetail; map: USGS Elk Creek Falls 7½'

This 125- to 150-foot cataract is the highest of the six along Elk Creek. Follow the directions to Upper Elk Falls (above), but at the canyon rim, follow the trail to the right among grassy slopes. There are many views of the falls during the next 0.25 mile. Elk Falls is 2.0 miles from the trailhead.

Middle Elk Falls
Type: punchbowl

This 20- to 30-foot waterfall 0.25 mile downstream from Elk Falls can be looked down on from near the trail. It is 2.25 miles from the trailhead.

Twin Falls and Small Falls
Type: tiered

These two waterfalls can be seen together from the trail. One is a 10- to 20-foot segmented drop; the other drops 10 to 20 feet in a punchbowl form. They are 0.1 mile past Middle Elk Falls, and 2.3 miles from the trailhead.

Lower Elk Falls
Type: plunge; map: USGS Elk Creek Falls 7½'

Walk to the end of the well-worn trail about 0.1 mile past Small Falls, 2.4 miles from the trailhead. Carefully follow the faint path to the top of the rocky basaltic outcrop for an excellent view. This 75- to 100-foot plunge is the most powerful of the Elk Creek falls. I recommend it only for cautious hikers who are not deterred by unfenced heights.

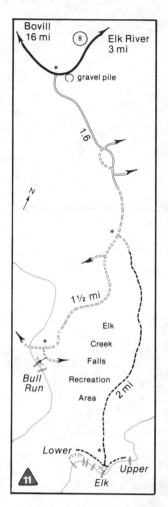

▲ *Elk Falls*

Bull Run Creek Falls
Type: cascade; map: USGS Elk Creek Falls 7½'

Instead of parking at the trailhead for Elk Creek Canyon, continue along the unnamed road, taking the forks as shown on the accompanying map. Park in 1.5 miles. A small, faint path leads shortly to these 75- to 100-foot cascades.

Lower Falls
Type: fan

Return to the road from Bull Run Creek Falls (above) and continue walking downstream along the ridge for 0.1 mile. After passing a small marshy area, scramble down the steep timbered slope to the creek below the base of the 30- to 50-foot falls. I recommend this waterfall for determined bushwhackers only.

Wilderness Areas of Central Idaho

The interior of Idaho is dominated by swift rivers cutting deep canyons through rugged mountains. This sparsely populated region contains the largest tracts of wilderness in the continental United States. Three million acres of primitive expanse are set aside for the adventurer: the Selway-Bitterroot, Frank Church River of No Return, Gospel Hump, and Sawtooth Wilderness Areas; the Hells Canyon and Sawtooth National Recreation Areas; and Wild and Scenic Salmon River.

The geology of this region is largely determined by the history of the *Idaho Batholith*. During the late Mesozoic era, 75 million to 100 million years ago, extensive intrusions of magma crystallized in the subsurface of central Idaho. Rocks ranging from igneous granite and diorite to metamorphic gneisses were formed. Over the next 50 million years, the batholith was uplifted into mountains.

The mountainous terrain of the Idaho interior has been shaped mostly by erosion. Alpine glaciers carved the batholith at least four times over the last 2 million years, sharpening peaks and widening valleys. Most waterfalls of the region were created by glaciation. *Warbonnet Falls* descends from a mountainside into a glacial valley. Other streams follow along valleys and encounter obstacles called *moraines* — linear rock deposits left by glacial activity. *Lady Face Falls*, for instance, breaks through and drops over a moraine.

Stream erosion also contributes to the configuration of the batholith. The Salmon, Snake, Selway, and Lochsa rivers have carved impressive canyons and gorges. Waterfalls tumble into these powerful waterways from tributaries that erode at a slower rate than the main rivers. *Fountain Creek Falls* and *Tumble Creek Falls* are examples. Cascades such as *Selway Falls* and *Carey Falls* are situations where heterogenous rock material is eroded unevenly by rivers.

Because of the wild nature of central Idaho, large descents remain to be found, described, and mapped. Many of these cataracts are accessible only by plane, but a good share await discovery by hikers and backpackers. This book describes 32 of the 67 falls recognized within the central interior.

1. SELWAY RIVER

The Selway River begins in the interior of the Selway-Bitterroot Wilderness. As it flows from the wilderness area, its waters become a

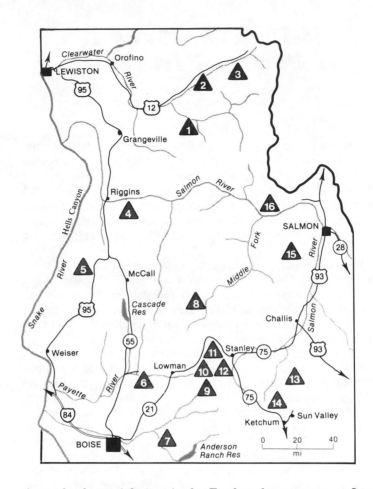

river of substantial magnitude. Farther downstream at Lowell, the Selway meets the Lochsa River to become Middle Fork Clearwater River.

Selway Falls
Type: segmented; map: USGS Selway Falls 7½'

Turn southeast off U.S. 12 at Lowell and drive 18 miles to the end of Selway River Road. The river cascades 50 feet down beside the gravel roadway.

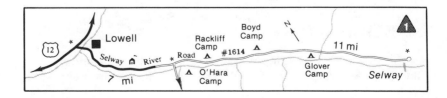

2. LOCHSA DRAINAGE

U.S. 12 faithfully parallels the Lochsa River from its beginning near Lolo Pass to its confluence with the Selway River 78 miles downstream. There are plenty of campsites along this stretch of the highway, but no vehicle service is available from Lolo Hot Springs to Lowell. Be sure your automobile has a full tank of gas before you start. Several waterfalls pour from tributary streams into the Lochsa within a 2-mile stretch 16 to 18 miles northeast of Lowell near U.S. 12.

Tumble Creek Falls
Type: fan

Tumble Creek veils 20 to 30 feet before flowing beneath the main highway into the Lochsa River. Look for this waterfall along the east side of U.S. 12 between mile markers 113 and 114. I've called this waterfall by the name of its creek.

Bimerick Falls
Map: USGS McLendon Butte 7½'

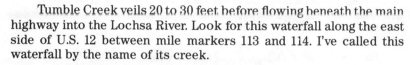

Park 0.8 mile north of Tumble Creek at the turnout for the start of Trail #257. The trail steeply ascends to Smoky Peak in 4 miles. Drop down to the drainage basin in 1 additional mile. The cataract is next to the trail. I recommend this trip for experienced hikers only, since my source indicated that the trail is not maintained annually by the Forest Service.

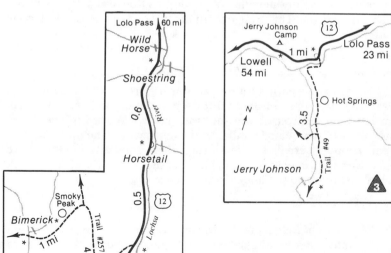

Horsetail Falls
Type: horsetail

At a sign by the road, look across the Lochsa to where Horsetail Falls descends 60 to 100 feet from an unnamed stream. Drive to a marked turnoff from the main highway between mile markers 114 and 115.

 ### Shoestring Falls
Type: tiered; map: USGS McLendon Butte 7½'

View this waterfall from across the river at the marked turnout between mile markers 115 and 116. Water stairsteps 150 to 200 feet in five sections where an unnamed creek drops into Lochsa River.

 ### Wild Horse Creek Falls
Type: tiered

Park at the Shoestring Falls turnout (above) and walk 0.1 mile along U.S. 12 to this double cataract from which water slides a total of 40 to 60 feet. I've named the waterfall after its stream.

3. WARM SPRINGS CREEK

Warm Springs Creek derives its name from thermal waters flowing into the stream from Jerry Johnson Hot Springs. Most hikers head for the rustic hot springs, whose waters are often entered *au naturel.* The scenery rapidly becomes secluded as you progress upstream past the springs. The trail eventually ascends past the following waterfall.

 ### Jerry Johnson Falls
Type: punchbowl; map: USGS Tom Beal Peak 7½'

Drive to the parking area for Warm Springs Creek Trail #49, located 1 mile east of Jerry Johnson Campground. A footbridge crosses Lochsa River before the trail reaches Warm Springs Creek and follows it upstream 1.5 miles to the hot springs. The trail crosses a small tributary creek 1 mile farther, then gradually climbs above Warm Springs Creek to trailside views of the falls in 1 mile. The creek below you roars 40 to 70 feet into a basin.

4. RIGGINS

The town of Riggins is the western gateway to the wild Salmon River. White-water boating is extremely exciting along this "River of

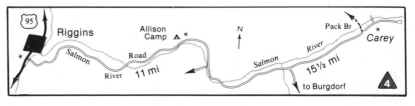

▲ *Wild Horse Creek Falls*

No Return." Riggins is downstream from most of the float "action," so jetboats carry visitors up and down the river. For more information on guided excursions, write: White Water, Bureau of Tourism and Industrial Promotion, Room 108, Capitol Building, Boise, ID 83720.

Carey Falls
Type: cascade

Turn off U.S. 95 onto Salmon River Road #1614. The junction is less than a mile south of Riggins. The road winds with the river for 26 miles to Wind River Pack Bridge. Carey Falls is about 0.5 mile farther upstream, or 1.5 miles before the end of the gravel road. This is the final waterfall along the Salmon River.

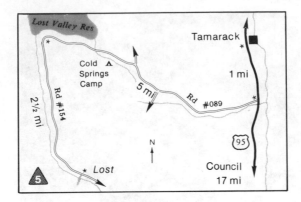

5. LOST VALLEY

Lost Creek Falls
Map: USGS Tamarack 7½'

Topographic maps suggest this entry should have roadside vantages. Depart U.S. 95 about 1 mile south of Tamarack, turning right (west) upon Road #089 for Lost Valley Reservoir. The reservoir's dam should be encountered after about 5 miles. Proceed south on Road #154, where the cataract occurs downstream in an estimated 2.5 miles.

6. GARDEN VALLEY

At the town of Banks, turn off S.R. 55 toward Lowman onto South Fork Road. Drive past the Garden Valley ranger station in 11 miles. The paved road turns to gravel after a total of 16 miles. Pass many hot springs next to the South Fork Payette River.

Little Falls
Type: block; map: USGS Garden Valley 15'

Drive 5.7 miles on the gravel surface of South Fork Road to this waterfall, which practically hugs the road. The 5- to 10-foot block falls is aptly named. Across the road from the falls is an abandoned mine shaft. Look, but don't enter!

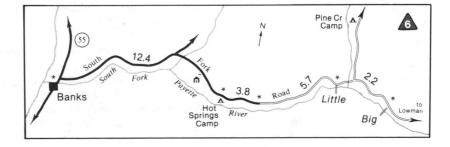

▲ *Mine Shaft near Little Falls*

Big Falls
Type: punchbowl; map: USGS Pine Flat 7½'

This 25- to 40-foot waterfall is "big" only in contrast with its downstream counterpart. Continue 2.2 miles past Little Falls (above). Park where the road widens and peer upstream to the canyon floor 100 to 150 feet below.

7. SOUTH FORK BOISE RIVER

Travel through rangeland, over the Danskin Mountains, and into South Fork Canyon. The 300- to 400-foot-deep gorge is rarely visited. Turn east off Interstate 84 10 miles south of Boise at the Blacks Creek Road/Kuna turnoff (Exit 64). Drive east (away from Kuna) along

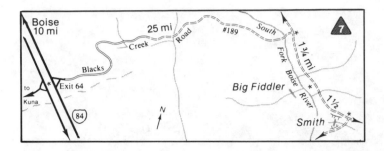

Blacks Creek Road #189. The road soon turns to gravel, then dirt after 10 miles. It is reliable from May to October, but not safe for passenger vehicles during the winter. Cross the Danskin Mountains and reach the South Fork in 21 miles. The road winds into the canyon and crosses the river 4 miles farther.

Big Fiddler Creek Falls
Type: horsetail

This 252-foot drop is the highest officially measured waterfall in Idaho. Unfortunately, the creek is seasonal, and its display is not very dramatic during the summer. After crossing South Fork Boise River on Blacks Creek Road #189, turn right (south) at the first junction and continue upstream on Road #189. The waterfall veils toward the South Fork in 1.75 miles on the opposite side of the river from the road.

Smith Creek Falls
Type: cascade; map: USGS Long Gulch 7½'

Drive about 1.5 miles past Big Fiddler Creek Falls (above) on Blacks Creek Road #189. Listen for the falls near where the road leaves the South Fork. The falls are 0.1 mile downstream from the first primitive road crossing the creek. Carefully make your way through sagebrush for clearer views of Smith Creek dropping steeply 150 to 200 feet.

8. MIDDLE FORK SALMON RIVER

Remoteness is the attraction of a vacation along the Wild and Scenic Middle Fork Salmon River. The river bisects the Idaho Primitive Area on its way to a confluence with the main fork of the Salmon. All but the initial entry can be reached only on extensive backcountry excursions. For river guide information, contact White Water, Bureau of Tourism and Industrial Promotion, Room 108, Capitol Building, Boise, ID 83720. Small craft air-service information can be obtained by writing the Idaho Department of Aeronautics, 2103 Airport Way, Boise, ID 83705.

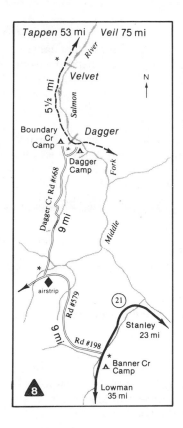

Dagger Falls

Type: tiered; map: USGS Chinook Mtn 15'

This is the only waterfall along the Middle Fork drainage readily accessible to travelers. Turn west off S.R. 21 onto Cape Horn Creek Road #198 just north of Banner Creek Camp. This route ascends over a pass in 3 miles and becomes Fir Creek Road #579. Six miles farther, across from Bruce Meadows Air Strip, turn right (north) on Dagger Creek Road #668. The campgrounds and the 15-foot falls are at the road's end in 13 miles.

Velvet Falls

This major cascade along the Middle Fork is accessible by water or trail. it is located 5.5 miles downstream from Dagger Falls (above).

Tappen Falls

This series of falls within a 0.5-mile stretch of Middle Fork Salmon River is located 8.5 miles downstream from Simplot Ranch, or 53 miles downstream past Velvet Falls (above).

Veil Falls

Look for this unnamed tributary descending on the east canyon wall about 2 miles past Big Creek, or 22.5 miles downstream from Tappen Falls (above).

9. SAWTOOTHS WEST

The rugged Sawtooth Mountains are a tribute to the sculpturing of past alpine glaciers. This section and the next three sections describe waterfalls in the Sawtooth Wilderness Area. To reach the following three cataracts near the western flank of the mountains, turn off S.R. 21 at the marked access road to Grandjean Camp. Drive 8 miles to trailheads at the end of the gravel road.

Goat Creek Falls

Type: tiered; map: USGS Warbonnet Peak 7½'

Start on South Fork Trail #452, which parallels South Fork Payette River. Reach the junction of Baron Creek Trail #101 in 1.25 miles; continue on Trail #452 to Goat Creek a moderate 1.25 miles farther. Scramble a short distance upstream to a series of cascades totaling 50 feet.

Fern Falls

Type: tiered; map: USGS Warbonnet Peak 7½'

Continue 7.5 miles past Goat Creek Falls (above) on South Fork Trail #452 to where South Fork Payette River tumbles twice in an attractive 30-foot display, 10 miles from the trailhead.

Smith Falls

Type: tiered; map: USGS Warbonnet Peak 7½'

Hike 1 mile upstream from Fern Falls (above) along South Fork Trail #452 to Elk Lake. The path crosses the South Fork Payette River 3.5 miles past the lake. Smith Falls, the last named waterfall on the South Fork Payette, is a short distance upstream, 14 miles from the trailhead.

10. BARON CREEK

Tohobit Creek Falls

Type: horsetail

Drive to the Grandjean area as described in the "Sawtooths West" section. Hike 1.25 miles along South Fork Trail #452 to Baron Creek Trail #101. Turn left and follow it 7 miles to trailside views across the canyon where Tohobit Creek descends into the glacial valley of Baron Creek.

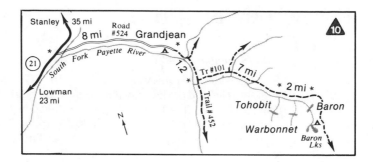

Warbonnet Falls
Type: horsetail

Continue 1 mile past the previous trailside vista to another waterfall hurtling from the lip of a hanging valley, 9.25 miles from the trailhead.

Baron Creek Falls
Type: segmented; map: USGS Warbonnet Peak 7½'

Baron Creek pours 50 feet down as the stream breaks through a glacial moraine of rock debris. Hike along Baron Creek Trail #101 for 1 mile past views of Warbonnet Falls (above) to this waterfall 10.25 miles from the trailhead. The trail continues up past the twin cataracts toward Baron Lakes.

11. STANLEY LAKE CREEK

Enter the Sawtooths from the north by driving 5 miles west of Stanley along S.R. 21. Turn left at Stanley Lake Road #455 and drive 3.5 miles to Inlet Camp. The trailhead for Stanley Lake Creek Trail #640 is near Area B of the campground.

Lady Face Falls
Type: punchbowl; map: USGS Stanley Lake 7½'

Stanley Lake Creek breaks through a moraine and falls 50 to 75 feet into a basin. Follow Stanley Lake Trail #640 for 2.5 miles. Look for a sign marking the falls. Retrace your steps if you've passed where the main trail crosses the creek.

Bridal Veil Falls
Map: USGS Stanley Lake 7½'

Hike 1.25 miles past Lady Face Falls (above) to the trail's junction with Hanson Lakes Trail. Nearby are trailside views of the outlet from Hanson Lakes cascading toward Stanley Lake Creek. The route continues up steeply to the lakes in 1.25 miles.

12. SAWTOOTHS EAST

Goat Falls
Type: fan; map: USGS Stanley Lake 7½'

Drive 2.25 miles west of Stanley on S.R. 21 to Iron Creek Road #619. Drive 4 miles to the end of the gravel road and the beginning of Alpine Lake/Sawtooth Lake Trail #640. Hike 1 mile, then turn left (southeast) at the junction with Alpine Trail #528. Continue 2.5 miles to full views of Goat Creek veiling 250 to 350 feet. *Note:* This is not the same Goat Creek described in "Sawtooths West."

13. HUNTER SUMMIT

East Pass Creek Falls
Map: USGS Meridian Peak 7½'

A backcountry waterfall deep within Sawtooth National Forest, whose parcels in this area are administered by Challis National Forest. Drive northeast from Ketchum and Sun Valley on Trail Creek Road #408, whose road designation changes to #208 after 10 miles or so at Trail Creek Summit. Continue for approximately 8 miles more to Road #128 and turn left (north). Take Road #128 an estimated 15 miles to its end at the start of Hunter Creek Trail #050. Embark upon the trail, hiking to Hunter Creek Summit in 3 miles. At the summit, the way turns into Trail #244, where the falls should be encountered 4.5 miles farther. Other routings are possible via S.R. 75 or U.S. 93; consult a map of Challis National Forest for additional information. I've named the falls after the creek.

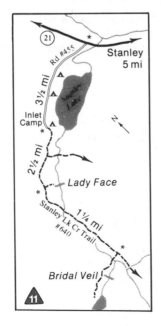

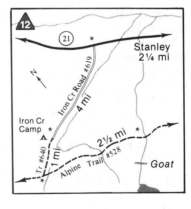

▲ *Goat Falls*

14. KETCHUM AREA

North Fork Falls
Type: segmented

A 50- to 75-foot slide along North Fork Big Wood River. Drive 8 miles north of Ketchum along S.R. 75 to the headquarters of Sawtooth National Recreation Area. Turn right (north) on North Fork Road #146. East Fork crosses the road after 3.5 miles; check the water level before attempting to ford the stream with your vehicle. Continue 1.5 miles to the end of the road, then begin hiking along North Fork Trail #115. Bear left (northwest) on Trail #128. After a total of 4 miles, the trail rises above the canyon floor at the falls.

15. SALMON NATIONAL FOREST

Two waterfalls tumble along Napias Creek deep in the mining country of Salmon National Forest. Napias is Shoshoni for "money." Prospectors named the stream when placer gold was discovered in it in 1866. Turn west off U.S. 93 at Williams Creek Road #021 about 5 miles south of Salmon.

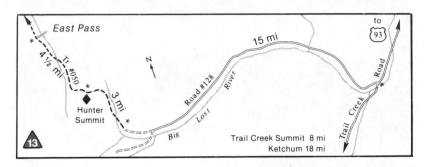

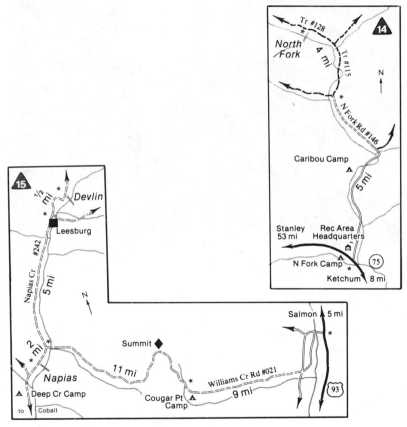

Napias Creek Falls
Type: tiered

Drive 20 miles on Williams Creek Road #021 to Napias Creek. Turn left (south) and continue on Road #021 as it follows the creek downstream. A series of cascades totaling 70 feet descends next to the road in about 2 miles.

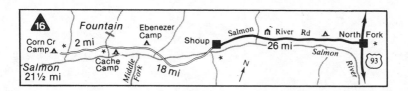

Devlin Falls

Map: USGS Leesburg 15'

Leave Williams Creek Road #021 at Napias Creek, turning right (north) on bumpy Napias Creek Road #242. The waterfall is next to the road 5.5 miles farther near the historic townsite of Leesburg. The community was born in the gold rush of 1866 and its population ballooned to 7,000 residents within 12 months. The rush soon subsided. By 1870 only 180 people lived in Leesburg. Today the site is a mining outpost at best.

16. SALMON RIVER

The Salmon River has carved a canyon over one mile deep as it flows 165 miles west through the Clearwater Mountains. Adventures await experienced rafters and boaters who accept the challenge of negotiating 40 stretches of rapids and cascades along the "River of No Return." Novices should not attempt to run this river. Secure the services of a licensed river guide or outfitter. For further information, write White Water, Bureau of Tourism and Industrial Promotion, Room 108, Capitol Building, Boise, ID 83720.

There are two named falls in the eastern half of the Salmon River Canyon. One is accessible to motorists, while the other can only be reached by river runners.

Fountain Creek Falls

Type: tiered

Turn west off U.S. 93 at North Fork and follow Salmon River Road westward. Drive to Shoup in 26 miles and Cache Bar Camp 18 miles farther. Look for falls 0.5 mile past the campground. Fountain Creek streams from a canyon wall toward the Salmon in a stairstep display. The road ends 2 miles beyond the falls.

Salmon Falls

Type: cascade; map: USGS Devils Teeth Rapids 7½'

Salmon Falls is 1.9 miles downstream from Corey Bar Camp on the Salmon River (water access only) or 21.5 miles west past where the road ends at the Corn Creek campsite. This cascade is one of many that test the boater's mettle. Corn Creek Camp is 46 miles west of U.S. 93, at the end of Salmon River Road.

The Snake River Plain of Southern Idaho

Southern Idaho presents the traveler with a dilemma. There is no best time of the year to visit its waterfalls. The prime viewing time for individual falls varies more dramatically here than in any other region of the Pacific Northwest.

Streams originating from springs are the least temperamental, since they flow continuously. Jump Creek and the Thousand Springs area offer examples. Some streamflows fluctuate with the demand for hydroelectric power. The falls near Hagerman and Clear Lakes are altered by the amount of water being diverted to the nearby power stations. The waterfalls along the Snake River near Twin Falls actually stop flowing most summers because Milner Dam, located farther upstream, impounds water for irrigation of agricultural lands. Some hydro projects along the Snake have destroyed waterfalls. American Falls Dam and Swan Falls Dam have replaced the original descents, and the waters of C. J. Strike Reservoir cover *Crane Falls.* The highland waterfalls northeast of Rexburg flow perennially, but are easily accessible during summer only. Cross-country skis or a snowmobile are required for travel from November to May.

The Snake River Plain has 41 recognized falls, of which 27 are described here. The majority of them were created by stream courses eroding across heterogeneous bedrock at varying rates. The falls along the Snake formed because bedrock such as rhyolite resists stream erosion more effectively than basalt, its igneous counterpart. Most of the falls in the eastern highland areas were shaped in the same way.

Waterfalls descend from the canyon rims of the Snake River for two reasons. Few streams flow into the river from the solidified lava flows of the Plain, and those that do cannot erode the underlying bedrock material as effectively as the Snake. As a result, waterfalls often drop where streams intersect the canyon rim. Other waterfalls descend from springs along the canyon walls.

1. JUMP CREEK CANYON

This small canyon is one of Idaho's hidden gems. Drive on U.S. 95 to Poison Creek Road, located 2.5 miles south of the junction with S.R. 55. In 3.5 miles, where the paved road takes a sharp right, turn left (south) on an unnamed gravel road. Follow it for 0.5 mile, then turn right (west) onto a dirt road. Do not be discouraged if you see a No Trespassing sign. This route is the correct public access to the

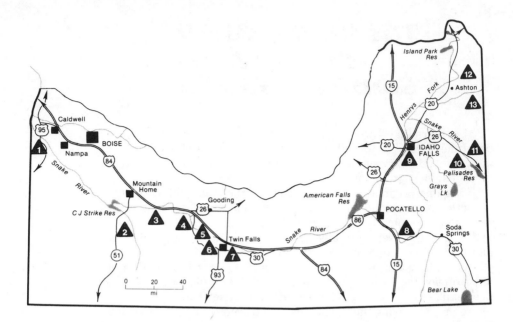

canyon. In 0.4 mile, the road forks. The low road leads to a private homestead and the high road to the right ends in front of the canyon in 1 additional mile. The land is administered by the Bureau of Land Management.

 ★ ★ / ★ ★

Jump Creek Falls
Type: horsetail; map: USGS Sands Basin 15'

Follow the pathway that begins at the end of the road to the canyon along the canyon's floor, hopping from stone to stone across the creek and climbing over, around, and under large boulders that have fallen into the gorge. At the trail's end in 0.2 mile, water splashes 40 to 60 feet into the canyon.

2. HOT SPRINGS

 ★

Indian Bathtub Falls
Type: punchbowl; map: USGS Hot Spring 7½'

Although the waterfall is unimpressive, the thermal springs of this area justify a visit. Drive on S.R. 51 to Bruneau, then continue southeast for 7.2 miles along Hot Spring Road. Turn right on the road marked Indian Bathtub, then left in 0.75 mile on the road marked Sugar Creek. In 2.9 miles, turn left (east) on a dirt road that leads 0.6 mile to the parking area near the hot springs.

Warm water trickles down 7 to 12 feet from adjacent bedrock into the basin. It's an excellent place to soak, but wear something on your feet. Careless visitors may have left broken glass at the bottom of the pool. Indian Bathtub is on land administered by the BLM.

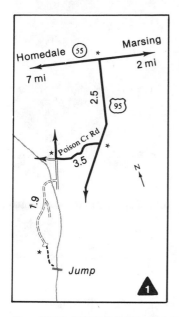

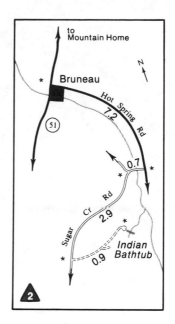

3. DEADMAN CANYON

Deadman Falls
Type: plunge; map: USGS Glenns Ferry 7½'

This gaping canyon was slowly carved by the erosive powers of seasonal Deadman Creek. Leave I-84 at Glenns Ferry. Drive 1.7 miles west of town along Frontage Road and turn left (south) onto Sailor Creek Road. Cross the bridge at the Snake River and continue 5.8 miles to the canyon rim.

These falls would be a sight worth seeing if only water flowed over the 125- to 175-foot escarpment. A small BLM dam prevents the creek from plunging into the canyon the majority of the year. Perhaps you could see a good show immediately after an intense rainstorm.

4. HAGERMAN AREA

The scenic quality of the falls along this section of the Snake River varies sporadically. There are dams and power plants next to each of the falls, and the amount of water allowed to flow over the natural course is determined by the region's electrical demand. The area is accessible via U.S. 30, also called Thousand Springs Scenic Route.

Lower Salmon Falls
Type: block; map: USGS Hagerman 7½'

Turn off U.S. 30 at the marked Lower Salmon Power Plant entrance, located 6.75 miles south of Gooding-Hagerman Exit 141 from I-84 or 1.5 miles north of downtown Hagerman. Drive about 0.75 mile

▲ *Upper Salmon Falls*

to the 10- to 15-foot waterfall. It is on the far side of the river below the power plant substation.

Upper Salmon Falls
Type: segmented; map: USGS Hagerman 7½'

Water diverges into four main blocks, each descending 15 to 25 feet along the Snake River. Drive 3.2 miles south of Hagerman on U.S. 30 and turn right (west) at the Upper Salmon Falls access sign. If you pass the rest area, you have missed the turnoff. Follow this secondary road 1.5 miles to the power plant. There are obscured views of the falls from a gravel road. For closer views, park at the east end of the gravel road and cross an unmarked catwalk to an island halfway across the Snake, then proceed down the cement walkway to the falls. Periodically, the walkway area is flooded by Idaho Power, and the company is not liable if unwary visitors are trapped on the island.

5. SNAKE PLAINS AQUIFER

The Snake River Plain northeast of Hagerman harbors one of the world's greatest groundwater resources. Mountain ranges southeast of central Idaho receive large amounts of precipitation, particularly during the winter. But the streams flowing south from these mountains fail to reach the Snake River because they sink into lava formations on the plain. Water collects in the pore spaces of the subsurface bedrock, and since these rock layers gently dip southwestward, gravity pushes the groundwater toward Hagerman.

The Snake River has eroded its course to intersect with this aquifer. As a result, numerous springs perennially gush from the river's north canyon wall. Most are above the canyon floor, so they are seen as waterfalls descending into the river.

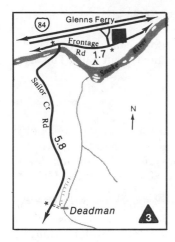

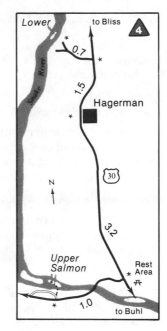

Falls of Thousand Springs

Type: horsetail; map: USGS Thousand Springs 7½'

There are eight major falls and many minor falls descending 40 to 100 feet from springs along the north wall on this 1-mile stretch of the Snake River Canyon located between 15 and 16 miles northwest of Buhl. Astoundingly, the river's volume increases up to tenfold at this point. All the falls can be seen from across the Snake on U.S. 30/ Thousand Springs Scenic Route. For a close-up view of the eastern-most falls, turn off from Clear Lakes Road at the sign to Thousand Springs Picnic Area.

Falls of Banbury Springs

Type: horsetail; map: USGS Thousand Springs 7½'

Some of these 30- to 80-foot falls can be seen from across the river, but most of them are obscured by the surrounding vegetation. Turn off U.S. 30 and drive to Banbury Hot Springs Resort at the marked access road 4 miles south of Thousand Springs. The resort is 1.5 miles from the main highway.

Devils Washboard Falls

Type: cascade; map: USGS Thousand Springs 7½'

This is a pretty 15- to 30-foot cascade when the adjacent power-house isn't diverting most of the water flow from spring-fed Clear Lakes. Drive along Clear Lakes Road to the Buhl Country Club, 7 miles north of Buhl and 12 miles south of Wendell. The waterfall is a short walk west of the country club parking area. At the entrance to the golf course is Clear Lakes Trout Company, reputed to be the world's largest trout farm.

6. SNAKE RIVER CANYON WEST

The Snake River has carved sharply through basaltic rock layers to create a narrow 400- to 500-foot canyon near Twin Falls. The area has several waterfalls.

Auger Falls

Type: cascade; map: USGS Jerome 7½'

Water churns over strange convolutions caused by rocky obstructions along the Snake River. Public views from the north rim are rapidly dwindling as rangeland is converted into housing developments. Turn off I-84 at Exit 168 and drive 3.3 miles south on Lincoln Road, or travel 4 miles west of U.S. 93 along Golf Course Road to the subdivision area. If you're lucky, you may find an undeveloped lot for sightseeing. Be careful near the rim. For closer views of these 25- to 50-foot cascades, drive about 5 miles from U.S. 93 along Canyon Springs Road.

Pillar Falls

Type: cascade; map: USGS Twin Falls 7½'

Towers of 30- to 70-foot rhyolitic rock rise between these 10- to 20-foot cascades along the Snake River. Turn east from U.S. 93 at the Golf Course Road sign. Continue along this dusty route for 0.9 mile, then park. Walk through the old dumping grounds for about 0.25 mile to the abrupt canyon rim. Pillar Falls is directly below. There is also a distant, yet stunning view of Shoshone Falls. You may wonder about the huge "sandpile" located along the south rim halfway between Pillar Falls and Shoshone Falls. It was the launch site for Evel Knievel's ill-fated attempt to jump the canyon on a "rocket-cycle" during the early 1970s.

Perrine Coulee Falls

Type: plunge; map: USGS Twin Falls 7½'

Agricultural activities cause this waterfall to flow year-round. In fact, its discharge actually increases during the dry summer! This occurs because the coulee collects the water that overflows from the irrigated upland. Turn west onto Canyon Springs Road from U.S. 93 and park at the undesignated turnout in less than 0.75 mile. The view is inspiring. A natural pathway goes behind the 197-foot plunge.

7. SNAKE RIVER CANYON EAST

Twin Falls

Type: segmented; map: USGS Kimberly 7½'

Only one of the twin waterfalls remains today. The larger portion has been dammed. Follow Falls Avenue 5 miles east from the city of Twin Falls, passing the junction to Shoshone Falls. Turn left (north) at the marked road leading 1 mile to the falls and adjacent picnic area.

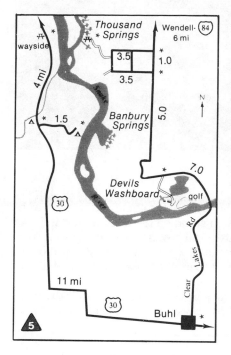

▲ *Perrine Coulee Falls*

A torrent of water hurtles down 125 feet during early spring, but becomes a trickle in summer months. Milner Dam farther upstream draws off a large part of the Snake River for irrigation during the midyear growing season.

Shoshone Falls

Type: block; map: USGS Twin Falls 7½'

This is the most famous waterfall in Idaho. It spans over 1,000 feet across and plunges 212 feet down. The awesome display is best viewed during springtime. Later in the year the river dries up and only large ledges of rhyolite can be seen. The water is diverted upstream for agricultural uses. Backtrack 3 miles from Twin Falls to the marked turn along Falls Avenue. Shoshone Falls Park is 2 miles farther.

The following Indian folklore about Shoshone Falls was told in pioneer days to J.S. Harrington by a Shoshoni Indian named Quish-in-demi. It is recorded in *Idaho: A Guide in Words and Pictures,* written in 1937 as part of a Federal Writers' Project:

"In the gloomy gorge above the falls there was, long ago, the trysting place of a deep-chested Shoshoni buck and the slender wild girl whom he loved. Their last meeting was here on a pile of rocks which overlooked the plunging waters. He went away to scalp with deft incisions and then to lift the shaggy mane of white men with a triumphant shout; and she came daily to stand by the thundering avalanche and remember him. That he would return unharmed she

▲ *Shoshone Falls*

did not, with the ageless resourcefulness of women, ever allow herself to doubt. But time passed, and the moons that came and ripened were many, and she still came nightly to stand on the brink and watch the changeless journeying of the water. And it was here that she stood one black night above the roar of the flood when a warrior stepped out of shadow and whispered to her and then disappeared. As quiet as the flat stone under her feet, she stood for a long while, looking down into the vault where the waters boiled up like seething white hills to fill the sky with dazzling curtains and roll away in convulsed tides. For an

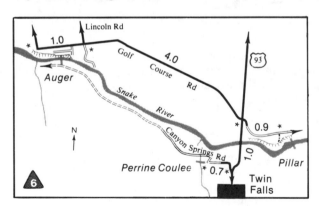

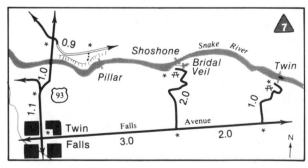

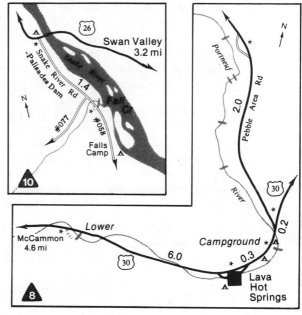

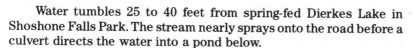

hour she gazed down there 200 feet to a mad pouring of motion and sound into a black graveyard of the dead. And then, slowly, she lifted her arms above her, listed her head to the fullest curve of her throat, and stood tiptoe for a moment, poised and beautiful, and then dived in a long swift arc against the falling white background....And the river at this point and since that hour has never been the same."

Bridal Veil Falls
Type: horsetail

Water tumbles 25 to 40 feet from spring-fed Dierkes Lake in Shoshone Falls Park. The stream nearly sprays onto the road before a culvert directs the water into a pond below.

8. LAVA HOT SPRINGS

Lower Portneuf Falls
Type: segmented; map: USGS McCammon 7½'

Portneuf River diverges into two 15- to 25-foot waterfalls: a cascade and a plunge. Drive 6 miles west of Lava Hot Springs along U.S. 30. Walk down an old jeep trail to the falls. They have not been previously named.

Campground Falls
Type: punchbowl

This 10- to 15-foot drop along the Portneuf is situated within a private campground, hence its name. It is located about 0.3 mile past the east side of Lava Hot Springs on U.S. 30.

Falls along the Portneuf
Type: cascade, block; map: USGS Haystack Mtn 7½'

Several small cataracts descend along a 1-mile reach of Portneuf River north of Lava Hot Springs. The farthest ones are 2 miles up Pebble Area Road. The ground tends to be marshy, so appropriate footwear is recommended on your cross-country trek.

9. CITY OF IDAHO FALLS

This low, turbulent descent on the Snake River shares its name with the surrounding community of 40,000. Turn off Interstate 15 at Broadway Street (Exit 118) and drive toward the city center. Immediately before the bridge crossing the Snake, turn left (north) on River Parkway. Stop and enjoy the falls from the adjacent city park.

Idaho Falls of the Snake River
Type: cascade

The 15- to 25-foot waterfall is over 0.25 mile wide and has the distinction of being man-made! Joe L. Marker, historical editor of the east Idaho tabloid *Post-Register*, explains:

"In the earlier days there were only rapids in the river at Idaho Falls. Then in 1909 during the administration of Mayor Ed Coltman, authorization was given by the city for William Walker Keefer to build a concrete dam in the river to channel some of the stream to the Eagle Rock power plant to generate the turbines for electricity.

"In recent years the dam started to deteriorate, and to assure adequate streamflow for the new bulb turbines in the river here, it was decided to tear out the old dam and rebuild it and the falls, which was undertaken and completed in 1981."

10. SWAN VALLEY

Fall Creek Falls
Type: fan; map: USGS Conant Valley 7½'

Drive 39 miles east of Idaho Falls or 3.25 miles west of Swan Valley along U.S. 26 to Snake River– Palisades Dam Road. Turn south and follow this gravel route 1.4 miles; park where the road widens. The best views of the falls are a short walk farther along the roadway. Fall Creek plunges 60 feet over travertine deposits into the Snake River. The water plumes upon either side of the central falls to form a natural fountain that must be seen to be believed.

11. UPPER PALISADE LAKE

Rainbow Falls
Type: tiered

Follow U.S. 26 for 2 miles northeast of the community of Palisades to Palisades Creek Road #254. Turn right and follow the

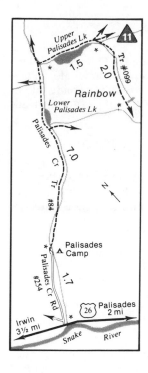

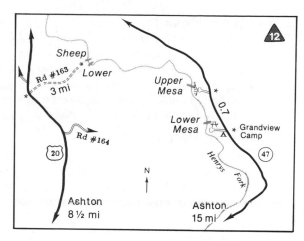

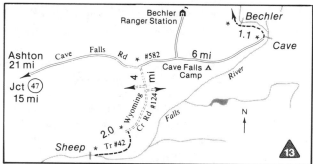

road 1.75 miles to its end at Palisades Campground. Start here on Palisades Creek Trail #84 and hike 7.5 miles to Upper Palisade Lake Trail #099. Bear right at subsequent trail junctions and proceed south into Waterfall Canyon, staying on Trail #099. The tiered waterfall with 80-foot and 30-foot descents is 2 miles farther.

Employees of the Palisades Ranger District, some of whom had lived in the area for 40 years, were surprised to learn that the waterfall has a name. I found it in the 1938 edition of *Idaho Encyclopedia*.

12. HENRYS FORK

Henrys Fork is a wild and scenic river in all but official federal designation. It winds through the Ashton Ranger District of Targhee National Forest.

Lower Mesa Falls
Type: block; map: USGS Snake River Butte 7½'

Peer from an overlook to the rushing water of Henrys Fork over 400 feet below. The river attains a chaotic state while thundering down this 65-foot waterfall. Drive 15 miles northeast to Ashton on S.R. 47 to the turnout appropriately titled Grandview.

Upper Mesa Falls

Type: block; map: USGS Snake River Butte 7½'

For side views of Henrys Fork plummeting 114 feet from a sheer wall of rhyolite rock, turn left (west) off S.R. 47 onto Upper Mesa Falls Road #295 about 0.75 mile past Grandview. Drive to the road's end in less than 1 mile. The waterfall, also known as *Big Falls*, is a short walk away. *Be careful at the canyon rim!*

Lower Sheep Falls

Type: cascade

Henrys Fork cascades 15 to 25 feet. Drive about 8.5 miles north of Ashton along U.S. 20 to Targhee National Forest Road #163; turn right. Follow Road #163 as far as your vehicle will allow, then hike the remaining 1.5 miles to the falls.

Sheep Falls

Type: cascade; USGS Lookout Butte 7½'

This 15- to 25-foot stairstep along Henrys Fork is less than 100 yards upstream from Lower Sheep Falls (above).

13. YELLOWSTONE

Although two of the following falls are actually in Wyoming, they have been included here because they can be most easily reached from just across the border in Idaho.

Sheep Falls

Type: block; map: USGS Warm River Butte 15'

The name of this 35-foot waterfall comes from the sheep drives that once occurred in this vicinity of the Falls River. Drive 6 miles from Ashton on S.R. 47 to the marked Cave Falls Road #582. Bear right, follow Road #582 for 15.25 miles, then turn right (south) at Wyoming Creek Road #124. This unimproved road ends in 4 miles at the beginning of Sheep Falls Trail #42. Hike almost 2 miles to the falls.

Cave Falls

Type: block; map: USGS Grassy Lake Reservoir 15'

This picturesque block waterfall descends 25 to 35 feet along Falls River within Yellowstone National Park. Travel as to Sheep Falls (above), but stay on Cave Falls Road #582 to its end at the falls, 20.5 miles from S.R. 47. The waterfall is named after a large recess beneath the stream's west bank.

Bechler Falls

Type: block; map: USGS Warm River Butte 15'

Follow the Bechler River Trail for 1.1 miles from Cave Falls (above) to this wide, low waterfall. The 15- to 25-foot cataract along Bechler River is in Yellowstone National Park.

INDEX

Names shown in parentheses refer to the general locations of waterfalls sharing the same name. These names correspond to the chapter headings in which discussions of the waterfalls are found. Pages with photographs of falls are indicated in italics.

Adam Creek Falls 200
Affi Falls 74
Alice Falls 61
Alpine Falls 23
Alsea Falls 146
American Falls 205
Annie Falls 190
Aputapat Falls 118
Asbestos Creek Falls 29
Auger Falls 236
Awbrey Falls 193
Banbury Springs, Falls of 235
Baron Creek Falls 225
Barr Creek Falls 189
Basin Creek Falls 40
Beach Creek Falls 50, *51*
Bear Creek Falls 189
Beaver Falls (Olympics) 49,
    (North Coast Range) 138
Bechler Falls 242
Benham Falls 196
Benson Falls 128
Big Creek Falls 92
Big Falls (Columbia Plateau) 194,
    (Central Idaho) 221
Big Fiddler Creek Falls 222
Bimerick Falls 217
Bird Creek Falls 102
Blister Creek Falls 163
Blue Grouse Falls 129
Bonnie Falls 137
Boulder Falls 29
Bridal Veil Falls (North Cascades,
    Mount Index) 24, (North
    Cascades, Stehekin) 39,
    (Columbia Gorge) 120, (Central
    Idaho) 225, (Snake River
    Plain) 239
Bridge Creek Falls 48
Bull Run Creek Falls 213

Butte Falls 191, *191*
Cabin Creek Falls 132
Campbell Falls 187
Campground Falls (Olympics) 53,
    (Snake River Plain) 239
Canadian Falls 205
Canton Creek Falls 184
Canyon Falls *16*, 23
Carbon Falls 61
Carey Falls 215, 219
Carter Falls 64
Carwash Falls 39
Cascade Falls 45
Cataract Falls 61
Cave Falls *230*, 242
Cavern Falls 45
Cavitt Falls 182
Cedar Creek Falls (North
    Cascades) 36, (Southern
    Cascade Range) 181
Chamokane Falls 108
Char Falls 205, *206*
Chenuis Falls 61
Chewack Falls 37
Chewuch Falls 37
Chichester Falls 176
Chinook Creek Falls 72
Christine Falls 66
Clarence Creek Falls 142
Clear Creek Falls 59, 78
Clear Lake Falls 78
Clearwater Falls 185
Cline Falls 194
Coal Creek Falls 171
Comet Falls 60, 66, *66*
Coopey Falls 120
Copper Creek Falls 93
Copper Falls 203, 210
Coquille River Falls 151, *152*
Cougar Falls 69

Cow Creek Falls 188
Cowlitz Falls 85
Crane Falls 231
Crooked Creek Falls 102
Crystal Falls (Inland Empire) *104*,
    109, (Cascade Range) 171
Curly Creek Falls *91*, 92
Cushing Falls 135
Dagger Falls 223
Dalles Falls 75
Davis Creek Falls 83
Dead Point Creek Falls 134
Deadman Falls 233
Deception Falls 22
Deep Creek Falls 202
Deer Creek Falls 72
Deer Lick Falls 187
Denman Falls 63
Devil Canyon Falls 157
Devil Creek Falls 78
Devils Washboard Falls 235
Devlin Falls 229
Dewey Lake Falls 75
Diamond Creek Falls *172*, 178
Dillon Falls 195, *196*
Dog Creek Falls 100
Domke Falls *38*, 39
Dosewallips Falls 54
Double Falls (Columbia Gorge) 124,
    (Cascade Range) 163
Doubtful Creek Falls 40
Dougan Falls 95
Douglas Falls 110
Downing Creek Falls 155, 168
Drake Falls 163
Drury Falls 21
Dry Creek Falls (Gifford
    Pinchot) 100, (Columbia
    Gorge) 129, *130*
Dry Falls 105, 116
Dutchman Falls 123
Duwee Falls 190
Eagle Creek Falls (Columbia
    Gorge) 129, (Cascade
    Range) 162
Eagle Falls 23
East Fork Falls 127
East Pass Creek Falls 226
Elk Creek Falls 145, 151

Elk Falls 212, *213*
Elowah Falls 125, *126*
Emile Falls 181
Entiat Falls 41
Ethania Falls 63
Explorer Falls 25
Fairy Falls (Mount Rainier) 68,
    (Columbia Gorge) 122
Fall Creek Falls (Mount Rainier) 71,
    (South Coast Range) 145,
    (Southern Cascade Range,
    Cascade Lake) 175, (Southern
    Cascade Range, Cavitt
    Creek) 183, (Snake River
    Plain) 240
Fall River Falls 196, *198*
Falls City Falls 144, *144*
Falls Creek Falls (North Cascades)
    36, *37*, (Olympics) 50, (Gifford
    Pinchot) *84*, 99, (Columbia
    Gorge) 130, (Southern Cascade
    Range) 178, (Columbia
    Plateau) 200, (Idaho
    Panhandle) 211
Falls View Falls 53
Fern Falls 224
Final Falls 157
First Falls 26
Fish Ladder Falls 80
Fishhawk Falls 140
Flattery Creek Falls 51
Flora Dell Falls 154
Foggy Dew Falls 37
Fountain Creek Falls 215, 229
Franklin Falls 20, *21*
Frustration Falls 157
Garda Falls 74
Gatch Falls 155, 168
Gate Creek Falls 17, 36
Gibson Falls 31
Goat Creek Falls 224
Goat Falls 226, *227*
Golden Falls 149
Gooch Falls 168
Goodman Falls 52
Gordon Falls 122
Gorge Creek Falls *34*, 35
Gorton Creek Falls 131
Granite Falls (North Cascades) 26,

(Idaho Panhandle) 205
Grant Purcell Falls 80
Grave Creek Falls 153
Green Peak Falls 146, *146*
Grotto Falls 173, 181
Grouse Creek Falls 89
Grouse Falls 207
Gunaldo Falls 142
Haines Falls 144
Hardy Falls 96
Harmony Falls 87, *87*
Hatana Falls 54
Hawk Creek Falls *113*, 114
Heather Creek Falls 27
Hellroaring Basin, Falls from 102
Hellroaring Falls 103
Hemlock Falls 181
Henline Falls 166
Hidden Falls (North Cascades) 40,
　　(Olympics) 45
Hideaway Falls 158
High Deck Falls 170
Hoko Falls 50
Hole in the Wall Falls 132
Hopkins Creek Falls 83
Horseshoe Basin, Falls of 17, 40
Horseshoe Falls 95
Horsetail Falls (Mount Rainier) 77,
　　(Columbia Gorge) 125, (Central
　　Idaho) 218
House Rock Falls 169
Huckleberry Creek Falls 74
Idaho Falls 240
Indian Bathtub Falls 232
Initial Falls 88
Ipsut Falls 61
Iron Creek Falls 86
Izee Falls 201
Jack Falls 184
Jerry Johnson Falls *214*, 218
Jeru Creek Falls 207
John Pierce Falls 35
Jump Creek Falls 232
Kalama Falls 90
Keekwulee Falls 20
Kelsey Falls 154
Kennedy Falls 55
Ketchum Creek Falls 35
Koosah Falls 168

Kotsuck Creek Falls 72
Ladder Creek Falls 35
Lady Face Falls 215, 225
Lancaster Falls 132
Langfield Falls 102
Larrupin Falls 63
Last Hope Falls 86
Latourell Falls 120
Lava Canyon, falls along 91
Lava Creek Falls 80
Lava Island Falls 195
Laverne Falls 149
Lee Falls *143*, 144
Lemolo Falls 185
Lillian Falls 176
Lindsey Creek Falls 132
Lithan Falls 176
Little Falls (Inland Empire) 108,
　　(North Coast Range) 140,
　　(Southern Cascade Range) 183,
　　(Central Idaho) 220
Little Goose Creek Falls 100
Little Lee Falls 143
Little Multnomah Falls 122
Little Niagara Falls 157
Little Palouse Falls 118
Little Wenatchee Falls 22
Loowit Falls 128
Lost Creek Falls 220
Lower Black Bar Falls 153
Lower Boulder Creek Falls 46, *47*
Lower Cataract Falls 61
Lower Copper Creek Falls 94
Lower Diamond Creek Falls 178
Lower Elk Falls 212
Lower Falls (South Coast
　　Range) 151, (Northern Cascade
　　Range) 170, (Southern Cascade
　　Range) 187, (Columbia Plateau,
　　Newberry Crater) 198,
　　(Columbia Plateau, Elk
　　Creek) 213
Lower Falls Creek Falls 178
Lower Kalama River Falls 90
Lower Kentucky Falls 148, *148*
Lower Lewis Falls 94, *94*
Lower Mesa Falls 241
Lower Multnomah Falls 122
Lower North Falls 164

Lower Oneonta Falls 124
Lower Portneuf Falls 239
Lower Red Blanket Falls 189
Lower Salmon Falls 233
Lower Sheep Falls 242
Lower Shellburg Falls 165
Lower Sherman Creek Falls 114
Lower Soda Falls 169
Lower South Falls 165
Lower Stevens Falls 59, 69
Lower Van Trump Falls 65
Lower Wells Creek Falls 33
Lucia Falls 95
Madcap Falls 64
Madison Creek Falls 46
Majestic Falls 171
Maple Falls 59, 69
Marble Creek Falls (Gifford
    Pinchot) 90, (Inland
    Empire) 110
Marie Falls 74
Marietta Falls (North Cascades) 31,
    (Gifford Pinchot) 89
Martha Falls 68
Mary Belle Falls 74
Marymere Falls 48
Mazama Falls 33
Mesatchee Creek Falls 76
Metlako Falls 128
Meyers Falls 111
Middle Elk Falls 212
Middle Falls 151
Middle Lewis Falls 94
Middle North Falls 163
Middle Tumwater Falls 57
Middle Van Trump Falls 65
Mill Creek Falls 189
Miller Creek Falls 92
Mission Falls 204
Mist Falls 121
Moon Falls 179
Mosier Creek Falls 134
Moulton Falls 95
Moyie Falls *208*, 209
Muir Creek Falls 187
Multnomah Falls 122, *123*
Munra Falls 127
Munson Creek Falls *136*, 141
Myrtle Falls *58*, 67

Napias Creek Falls 228
Narada Falls 64, *65*
National Creek Falls 187
Necktie Falls 122
Nehalem Falls 140
Niagara Falls 142
Ninemile Falls 114
Nooksack Falls *32*, 33
North Falls 163
North Fork Falls (North
    Cascades) 29, *30*, (Central
    Idaho) 227
North Fork Smith Falls 148
Nuhunta Falls 67
Odin Falls 194
Ohanapecosh Falls 72, *73*
Ohanapecosh Park, Falls of 74
Olallie Creek Falls 71
Olympia Falls 57
Oneonta Falls 124
Outlet Falls 103, *103*
Pacific Crest Falls 129
Palouse Falls 107, 118
Panther Creek Falls 99
Paradise Falls 67
Paulina Creek Falls 199, *199*
Pearsoney Falls 189
Pegleg Falls 162, *162*
Pencil Falls 158
Periwee Falls 109
Perrine Coulee Falls 236, *237*
Petersburg Falls 135
Pewee Falls *108*, 109
Pillar Falls 236
Ponytail Falls 125
Portneuf, Falls along the 240
Preston Falls 17, 40
Pringle Falls 196
Prospect Falls 189
Proxy Falls 173, 175
Puff Falls 100, *101*
Puget Sound Falls 57
Punch Bowl Falls 128
Punchbowl Falls 133, *133*
Quillisascut Creek Falls *112*, 113
Rainbow Falls (North Cascades,
    Mount Baker) 32, (North
    Cascades, Lake Chelan) 38,
    (Olympics) 57, (Mount

Rainier) 83, (Northern Cascade
Range) 170, (Southern Cascade
Range) 173, (Snake River
Plain) 240
Rainie Falls 153
Ramona Falls 156
Ranger Falls 60
Rapid Lightning Falls 205
Red Blanket Falls 190
Rock Creek Falls (Gifford Pinchot,
Lake Merwin) 90, (Gifford
Pinchot, Rock Creek) 97, *97*,
(Inland Empire) 117, *117*
Rocky Brook Falls 54
Rodney Falls 96
Royal Terrace Falls 171
Ruckel Creek Falls 128
Rush Creek Falls 92
Rustic Falls 44
Ryan Falls 29
Sahalie Falls (Northern Cascade
Range, Bennett Pass) 158,
(Northern Cascade Range,
McKenzie River) 168, *169*
Salmon Creek Falls 176
Salmon Falls (Inland Empire) 115,
115, (Northern Cascade
Range) 166, (Central
Idaho) 229
Salmon River, Falls along 157
Salt Creek Falls 177, *177*
Selway Falls 215, 216
Sevenmile Creek Falls 167
Shadow Falls 183
Sheep Creek Falls 111
Sheep Falls (2) 242
Shellburg Falls 165
Sheppards Dell Falls 120
Shipherd Falls 98
Shoestring Falls 218
Shoshone Falls 236, 237, *238*
Shute's River Falls 57
Silver Falls (North Cascades) 40, *41*,
(Mount Rainier) 70, *70*, (South
Coast Range) 149
Siuslaw Falls 149
Skookum Falls 75
Skoonichuk Falls 129
Skymo Creek Falls 35

Slide Creek Falls 131
Slide Falls 202
Sluiskin Falls 68
Small Falls 212
Smith Creek Falls 222
Smith Falls (Southern Cascade
Range) 179, (Idaho
Panhandle) 209, (Central
Idaho) 224
Smith River Falls 147
Snoqualmie Falls 19
Snoquera Falls 75
Snow Creek Falls 203, *200*
Snowshoe Falls 20
Soleduck Falls *42*, 48
South Falls 165
South Fork Falls (Mount Rainier) 78,
79, (Columbia Plateau) 201
South Umpqua Falls 187
Spirit Falls 179, *180*
Split Falls 158
Spokane Falls 107
Spray Falls 60, 62, *63*
Stafford Falls 72
Stair Creek Falls 154
Starvation Creek Falls 132
Stasel Falls 165
Steamboat Falls 183
Steelhead Falls 194
Steep Creek Falls 98
Stein Falls 158
Stevens Lake Falls 210
Straight Creek Falls 93
Strawberry Bay Falls 52
Strawberry Falls 201
Stuart Falls 190
Suiattle Falls 30
Sullivan Creek Falls 166
Summer Falls 106, 116
Summit Creek Falls 133
Sunset Falls (North Cascades) 24,
(Gifford Pinchot) 95
Susan Creek Falls 183
Swan Falls 231
Switchback Falls 155, 158
Sylvia Falls 60, 69
Tamanawas Falls 159, *159*
Tamolitch Falls 168
Tanner Falls 127

Tappen Falls 223
Tate Creek Falls 154
Tato Falls 67
Teepee Falls 18, 31
Tenas Falls 129
The Falls 162
Thousand Springs, Falls of 235
Thunder Falls 80, *81*
Titacoclos Falls 51
Tohobit Creek Falls 224
Toketee Falls 173, 184
Torrelle Falls 203
Triple Creek Falls 27
Triple Falls 125
Tumalo Falls *192*, 195
Tumble Creek Falls 215, 217
Tumwater Falls *56*, 57
Tunnel Falls 129
Twentytwo Creek Falls 27, *27*
Twin Falls (North Cascades, North
    Bend) 19, (North Cascades,
    Twin Falls Lake) 28, (Gifford
    Pinchot) 93, (Northern
    Cascade Range) 163, (Idaho
    Panhandle) 212, (Snake River
    Plain) 236
Umbrella Falls 158
Union Creek Falls 77, *77*
Upper Black Bar Falls 153
Upper Boulder Creek Falls 47
Upper Clear Creek Falls 80
Upper Elk Falls 212
Upper Falls (Mount Rainier) 80,
    (Inland Empire, Spokane) 107,
    (Inland Empire, Northport) 111,
    (North Coast Range) 138,
    (South Coast Range) 151,
    (Southern Cascade Range,
    Cascade Lake) 175, (Southern
    Cascade Range, Upper
    Rogue) 186, (Columbia
    Plateau) 199, (Idaho
    Panhandle) 209
Upper Falls Creek Falls 179
Upper Hellroaring Falls 103
Upper Horsetail Falls 125
Upper Kentucky Falls 147
Upper Latourell Falls 120
Upper Lewis Falls 93

Upper McCord Creek Falls 125
Upper Mesa Falls 242
Upper Multnomah Falls 124
Upper North Falls 163
Upper Palouse Falls 118
Upper Priest Falls 205
Upper Salmon Falls 234, *234*
Upper Sherman Creek Falls 114
Upper Snoqualmie Falls 19
Upper Soda Falls 170
Upper Stevens Falls 68
Upper Tumwater Falls 56
Valley of 10,000 Waterfalls 53
Van Horn Falls 74
Van Trump Falls 65
Vanishing Falls 157
Veil Falls 224
Velvet Falls 223
Vidae Falls 173, 190
Wah Gwin Gwin Falls 133
Wahclella Falls 127, *127*
Wahkeena Falls 122
Wallace Falls 17, 24, *25*
Wallalute Falls 160, *161*
Wallowa Falls 200
Warbonnet Falls 225
Warm Springs Falls 185, *186*
Warren Falls 132
Watson Falls 185
Wauhaukaupauken Falls 74
Wauna Falls 128
Weeks Falls 19
Wellington Creek Falls 206
Wells Creek Falls 33
Whispering Falls 167
White River Falls 22
Whitehorse Falls 185
Wild Horse Creek Falls 218, *219*
Wildwood Falls 179
Willow Creek Falls 210
Wilmont Creek Falls 114
Winter Falls 164
Wolf Creek Falls (Olympics) 46,
    (Southern Cascade Range) 181
Wy'east Falls 129
Yakso Falls 181
Yocum Falls 157
Youngs River Falls 139, *139*
Yozoo Creek Falls 89

About the author:

Gregory A. Plumb, a native of Michigan, is an assistant professor of geography at the University of Oklahoma. He lived in the Pacific Northwest for five years while pursuing advanced degrees, spending his spare time in the wilds searching out the many waterfalls in the region. It was then that he discovered no guidebook existed for waterfall fans, and so combined his love for the subject with his knowledge of geography to create one. Plumb continues to vacation in the Northwest each summer, searching out ever more waterfalls. Plumb is a member of the board of directors of the Beer Can Collectors of America and has written a book published by the association, titled *BCCA Guide to U.S. Beer Cans: 1975-1988.*

Look for these other Northwest hiking guides from The Mountaineers:

50 Hikes in OREGON'S COAST RANGE & SISKIYOUS
By Rhonda and George Ostertag. Some of Oregon's most magnificent and varied scenery is in the mountainous corridor between Interstate 5 and coastal Highway 101. This book presents hikes for a wide range of skill levels, showing off the best of these mountains in hikes from a 1.5-mile nature trail to a 47-mile backpack. Fully detailed trail descriptions, maps, photos. $12.95

50 Hikes in MOUNT RAINIER NATIONAL PARK
Ira Spring, Harvey Manning. Up-to-the-minute information on all the hiker trails in this popular park, including the Wonderland Trail. $9.95

100 Hikes in the SOUTH CASCADES AND OLYMPICS
Ira Spring, Harvey Manning. From the Columbia River to Snoqualmie Pass, here are trail hikes for every level of hiker-skill. Many hikes in the newer wilderness area, plus the wild Olympic Mountains. $9.95

100 Hikes in the ALPINE LAKES
Ira Spring, Vicky Spring, Harvey Manning. Wonderful collection of mountain-trail hikes from Snoqualmie Pass to Stevens Pass in the Cascades. Covers both the magnificent Alpine Lakes Wilderness Area and miles of roaming on either side. $9.95

100 Hikes in the GLACIER PEAK REGION
Ira Spring, Harvey Manning. More intriguing hikes, from Stevens Pass to the north end of Lake Chelan. Includes the Darrington-Monte Cristo area and Glacier Peak Wilderness Area. $10.95

100 Hikes in the NORTH CASCADES
Ira Spring, Harvey Manning. Short hikes, long day trips, backpacks — all here, ready to be hiked. Covers from north of Lake Chelan to the Canadian Border, including Mt. Baker area, North Cascades National Park, Pasayten Wilderness. $10.95

100 Hikes in the INLAND NORTHWEST
Rich Landers, Ida Rowe Dolphin. Detailed descriptions, maps, photos on the best hikes within a three-hour drive of Spokane, WA. Stretches from the Yakima Rim in Eastern Washington the the Whitefish Mountains of Northwestern Montana, from Oregon's Wallowa Mountains to B.C.'s Selkirks. $10.95

BEST HIKES WITH CHILDREN in Western Washington & the Cascades
Joan Burton, Ira Spring, Harvey Manning. Describes 102 hikes of particular interest to children under 12, in the Cascades, Olympics, and Puget Sound foothills of Washington. Short and long hikes, some great for backpacking, all with "turnarounds" short of the end. $12.95

Ask for these at your book or outdoor store, or phone order toll-free at 1-800-553-4453 with VISA/MasterCard. Mail order by sending check or money order (add $2.00 per order for shipping and handling) to:

> The Mountaineers
> 306 2nd Ave. W., Seattle WA 98119

Ask for free catalog